# multiple
# choice
# chess II

## GRAEME BUCKLEY

EVERYMAN CHESS

Everyman Publishers plc  www.everymanbooks.com

First published in 2002 by Everyman Publishers plc, formerly Cadogan Books plc, Gloucester Mansions, 140A Shaftesbury Avenue, London WC2H 8HD

**British Library Cataloguing-in-Publication Data**
A catalogue record for this book is available from the British Library.

ISBN 1 85744 309 8

Distributed in North America by The Globe Pequot Press, P.O Box 480, 246 Goose Lane, Guilford, CT 06437-0480.

All other sales enquiries should be directed to Everyman Chess, Gloucester Mansions, 140A Shaftesbury Avenue, London WC2H 8HD
tel: 020 7539 7600  fax: 020 7379 4060
email: dan@everyman.uk.com
website: www.everyman.uk.com

**EVERYMAN CHESS SERIES** (formerly Cadogan Chess)
Chief advisor: Garry Kasparov
Commissioning editor: Byron Jacobs

Typeset and edited by First Rank Publishing, Brighton.
Production by Book Production Services.
Printed and bound in Great Britain by The Cromwell Press Ltd., Trowbridge, Wiltshire.

# Everyman Chess

## Popular opening books:

| | | |
|---|---|---|
| 1 85744 218 0 | Unusual QG Declined | Chris Ward |
| 1 85744 253 9 | Alekhine's Defence | Nigel Davies |
| 1 85744 256 4 | Queen's Gambit Declined | Matthew Sadler |
| 1 85744 232 6 | French Classical | Byron Jacobs |
| 1 85744 281 4 | Modern Defence | Speelman & McDonald |
| 1 85744 292 X | Symmetrical English | David Cummings |
| 1 85744 290 3 | c3 Sicilian | Joe Gallagher |
| 1 85744 239 3 | Grunfeld Defence | Nigel Davies |
| 1 85744 242 3 | Offbeat Spanish | Glenn Flear |
| 1 85744 262 8 | Classical Nimzo-Indian | Bogdan Lalic |
| 1 85744 291 1 | Sicilian Grand Prix Attack | James Plaskett |
| 1 85744 252 0 | Dutch Stonewall | Jacob Aagaard |
| 1 85744 257 1 | Sicilian Kalashnikov | Pinski & Aagaard |
| 1 85744 276 8 | French Winawer | Neil McDonald |

## Books for players serious about improving their game:

| | | |
|---|---|---|
| 1 85744 226 1 | Starting Out in Chess | Byron Jacobs |
| 1 85744 231 8 | Tips for Young Players | Matthew Sadler |
| 1 85744 236 9 | Improve Your Opening Play | Chris Ward |
| 1 85744 241 5 | Improve Your Middlegame Play | Andrew Kinsman |
| 1 85744 246 6 | Improve Your Endgame Play | Glenn Flear |
| 1 85744 223 7 | Mastering the Opening | Byron Jacobs |
| 1 85744 228 8 | Mastering the Middlegame | Angus Dunnington |
| 1 85744 233 4 | Mastering the Endgame | Glenn Flear |
| 1 85744 238 5 | Simple Chess | John Emms |

## Books for the more advanced player:

| | | |
|---|---|---|
| 1 85744 233 4 | Attacking with 1 e4 | John Emms |
| 1 85744 233 4 | Attacking with 1 d4 | Angus Dunnington |
| 1 85744 219 9 | Meeting 1 e4 | Alexander Raetsky |
| 1 85744 224 5 | Meeting 1 d4 | Aagaard and Lund |
| 1 85744 273 3 | Excelling at Chess | Jacob Aagaard |

# multiple choice chess II

## GRAEME BUCKLEY

Everyman Publishers plc   www.everymanbooks.com

# CONTENTS

# BIBLIOGRAPHY

---

**Books**

*Encyclopaedia of Chess Openings A-E* (Sahovski Informator)

**Periodicals**

*Informator*
*New in Chess Yearbook*
*New in Chess Magazine*
*Chess Life*
*Chess Monthly*
*British Chess Magazine*

**Electronic**

Chess Assistant
ChessBase

# INTRODUCTION

## How to use this Book

I hope you do not object if I am brief and perhaps slightly cheeky in this book. I will begin by advising that readers can treat *Multiple Choice Chess 2* in a similar way to *Multiple Choice Chess*. This implies that readers will have already examined the material in the first book of this series, and if that is so then all is well and good. I also need to add, however, as a reminder and for new players trying their hand at this type of book that I hope, young or old, everyone will find that this is a fun, interactive book with plenty of useful advice and tips for both beginner and advanced player.

The book can be treated either as a series of exercises or as informative games. The exercises are of the form 'guess the next move', but there's always a list of alternatives so that the reader cannot be floundering in a plausible but wrong direction. In this way, I hope nobody gets frustrated.

I should also reiterate that if the book is treated as a series of exercises, then safe moves, that is any moves that do not give away any material, are rewarded more often than not. In this book there is more emphasis than in the first book on looking ahead, anticipating the next move and on calculating variations. In this way, I hope the book continues to cater for the more elite players.

On playing through the games it should always be borne in mind that the competitors, in the majority of cases, were playing 40 moves during a four-hour period. On top of that, professional players are well trained in all phases of the game. Therefore, one must spend a decent amount of time on the games if one is to have a chance of achieving a high score. If you are of a lower grade or rating then you should not be disappointed with a lower point score. This will leave you room for improvement for when you become stronger. It will also give more experienced players a chance to score higher than you. The highest scores can only be obtained with the right approach (and a careful reading of the explanations for each move so as not to miss any bonus points which all add to your score!). If you wish to make the exercises more difficult, then you can cover up the list of choices and choose your own move, just as you did in the first book. Remember that if you do this, then before you read on in that exercise it is best to verify that the move you have chosen was in the list. In this way you can adjust your thoughts if you need to and you can have a 'second go' without having revealed any 'answers'.

Okay, you'd better get your chess set out, your brain in gear and make a start. Please do not forget to have something at hand in order to cover up the part of the page with the 'answers' on so that you cannot be accused of cheating (inadvertently, of course). Work hard and have fun!

Graeme Buckley
Sutton
November 2002

# CHAPTER ONE

## Mating Attacks

It is always a satisfying feeling to conclude a game of chess with mate. On other occasions one could almost argue that a player is being unsporting if they give up a piece to avoid being mated, only to have a completely lost game but be able to last ten or fifteen moves longer!

The following games are four examples of ruthless pursuits of the enemy king, with many complicated but nevertheless engaging variations as one monarch is caught in a well-prepared net.

In the first game, which is an old one, White asserts his advantage from having the superior minor piece. One could argue that this game belonged in Chapter 3, but I would never encourage that the ideas in chess are contained in separate boxes, rather that they all overlap and intermingle.

In this chapter there is an assortment of openings to illustrate that this style of chess can materialise from many positions. It is in only the last game of this chapter that both sides castle in the more traditional kingside manner. The first two are games that contain provocative opposite-wing castling and

the third is an encounter with a very special type of attack. Interestingly, Black scores 75% of the victories here, although it is a recognised feature at top-level chess that the white pieces are advantageous to a degree. Perhaps it is for this reason that black openings are getting more and more aggressive as Black strives to counterbalance his opponent's first move with a sharp response.

Especially towards the end of the encounters, try to work out mating lines to the very end, as there will be bonus points for how far ahead you see. Forcing variations, with perhaps checks all the way, are not as intimidating as they first appear.

Also, it is worth bearing in mind that these players are not going to go all out for mate as a gamble while the rest of their army is obliterated on the opposite wing. There may be times when some defensive moves are in order to maintain total control of the situation.

There is little emphasis on the opening to give everyone an equal chance and I hope you enjoy hunting down the grandmaster moves and the enemy king!

---

## Game 1
# Taimanov-Petrosian
### Leningrad 1959

**1 d4 e6 2 c4**

This is an example of grandmaster psychology. The invitation to transpose to an e4 opening is declined.

**2...d5 3 ♘c3 ♗e7 4 ♘f3 ♘f6 5 ♗g5 0-0 6 e3 b6**

Nowadays the precise move order is 6...h6 and only after 7 ♗h4 does Black decide to develop his bishop with...b7-b6.

**7 cxd5 exd5**

The line 7...♘xd5 8 ♘xd5 exd5 9 ♗xe7 ♕xe7 10 ♗d3 ♗e6 11 ♕c2 secures White a tiny edge because Black has to waste a tempo so as not to lose the h7-pawn. You can recall that Black should have played 6...h6.

**8 ♗d3 ♗b7 9 ♕c2 h6 10 ♗xf6 ♗xf6 11 h4**

White announces his aggressive intentions. Castling kingside leads to far more restrained positions where White seeks to execute a 'minority attack' on the queenside and leave his opponent with weaker pawns.

**11...c5 12 0-0-0 ♘c6**

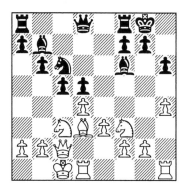

Taimanov was proud of this encounter and even selected it as one of his favourite games. Can you duplicate any of his moves?

Over to you...

| a) 13 dxc5 |
| b) 13 ♘xd5 |
| c) 13 ♗h7+ |
| d) 13 g4 |

13 dxc5 (a) is wrong in principle as it opens up the queenside for Black to launch an attack. However, if you spotted the possibility to win a pawn and come crashing down the centre with 13 dxc5 bxc5 14 ♘xd5, when 14...♕xd5 fails to 15 ♗h7+, score one point. This type of tactic is invaluable to many positions. However, in the same breath, take an extra point if you realised that 13 dxc5 does not force the recapture 13...bxc5, and indeed Black stands well after 13...♘b4.

13 ♘xd5 (b) drops the knight and two points.

13 ♗h7+ (c) ♔h8 could lead to White getting his bishop trapped after a later ...g7-g6. If you had planned to grab the d-pawn with 14 dxc5 etc. take one point as your intentions are positive, but again a crucial extra point is for those who passed on this idea due to the intermezzo 14...♘b4. You can have bonuses for the variations in (a) and (c) if you saw them, as they are slightly different in character.

13 g4 (d) is our star contender for three points. White leaves the centre and queenside alone and begins to aim at the enemy fortress.

**13 g4 cxd4**

| a) 14 exd4 |
| b) 14 ♘xd4 |
| c) 14 g5 |
| d) 14 ♗h7+ |

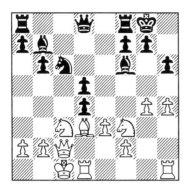

14 exd4 (a) is the correct way to regain the pawn and scores two points.

14 ♘xd4 (b) scores one but only if you had judged that 14...♘xd4 15 exd4 ♗xh4 16 f4 would be too dangerous for Black to seriously contemplate.

Remember the old saying that 'the threat is worse than the execution'. In this case 14 g5 (c) would definitely be premature as Black can ease the tension with 14...dxc3 15 gxf6 ♕xf6.

Deduct two points for 14 ♗h7+ (d) ♔h8 15 exd4 g6 16 ♗xg6 fxg6 17 ♕xg6 ♗g7.

**14 exd4 ♕d6**

At this stage there is a bonus for those who are aware that White's d4-pawn is 'safe' from capture as there is ♗h7+ at the end of any sequence where Black's minor pieces go snaffling.

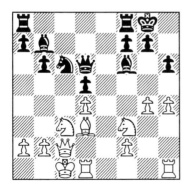

a) 15 ♘b5
b) 15 ♔b1
c) 15 g5
d) 15 ♖hg1

15 ♘b5 (a) rather walks into Black's 'trap' and costs you two points. Typically, 15...♕f4+ 16 ♘d2 a6 17 ♘c3 ♘xd4 would follow.

It takes plenty of patience and experience to take time out from an attack to quietly place your monarch out of danger. 15 ♔b1 (b) scores three.

15 g5 (c) can have one point, although Black has the better prospects after 15...♕f4+ 16 ♔b1 ♕xf3 17 gxf6 ♕xf6 18 ♘xd5 ♕d6. Admittedly, opening up the h-file with 15...hxg5 would have spelt disaster for Black due to 16 hxg5 ♕f4+ 17 ♔b1 ♗xg5 18 ♗h7+ ♔h8 19 ♗g8+ ♗h6 20 ♕h7 mate. You can have a bonus for spotting that.

15 ♖hg1 (d) again fails to appreciate the point behind Black's previous move so deduct one for permitting 15...♕f4+ 16 ♘d2 ♘xd4.

**15 ♔b1 ♘b4**

If anyone was thorough enough to wonder what White was intending to do about 15...♕f4 here, award yourself a bonus with a further on offer for those who calculated 16 ♘xd5 ♕xf3 17 ♗e4 as a powerful course of action.

It is also worth pointing out that, although Black is about to secure the bishop pair here, the position is significantly blocked so this should suit White, who will have two knights, fine.

a) 16 ♕b3
b) 16 ♕a4
c) 16 ♕d2
d) 16 ♘b5

16 ♕d2 (c) remains central and flexible and scores the maximum of two.

In descending order, 16 ♕b3 (a) nets

one, while 16 ♕a4 (b) ♘xd3 17 ♖xd3 ♖fe8 posts White's army on slightly unusual squares for zero and 16 ♘b5 (d) looks decidedly awkward after 16...♕d7 17 ♕b3 ♘xd3 18 ♖xd3 ♗a6 (or even 18...♕xg4) and scores minus one.

**16 ♕d2 ♘xd3**

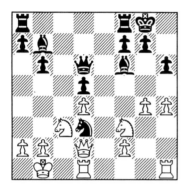

a) 17 ♕xd3
b) 17 g5
c) 17 ♘b5
d) 17 ♘e4

17 ♕xd3 (a) is the only one on the list to score here with one point.

As I try and drum into my pupils, 98% of chess is made up of good, solid, logical moves. 17 g5 (b) ♘f4 and 17 ♘b5 (c) ♕d7 both drop one point and 17 ♘e4 (d) loses you three.

**17 ♕xd3 g6**

a) 18 g5
b) 18 h5
c) 18 ♕e3
d) 18 a3

18 g5 (a) seeks to open files on the kingside and is worth three points. 18 h5 (b), with similar intentions, scores one, but allows Black to blockade with 18...g5.

Nothing for 18 ♕e3 (c) or 18 a3 (d); the former permits Black to consolidate his position with 18...♗g7 19 g5 h5 and the latter is pointless.

**18 g5 ♗c8**

a) 19 gxf6
b) 19 gxh6
c) 19 h5
d) 19 ♔a1

Minus five for 19 gxf6 (a), which falls for 19...♗f5. Don't forget that your opponent is the infamous Petrosian, who is not going to relinquish pieces without good reason.

As long as you gave Black's previous move the respect it deserves, you should not have fallen for 19 gxh6 (b) ♗f5 either. If you did, you have learnt a valuable lesson in the necessity to always consider what your opponent is up to, and on this occasion it costs you seven points. For the same reason, 19 h5 (c) ♗f5 reduces your total by six.

Again it is the gentle but logical sidestep by the monarch, 19 ♔a1 (d), which merits top marks of one point.

**19 ♔a1 ♗f5**

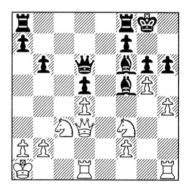

a) 20 ♕e3
b) 20 ♕d2
c) 20 ♘b5
d) 20 ♘e5

Heading the list is the accurate 20 ♕d2 (b), which scores two.

The move 20 ♘b5 (c) fails tactically to 20...♗xd3 21 ♘xd6 ♗e2 22 gxf6 ♗xf3 and diminishes your total by two. Notice here how Black captures the lower valued piece, the knight, in order to make a fork and win an exchange on the following move.

No points for 20 ♕e3 (a) as Black will gain a tempo on the queen with 20...♖fe8. The outright blunder of 20 ♘e5 (d) ♗xd3 sets you back seven points.

**20 ♕d2 ♗g4**

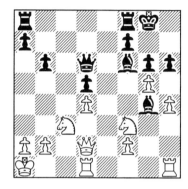

> **a) 21 ♕d3**
> **b) 21 ♕e3**
> **c) 21 gxf6**
> **d) 21 ♘b5**

I'm not sure how you plan to avoid the repetition after 21 ♕d3 (a) ♗f5, but take one for this. The move 21 ♕e3 (b) again cannot be right due to 21...♖fe8 – no points for this. On the other hand, 21 gxf6 (c) ♗xf3 22 ♕xh6 looks promising – take one for this, another for spotting ♕g7 mate and one more for 22...♕xf6 23 h5. A bonus is awarded for anyone rejecting 21 gxf6 on account of a timely ...♕g7.

That leaves 21 ♘b5 (d) to score two points. As discussed in the lines above, the black queen is required to cover the mate threats so 21 ♘b5 causes Black to be extra careful where he moves the great lady. You score two bonus points if you realised this.

**21 ♘b5 ♕e6**

Take one bonus point if you had calculated 21...♕d8 22 ♕f4 ♗xf3 23 ♕xf3 hxg5 24 hxg5 ♗xg5 and another if you saw 25

♕h3 ♔g7 26 f4 with a huge advantage.

> **a) 22 ♖de1**
> **b) 22 ♖he1**
> **c) 22 ♕e3**
> **d) 22 gxf6**

This may seem harsh, but with 22 ♖he1 (b) you must dock yourself one point as 22...♕f5 leaves White with a problem to solve. Sometimes it matters little which rook we move, but in this instance it is necessary to remove the pin on the knight and therefore 22 ♖de1 (a) nets two points.

As the attacking side, we don't want to exchange queens. The sequence 22 ♕e3 (c) ♕xe3 23 fxe3 ♗xf3 24 gxf6 backs up this fact and reduces your score by two.

22 gxf6 (d) ♗xf3 23 ♕xh6 again misses its target due to 23...♕xf6 – you must lose three points for this error as it has already been pointed out.

**22 ♖de1 ♕f5**

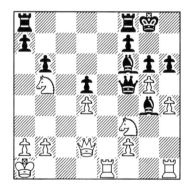

> **a) 23 gxf6**
> **b) 23 gxh6**
> **c) 23 h5**
> **d) 23 ♘e5**

The variation 23 gxf6 (a) ♗xf3 24 ♖hg1 ♕xf6 25 ♕xh6 ♖fe8 is good enough for one point but it favours Black because he has covered White's attack. Although he can snatch a pawn beginning with 25...a6, the move 25...♖fe8 is stronger.

I lack enthusiasm for 23 gxh6 (b) ♗xf3, which costs you two points, and 23 h5 (c) ♗xf3 has the same fate.

23 ♘e5 (d) feels right, looks right and is right (score three points). Black now has to watch out for 23...hxg5 24 ♘d6, which earns you a bonus of two if you saw it because White wins material. The coordination of White's pieces now points to a successfully executed opening. An interesting observation at this stage is that the black bishop has been under fire from the pawn on g5 for four moves and only now is White finally threatening to capture it.

**23 ♘e5 ♗xe5**

a) 24 ♖xe5
b) 24 dxe5
c) 24 gxh6
d) 24 f3

If you went for 24 ♖xe5 take two points and join the club. Players often prefer to make moves which attack the enemy queen, but here Taimanov assessed 24 dxe5 (b) to be stronger and one has to agree that the d4-square and the d6-square appear extremely inviting for the white knight. Take four points for this move.

24 gxh6 (c) ♗f4 loses the plot and four points, while the wayward 24 f3 (d) ♗xf3 25 ♖xe5 ♕d7 26 ♖f1 limits the damage to minus two.

**24 dxe5 h5**

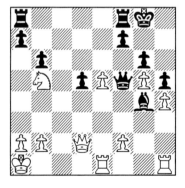

a) 25 ♘d4
b) 25 ♘d6
c) 25 ♕xd5
d) 25 f4

25 ♘d4 (a) is tasty for two points, but the text choice 25 ♘d6 (b) is awarded the token top score of three.

25 ♕xd5 (c) prematurely grabs the d-pawn since 25...♗f3 sets up a nasty fork and costs you two points. If you saw and rejected this then add one to your score.

Lastly, 25 f4 (d) is fine for one point.

**25 ♘d6 ♕e6**

The question for White now is how to proceed? He has the better pawn structure, the more useful minor piece, greater development and the slightly safer king. All well and good, but how to make the most of the various assets?

a) 26 ♖e3
b) 26 ♖hg1
c) 26 f4
d) 26 f3

26 ♖e3 (a) sets up a selection of possibilities and scores two points. White can slowly round up the d-pawn or invade down the c-file at his leisure.

26 ♖hg1 (b) is sufficient for one point, as is 26 f4 (c). There is no need to rush with 26 f3 (d) ♗xf3, so drop one there.

**26 ♖e3 ♖ad8**

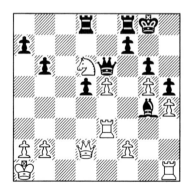

a) 27 ♕d3
b) 27 ♖d3
c) 27 f3
d) 27 ♖c1

27 ♕d3 (a) and 27 f3 (c) are sensible for one point apiece. Although 27 ♖d3 (b) ♕xe5 28 ♖xd5 maintains material equality, it lets Black off the hook and therefore fails to score.

27 ♖c1 (d), however, is guaranteed to limit Black's play and scores three. Notice how all of White's pieces occupy dark squares, in contrast to the colour of the opposing bishop.

**27 ♖c1 ♖d7**

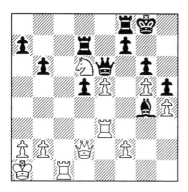

a) 28 f3
b) 28 ♕d4
c) 28 ♖ec3
d) 28 ♘b5

28 ♕d4 (b) is awarded the top score of two as White calmly inches forward.

28 f3 (a) and 28 ♘b5 (d) are safe enough for one point. Abandoning the e-pawn, however, with 28 ♖ec3 (c) ♕xe5 inches your total back by one.

**28 ♕d4 ♗h3**

a) 29 ♖d1
b) 29 ♖xh3
c) 29 ♘xf7
d) 29 ♖f3

29 ♖f3 (d) further seeks to infiltrate on the dark squares (that f6-square is asking for it!) and scores three. 29 ♖d1 (a) must also come under consideration and scores two.

It is a pity if you considered at any length 29 ♖xh3 (b) ♕xh3 – this scores minus two. 29 ♘xf7 (c) also sets you back two points as 29...♖dxf7 leaves you wishing you still had your glorious knight on the board.

**29 ♖f3 ♖e7**

a) 30 ♖f6
b) 30 ♖e1
c) 30 ♖d1
d) 30 a3

I certainly hinted that the white rook might be heading for f6, but not at the price of the e5-pawn so one away for 30 ♖f6 (a) ♕xe5.

30 ♖e1 (b) spoils all of Taimanov's work in one fell swoop but illustrates a typical theme of swindling in the latter stages of a middlegame. Deduct three for missing 30...♕xd6 31 exd6 ♖xe1+, but a bonus is available for the smart cookies who saw that coming. 30 ♖d1 (c) also falls tactically to 30...♗g4 31 ♖f6 ♕xe5 and therefore you must take off one point.

So that leaves the apparently insignificant, but in fact masterly, 30 a3 (d) to merit three points. A further bonus is yours if you are fully aware that Black cannot immediately munch your e-pawn since the bishop on h3 would be hanging, i.e. 30 a3 ♕xe5 31 ♕xe5 ♖xe5 32 ♖xh3.

**30 a3 ♖d8**

a) 31 ♖fc3
b) 31 ♖f6
c) 31 ♘b5
d) 31 ♖e1

31 ♖f6 (b) heads directly for a decisive assault – please add two to your score. A further bonus of one can be added if you calculated that 31...♕xe5 32 ♕xe5 ♖xe5 33 ♘xf7 is painful for Black.

One point for indirectly defending the d-pawn with 31 ♘b5 (c) since 31...♕xe5 32 ♕xe5 ♖xe5 33 ♖xh3 is still on.

31 ♖e1 (d) ♖xd6 32 exd6 ♕xe1+ was another trick to watch out for – lose a point for this. Again, a bonus is reserved for those who rejected 31 ♖e1 for this reason.

31 ♖fc3 (a) does now drop the e-pawn to 31...♕xe5 since the knight on d6 is as loose as the bishop on h3. Drop one point from your total.

**31 ♖f6**

Notice how White occupies both the d6- and f6-outposts and that the square in front of the isolated d-pawn is also occupied. Here White has demonstrated why his knight can triumph over a bishop.

**31...♕g4**

a) 32 f4
b) 32 ♖f4
c) 32 ♕xg4
d) 32 ♕xd5

32 f4 (a) and 32 ♕xg4 (c) are reasonable for one. 32 ♖f4 (b) seems to be a backward step and scores zero, but the timely winning of the d-pawn with 32 ♕xd5 (d) is natural and strong for two points.

**32 ♕xd5 ♕xh4**

a) 33 ♘xf7
b) 33 ♖xf7
c) 33 ♖xg6+
d) 33 e6

33 ♖xg6+ (c) merits two points, with one extra if you saw that this was a threat when you captured on d5 with the queen.

Capturing on f7 backfires badly in all situations. For example, 33 ♘xf7 (a) ♖xd5 sets you back eight, while 33 ♖xf7 (b) scores minus two due to 33...♖xd6 34 ♖xe7+ (34 exd6 ♖xf7) 34...♖xd5. If you had a rush of blood and intended to mate Black with 33 ♖xf7 ♖xd6 34 ♖c8+, you have my sympathies as it is easy to forget that the bishop on h3 exists.

Finally, letting the bishop have his pride back with 33 e6 (d) ♗xe6 costs you one point.

**33 ♖xg6+ ♔f8**

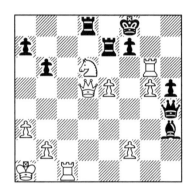

There are some beautiful variations if Black plays 33...♔h7 instead. Either enjoy them or try and work out what happens before you look below.

Three bonus points are up for grabs if you find the key move and pursue the three black responses to an adequate conclusion. 34 ♘f5! and now:

1) 34...♖xd5 35 ♖g7+ ♔h8 36 ♖c8+ leads to mate.

2) 34...♗xf5 35 ♖h6+ ♔g7 36 ♕xd8 ♖xe5 37 ♕h8 mate.

3) 34...fxg6 35 ♕xd8 ♖f7 36 ♖c8.

a) 34 ♘f5
b) 34 ♖f6
c) 34 ♕f3
d) 34 ♖e1

Just because it worked after 33...♔h7 in the notes, doesn't mean it isn't garbage here. Take off five for 34 ♘f5 (a) since after 34...♖xd5 35 ♖c8+ the move 35...♖e8 defends, while if 35 ♘xh4 then 35...fxg6 leaves Black material ahead.

34 ♖f6 (b) scores two and sets the trap 34...♕xg5 35 ♖xf7+, but this move was probably passed over due to 34...♗e6.

34 ♕f3 (c) is a dreadfully difficult move for Black to meet whether in time trouble

or not. I say this because it is quite usual for time pressure to begin to affect games around this stage as the first time limit was invariably set at 40 moves in a certain amount of time. To name a few of Black's headaches: he cannot capture with 34...♖xe5 due to 35 ♕xf7 mate; he is unable to shore up his kingside with 34 ♗e6 since 35 ♖xe6 ♖xe6 also allows 36 ♕xf7 mate; and the white queen, if left to her own devices, will invade on f6 with an unstoppable mate. I'm sorry, I have been so carried away by the elegance of 34 ♕f3 that I have forgotten to award it four points.

I'm sure no one risked losing five hard-earned points with 34 ♖e1 (d) fxg6.

**34 ♕f3 ♕d4**

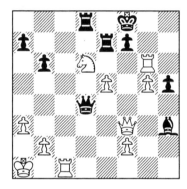

a) 35 ♕f6
b) 35 ♕xh5
c) 35 ♖f6
d) 35 ♖h6

I did say the white queen fancied a flurry with 35 ♕f6 (a), but Black's last nearly put

Let us see how you did.

paid to that by setting up a temporary defence of 35...♕xe5. No score if you missed that, but if you carried on and worked out that 36 ♖h6! ♕xf6 37 gxf6 also wins due to the mate on h8 and the threat to the black rook on e7, award yourself five points.

35 ♕xh5 (b) encourages instant resignation so award yourself two points for this. If you saw that you were exposing yourself to 35...fxg6 (yes, a whole rook for the blissfully unaware) and had 36 ♕h8 mate in store, then score an extra one.

Everyone is welcome to work out all the attempts at black defence and the way for White to combat them. I can tempt you with a bonus for each variation you can work out listed below.

If you are not sure how Black can even try to stop mate, then sneak a look at Black's 35th moves and then go from there. Don't be afraid if a line appears long because a 'forced' variation, where one side is making only moves (often out of check), is not difficult to unravel.

1) 35...♖xd6 36 ♕h8 mate.
2) 35...♕xe5 36 ♕h6+ ♕g7 37 ♕xg7 mate.
3) 35...♖e6 36 ♕h8+ ♔e7 37 ♖c7+ ♖d7 38 ♕e8 mate.
4) 35...♖ed7 36 ♕h8+ ♔e7 37 ♘c8+ ♖xc8 38 ♕f6+ ♔f8 39 ♖xc8+ ♖d8 40 ♖xd8+ ♕xd8 41 ♕xd8 mate.

35 ♖f6 (c) scores one, as does 35 ♖h6 (d) ♕xe5, which transposes to (a) after 36 ♕f6!. To be consistent, there are four bonus points for appreciating that 36 ♕f6 scuppers Black's chances of survival.

**35 ♕xh5 1-0**

Less than 14: You could almost double your score if you steered clear of the traps.
14-27: Your score is healthy, but try to spend more time calculating the tactics.
28-41: You are a well-rounded player. I hope your region has signed you up this season.
42-54: Excellent play. A dangerous opponent, no doubt.
55+: You have thrived with this attacking masterpiece. Does your opening repertoire feature other lines with castling on opposite wings?

---

## Game 2
## Nijboer-Korchnoi
### Arnhem 1999

---

**1 e4 e6 2 d4 d5 3 ♘c3 ♘f6**

The Winawer with 3...♗b4 leads to completely different types of positions. Here Korchnoi chooses the Classical Variation.

**4 e5 ♘fd7 5 f4 c5 6 ♘f3 ♘c6 7 ♗e3 a6 8 ♕d2 cxd4 9 ♘xd4**

Maintaining control over d4 is central to White's strategy.

**9...♗c5 10 0-0-0 0-0 11 h4**

The position is no doubt familiar to French Defence followers. Even if the structure is new to you, castling on opposite wings must generate an instinct to attack the enemy monarch before you are overrun. Black to play...

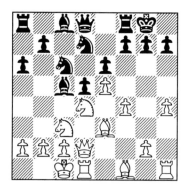

a) **11...♘xd4**
b) **11...♗xd4**
c) **11...♕c7**
d) **11...h5**

11...♘xd4 (a) scores two, although I don't want to give away the follow-up. 11...♗xd4 (b) is also playable and scores one, as does 11...♕c7 (c).

No score, however, for 11...h5 (d) as Black must try and keep it 'tight at the back'.

**11...♘xd4 12 ♗xd4**

a) **12...♗xd4**
b) **12...h5**
c) **12...b5**
d) **12...♗b4**

Take one point for 12...♗xd4 (a) and the interesting 12...♗b4 (d).

Again 12...h5 (b) will only encourage White to prise open the kingside with g2-g4 at some stage, so no points there.

12...b5 (c) top scores with two points Now we can appreciate the necessity for the previous 11...♘xd4 in order for Black to expand on the queenside. (The knight would have been loose on c6 for those who do this quiz over breakfast and are not yet in the land of the living.)

**12...b5 13 ♖h3**

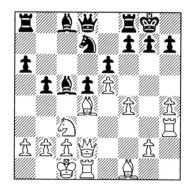

a) **13...h5**
b) **13...♗xd4**
c) **13...b4**
d) **13...♕a5**

Sorry, 13...h5 (a) is still out of bounds and loses one point this time.

Again there is nothing wrong with

---

13...♗xd4 (b) for one point, while 13...♕a5 (d) also scores one. Take a bonus if you realised that you would then be threatening ...b4 followed by ...♕xa2. Korchnoi prefers to push on with 13...b4 (c) as he might well wish to occupy the a5-square with his pawn, thus allowing his 'bad' bishop to come alive via a6. Take two points for this.

**13...b4 14 ♘a4**

> a) 14...♗a7
> b) 14...♗e7
> c) 14...♗xd4
> d) 14...♕a5

14...♗e7 (b) and 14...♕a5 (d) are safe enough for one point, but it is 14...♗xd4 (c) which scores the maximum of two. The move 14...♗a7 (a) loses a pawn to 15 ♗xa7 ♖xa7 16 ♕xb4, so it's minus one for this.

**14...♗xd4 15 ♕xd4**

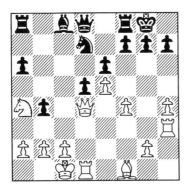

> a) 15...f6
> b) 15...a5
> c) 15...♖b8
> d) 15...♕e7

I cannot be too harsh on 15...f6 (a), which scores two points, since it was seen in Kasparov-Short, Amsterdam 1994. Needless to say, Korchnoi did not fancy the outcome after 16 ♕xb4 fxe5 17 ♕d6 ♕f6 18 f5 and hence he had an alternative prepared.

Korchnoi's choice of 15...a5 (b) scores three, while 15...♖b8 (c) and 15...♕e7 (d)

net a creditable one.

**15...a5 16 c4**

> a) 16...♗b7
> b) 16...dxc4
> c) 16...bxc3
> d) 16...♕e8

Two points for bolstering up the centre with 16...♗b7 (a). But nothing for 16...dxc4 (b), which runs into 17 ♘c5 ♖a7 18 ♘xe6. Take a bonus point if you rejected 16...dxc4 for this tactical reason.

16...bxc3 (c) uses the *en passant* rule and logically opens lines on the queenside, scoring three points. There may be one or two of you who have not come across en passant so do take time out to learn it. I am keen to assure my pupils that this is the last and hardest rule they will have to learn.

Deduct one for 16...♕e8 (d), but if you intended the flashy 17 cxd5 ♘xe5 followed by 18...♕xa4 you'll have to lose a further two since you overlooked 18 ♘b6. If it is any consolation, I am impressed that you had the imagination to set up the discovered attack on the white knight. Next time it might be sound!

**16...bxc3 17 ♖xc3**

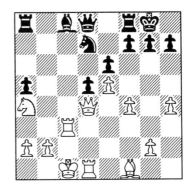

> a) 17...♕xh4
> b) 17...♗b7
> c) 17...♖b8
> d) 17...♘b8

Perhaps it's a risky pawn to take, but Korchnoi has a vast wealth of experience. So 17...♕xh4 (a) scores two points.

17...♗b7 (b) and 17...♖b8 (c) are sensible and score one point, with a bonus point if you saw that 18...♖b4 constitutes a nasty threat.

Finally, nothing for 17...♘b8 (d), which invites 18 ♘b6 and, after 17 moves, leaves all of Black's pieces confined to the back rank!

**17...♕xh4 18 g3**

a) 18...♕e7
b) 18...♕d8
c) 18...♕h5
d) 18...♕h6

One point for retreating with 18...♕e7 (a), but two for Korchnoi's choice of 18...♕d8 (b).

I mistrust both 18...♕h5 (c) and 18...♕h6 (d) as White can gain a vital tempo against the black queen with ♗g2 and ♖h1. These moves also leave her majesty short of squares and score no points.

**18...♕d8 19 ♔b1**

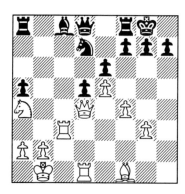

a) 19...♗a6
b) 19...♗b7
c) 19...♖b8
d) 19...♖e8

19...♗a6 (a) seeks to exchange the light-squared bishops before White can use his to

target h7. Score two points for this selection.

19...♗b7 (b) and 19...♖b8 (c) are good enough for one point, but 19...♖e8 (d) is too irrelevant to merit a score here.

**19...♗a6 20 ♗xa6 ♖xa6 21 ♖h1**

a) 21...h6
b) 21...f5
c) 21...♕b8
d) 21...♖a8

First of all, there are two bonus points for appreciating that White is now lined up to hit you with 22 ♕d3, targeting mate on h7 and the rook on a6. 21...h6 (a) prevents the main threat and scores one, but a bonus is available if you were uneasy about this due to 22 g4, with g4-g5 in the air. 21...f5 (b) is a serious attempt to hold White up and scores two, but this is conditional on you being aware that 22 exf6 was on the cards and that you intended to recapture with 22...♘xf6 to take the sting out of 23 ♕d3.

21...♕b8 (c) fails to meet the threat of 22 ♕d3 and therefore costs you five points. It is 21...♖a8 (d) which proves to be most effective – score three for this.

**21...♖a8 22 g4**

a) 22...g6
b) 22...♖b8
c) 22...♖c8
d) 22...g5

22...g6 (a) 23 ♖ch3 is the start of a powerful attack for White, so drop three if you allowed White this luxury.

22...♖b8 (b) is worth two, but how did you plan to meet 23 ♖ch3? If you assumed 23...♖b4 was enough to put White off, you must deduct one as 24 ♖xh7 is lethal. If you intended 23...h6 24 g5 ♖b4, you may keep your points intact and add a bonus one to your score. You may even earn a further bonus if you calculated 22...♖b8 23 ♕d3 h6 24 g5 ♖b4 25 gxh6 g6 as a way to sustain the shelter around the black king.

22...♖c8 (c) scores one point, but the drastic 22...g5 (d) drops four on the strength of 23 ♖ch3.

**22...♖b8 23 a3**

> a) 23...♖b7
> b) 23...♖c8
> c) 23...♘b6
> d) 23...♔h8

The rook may be needed to defend along the seventh rank, or Black may want to double rooks later; so one point for 23...♖b7 (a). Attempting to exchange a pair of rooks with 23...♖c8 (b) also scores one, but top marks of two goes to Korchnoi's 23...♘b6 (c). Take a bonus if you backed this up mentally by trying to eliminate the defence of the b2-square.

Zero points for 23...♔h8 (d), which is worse than a waiting move as mate beckons.

**23...♘b6 24 g5**

> a) 24...♘c4
> b) 24...♘xa4
> c) 24...♕d7
> d) 24...f6

24...♘xa4 (b) scores two points, but for a bonus you need to have analysed the critical 25 ♖ch3 ♖xb2+ 26 ♕xb2 ♘xb2 27 ♖xh7 and now:

1) 27...f5 28 g6 earns you another point because White still wins.

2) 27...g6 28 ♖h8+ ♔g7 29 ♖1h7 mate credits you with another point.

3) A further bonus for 25...h6! 26 gxh6 g6 27 ♕xa4, which is an escape route to a more than adequate position for Black.

Minus two for 24...♘c4 (a), which proves to be rather slow after 25 ♖ch3. The move 24...♕d7 (c) slips up to 25 ♘xb6 and slips your score back by three. Finally, 24...f6 (d) also fails badly to 25 gxf6 gxf6 26 ♕g1+ ♔h8 27 ♖xh7+ ♔xh7 28 ♖h3 mate – lose four for this.

**24...♘xa4 25 ♕xa4**

> a) 25...♕b6
> b) 25...♖b6
> c) 25...♖c8
> d) 25...d4

It must be a relief for Black to create his own threats with 25...♕b6 (a) – this scores three points. If you were not aware that this threatens a mate in one, then do not add a bonus of one to your score.

The alternative moves all receive one point as long as you are resting your hopes of defence on, for example, 26 ♖ch3 h6 27 gxh6 g6.

**25...♕b6 26 ♕c2**

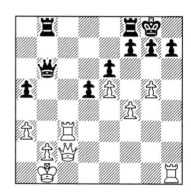

> a) 26...♖b7
> b) 26...d4
> c) 26...♖fd8
> d) 26...g6

26...♖b7 (a) and 26...d4 (b) both allow White to end the game prematurely with 27 ♕xh7 mate – score minus five for these two moves.

c) 26...♖fd8, whether by design or not, allows the king to run with 27 ♕xh7+ ♔f8. However, after 28 ♖c2 (to defend the mate on b2) it is hardly pleasant for Black, so score minus three for this.

26...g6 (d) affords the best resistance and scores one point, with an important bonus if you found 27 ♕h2 h5 to keep the king-side blocked. I haven't forgotten about en

passant; 28 gxh6 ♔h7 is still secure.
**26...g6 27 ♖h6**

---
a) 27...♕b7
b) 27...♖b7
c) 27...d4
d) 27...♖fd8
---

One point for 27...♕b7 (a) and two for 27...♖b7 (b), with a further one if you saw the idea of White doubling rooks on the h-file in order to pressurise h7.

27...d4 (c), in combination with 28 ♖ch3 ♖fd8 29 ♖xh7 ♔f8, and 27...♖fd8 (d) 28 ♖ch3 d4 29 ♖xh7 ♔f8 transpose to the same position and are both awarded one point. However, if you did not anticipate the necessity for ...♔f8 in advance, no points.

**27...♖b7 28 ♕h2**

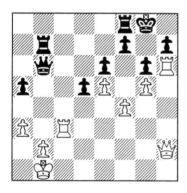

---
a) 28...d4
b) 28...♕d4
c) 28...a4
d) 28...♖fb8
---

One point for 28...d4 (a), but it does not end there. What is your idea against 29 ♖xh7? If 29...f5 is the best you can come up with, drop two points and play out the consequences of 30 ♖h8+ ♔f7 31 ♕h7+ ♔e8 32 ♖c8+. If, however, you spotted the resourceful 29...♕xb2+ 30 ♕xb2 ♖xb2+ 31 ♔xb2 dxc3+ 32 ♔xc3 ♔xh7 take three bonus points. I haven't quite finished the

Spanish Inquisition... If faced with 29 ♖ch3, how do you continue? One bonus for 29...♖fb8; nothing for anything else.

28...♕d4 (b) scores two points, plus another for realising that 29 ♖xh7 ♕d1+ 30 ♖c1 ♖xb2+! is okay for Black.

28...a4 (c) may be okay if White rushes in with 29 ♖xh7, when again 29...♕xb2+ 30 ♕xb2 ♖xb2+ 31 ♔xb2 ♔xh7 saves the day. However, it is 29 ♖c2 f5 30 gxf6 ♖ff7 31 ♖g2 which causes concern and therefore costs you three points.

28...♖fb8 (d) sees Black coordinating his pieces to maximum effect and collects three points.

**28...♖fb8 29 ♖c2**

---
a) 29...♕d4
b) 29...♔f8
c) 29...♕e3
d) 29...f5
---

This is perhaps the key point of the encounter. 29...♕d4 (d) merits five points. The main defence lies in 30 ♖xh7 ♖xb2+ 31 ♖xb2 ♖xb2+ 32 ♕xb2 ♕d1+ 33. ♕c1 ♕xc1+ 34 ♔xc1 ♔xh7 35 ♔c2 ♔g7 etc., which heads for a drawn king and pawn ending.

29...♕e3 (c) is worth three points as 30 ♖xh7 can again be met by 30...♖xb2+! 31 ♖xb2 ♕d3+ 32 ♔a2 ♕c4+ with a draw by perpetual check.

Neither 29...♔f8 (b) 30 ♖xh7 nor 29...f5 (d) 30 gxf6 inspires confidence – score zero for these options.

**29...♕d4 30 ♔a1**

---
a) 30...♕d1+
b) 30...a4
c) 30...♖b3
d) 30...♖xb2
---

This is actually a classic case of the attacker's reduced sense of danger. He has spent all game conjuring up mates and plots to trap the enemy king, so much so that he has not concentrated on the fact that his opponent might also have ambitions. Korchnoi does not miss his opportunity...did you?

30...♛d1+ (a) scores four points, but only if you planned to meet 31 ♔a2 with 31...♜b3, threatening 32...♜xa3+!. The immediate 30...♜b3 (c) also takes full advantage of White's dubious manoeuvre and scores four points (but only three if you did not realise that you were threatening ...♜xa3+).

30...a4 (b) justifies White snuggling up in the corner of the board and permits 31 ♜xh7 – lose one point. 30...♜xb2 (d) loses material and four points.

### 30...♜b3 31 ♔a2

First of all, if you considered the defence 31 ♜h3 but worked out the forcing line 31...♛d1+ 32 ♔a2 ♜xh3 33 ♛xh3 ♛xc2 as a win for Black award yourself a bonus.

If you also thought White might try 31 ♜xh7 and discovered the beautiful finish 31...♜xa3+ 32 ♔b1 ♜xb2+ 33 ♜xb2 ♛d1 mate have an extra bonus.

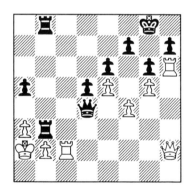

What was your final total?

---

| a) 31...f5 |
| b) 31...♜c3 |
| c) 31...♜xa3+ |
| d) 31...♛a4 |

31...f5 (a) misses the boat and scores minus one.

31...♜c3 (b) may be a bolt of inspiration if White obliges with 32 bxc3 ♛c4+ 33 ♔a1 ♛f1+ 34 ♔a2 ♛b1 mate, but what if White calmly captures your rook with 32 ♜xc3 instead? Okay, one point for the clever idea, minus five for the fact that it hangs a rook. This leaves a grand total of minus four (or the full minus five for those who went for 31...♜c3 without having the unlikely mate to back it up).

31...♜xa3+ (c) forces many different perpetual checks but no more. For example, 32 ♔xa3 ♛b4+ 33 ♔a2 ♛a4+ 34 ♔b1 ♜xb2+ 35 ♔xb2 ♛b4+ 36 ♔c1 ♛e1+ 37 ♔b2 ♛b4+ or 32 bxa3 ♛d3 33 ♜b2 ♛c4+ 34 ♔b1 ♛f1+ 35 ♔c2 ♛c4+ 36 ♔d1 ♛f1+. One bonus point for each line you established ending in a draw (a maximum of three) but minus two if you did not realise the outcome.

31...♛a4 (d) takes top honours as the strike to cause White to pack his bags – take five points for this.

### 31...♛a4 0-1

White actually resigned here. Let us assume White's next move to be 32 ♜xh7 so you can have the experience of working out the forced win.

Three bonus points for 32 ♜xh7 ♜xa3+ 33 bxa3 ♛b3+ 34 ♔a1 ♛b1 mate. There was no adequate defence.

---

Less than 10: You will lift your total by checking any tactics and tricks in the position.

11-20: You failed to get to grips with this game but, on the positive side, you must have found a handful of decent moves.

21-32: An estimable result. Most of your choices make a lot of sense.

33-44: A sterling performance. You are a formidable opponent for anyone.

45+: Phenomenal. You played like Korchnoi in less time than he took for the game.

# Game 3
## Nunn-Nataf
France 1999

**1 e4 c5 2 ♘f3 ♘c6 3 d4 cxd4 4 ♘xd4 e5**

The Kalashnikov – a sharp line.

**5 ♘b5 d6 6 c4 ♗e7 7 ♘1c3 a6 8 ♘a3 f5 9 ♗d3 f4 10 g3**

De Firmian-Shabalov, Denver 1998 continued more quietly with 10 ♘c2 ♘f6 11 b3 0-0 12 ♗b2 ♔h8 13 ♕e2 ♗e6 14 ♘d5 etc., but Nunn can always be relied upon to test the most critical variations.

**10...♘f6 11 gxf4 exf4 12 ♗xf4 0-0 13 ♗g3**

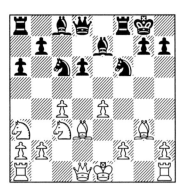

You are a pawn down but with plenty of activity and development to compensate for the slight material deficit. Now take over the pieces of the French Grandmaster Igor-Alexandre Nataf, well known for his confidence and lively ideas. Maybe I should emphasise that, as this is a short game, you may wish to play extra vigilantly in order to catch any bonus points going.

a) 13...♗g4
b) 13...♘g4
c) 13...♗e6
d) 13...♘e5

13...♗g4 (a) is a sensible way to bring the

last minor piece into play and scores two points. There might follow 14 f3, when 14...♗e6 or 14...♗h5 is possible.

It is normally correct to develop all your pieces before moving a piece for the second time, so if that was your reason for dismissing 13...♘g4 (b), you may take a bonus point. However, here Nataf judges that he should begin to harass White before he has time to consolidate his position. Take three points if you chose 13...♘g4.

13...♗e6 (c) scores two as it is a good habit to obey opening principles, while 13...♘e5 (d) is worth one but has limited attacking possibilities after 14 ♗e2 ♗g4 15 f3 ♗h3 16 ♖g1 or 16 f4.

**13...♘g4 14 ♗e2**

a) 14...h5
b) 14...♘ce5
c) 14...♘f6
d) 14...♘xf2

14...h5 (a) allows the nasty 15 ♕d5+, so lose two points if you chose this.

14...♘ce5 (b) receives two different scores. Lose one point if you missed 15 f4 and now think you are dropping a piece. However, if you are totally aware that your knights are in a spot of bother and you justified Black's knight sorties with 15 f4 ♘e3 16 ♕d2 ♘g2+ then give yourself a point. If you saw 17 ♔d1 ♘g6, then take a bonus point, plus another two for 17 ♔f2 ♘xf4 18 ♗xf4 ♗g5.

14...♘f6 (c) is okay for one, but the star move is the forthright 14...♘xf2 (d) – take three points for this.

**14...♘xf2 15 ♕d5+**

Firstly, did you work out why White avoided the immediate capture of the knight?

Two bonus points if you analysed 15 ♗xf2 ♖xf2 16 ♔xf2 ♗h4+ 17 ♔e3 (amazingly the computer programme *Fritz* suggested 17 ♔g2 ♕g5+ 18 ♗g4 ♗xg4 19 ♕d5+ as better for White, but fortunately these are a pair of humans...) 17...♕g5+ 18 ♔d3 ♘b4+ 19 ♔d4 ♗f2 mate.

a) 15...♗e6
b) 15...♖f7
c) 15...♔h8
d) 15...♘xh1

There are superior ways to get out of check than 15...♗e6 (a), which loses three points.

Nothing for 15...♖f7 (b) as 16 ♗xf2 leaves your rook pinned on f7. However, if you intended to follow up with 16...♘b4, chasing the queen away, you can have one point.

15...♔h8 (c) is Nataf's choice and is worth two points, while 15...♘xh1 is illegal and shall therefore be ignored.

**15...♔h8 16 ♗xf2**

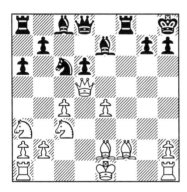

a) 16...♖xf2
b) 16...♗h4
c) 16...♘b4
d) 16...♕a5

16...♘b4 (c) is a must as Black drives away the dominant queen. Take four points for this.

16...♖xf2 (a) 17 ♔xf2 ♗h4+ 18 ♔g2 loses much of its appeal (and two points) as there are no further checks worth considering.

Nothing for 16...♗h4 (b) 17 ♗g3 which, with Black being a piece down, seems rather slow.

Exchanging queens would head for an ending when White is a piece to the good, so minus one for 16...♕a5 (d).

**16...♘b4 17 ♕h5**

Two bonus points if you relished the prospect of 17 ♕d4 ♖xf2 18 ♔xf2 ♗h4+ 19 ♔f3 ♗h3, when Black has a vicious assault against the enemy king. Your score increments by one for calculating 19 ♕xf2 ♗h4.

a) 17...♘c2+
b) 17...g6
c) 17...♖xf2
d) 17...♗e6

The knight on a3 covers the c2-square, so lose three points for choosing 17...♘c2+ (a).

17...g6 (b) seeks to send the white queen packing but actually opens up the diagonal to allow White some respite with 18 ♗d4+, so no score there.

17...♖xf2 (c) is still high on the list of Nataf's strategy to expose the white monarch, so this gets three points.

Maintaining some pressure with 17...♗e6 (d) is worth one point.

**17...♖xf2 18 ♔xf2**

a) 18...♗h4+
b) 18...♕f8+
c) 18...g6
d) 18...♕b6+

Nataf saw fit to continue his attack with 18...♗h4+ (a) – score three points for this. The three alternatives are also good enough for one point apiece.

**18...♗h4+ 19 ♔g2**

a) 19...♕g5+
b) 19...♗h3+
c) 19...♕d7
d) 19...g6

The attacking side wants to maintain queens on the board so 19...♕g5+ (a) must be wrong. This scores no points.

Minus three for 19...♗h3+ (b) 20 ♔xh3. If you thought you had a follow-up, I'm afraid you don't. 19...♕d7 (c) also lets White off the hook with 20 ♕xh4 and scores minus three.

Last, but not least, it is 19...g6 (d) which gets two points. Take a bonus if you have already assessed that the white queen now has only two safe squares, and a further one if you dismissed 20 ♕h6 due to 20...♗g5, when her majesty runs out of space.

**19...g6 20 ♕f3**

a) 20...♕g5+
b) 20...♕f6
c) 20...d5
d) 20...♗e6

20...♕g5+ (a) causes the king to be inconvenienced again so please add two to your score. Add two more if you had realised that the significance of chasing the white queen away from h5 was to allow Black this notable check on g5.

It is still not in Black's interest to exchange queens, so nothing for 20...♕f6 (b). The sequence 20...d5 (c) 21 ♘xd5 does not aid Black in the slightest and hinders your score by one. On the contrary, 20...♗e6 (d) does no harm and is worth one point.

**20...♕g5+ 21 ♔f1**

Now try and work out a forced win for Black. It is harder in your own games because you do not know exactly when the lightning strikes are there, but after years of experience one starts to sense when a mate might be imminent and there is the temptation to look that little bit harder.

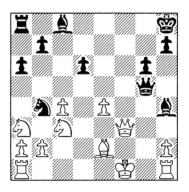

Unfortunately for Nunn, who has one of the best analytical minds in the business, he no doubt saw it all coming...

a) 21...♕h6
b) 21...♔g7
c) 21...♗h3+
d) 21...♕d2

I suppose I should congratulate you for preventing the mate threat of 22 ♕f8, so one point for 21...♕h6 (a), but you are hardly causing Nunn to sweat. 21...♔g7 (b) is also worth one for the same reason, but the same comments apply to you, too .

21...♗h3+ (c) takes top honours with five points, but you need to be aware that White can capture your bishop with 22 ♕xh3 and have at least the next move up your sleeve. If it turns out that your intention is not carried out, you must only take three points for correctly 'guessing' Nataf's 21st, rather than working it all out.

Whoops! 21...♕d2 (d) allows 22 ♕f8 mate, but only lose two points as I have obviously dragged you into a game that you are not comfortable with.

**21...♗h3+ 22 ♕xh3**

a) 22...♖f8+
b) 22...♕f4+
c) 22...♕f6+
d) 22...♕d2

22...♖f8+ (a) is the correct follow-up and scores three points.

22...♕f4+ (b) and 22...♕f6+ (c) can have one if you saw 23 ♔g2 falls foul of 23...♕f2 mate. If, however, you rejected these on the basis that White could interpose both checks with bishop or queen, have a bonus.

22...♕d2 (d) loses one point and the whole plot after 23 ♔g2 ♕xb2 24 ♖ab1 ♕xa3 25 ♖b3 ♕a5 26 ♕xh4.

**22...♖f8+ 23 ♗f3**

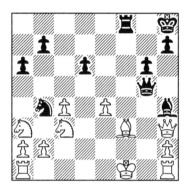

Award yourself two bonuses if you saw the attack starting with 23 ♕f3 ♖xf3+ 24 ♗xf3 ♕e3. Add another for the sequence 25 ♔g2 ♕f2+ 26 ♔h3 ♕xf3+ 27 ♔xh4 h6, with the idea of 28...g5 mate.

|         |
|---------|
| a) 23...♕d2 |
| b) 23...♕e3 |
| c) 23...♕h5 |
| d) 23...♗g3 |

23...♕d2 (a) is tempting for two but allows White to resist with 24 ♘e2.

23...♕e3 (b) really puts the boot in for four points.

23...♕h5 (c) tries to make use of the fact that the bishop is pinned but, with best play by White, Black cannot break through after 24 ♔e2. Score one point for 23...♕h5.

Black has given away material and cannot afford exchanges in the variation 23...♗g3 (d) 24 ♕xg3 ♕xg3 25 hxg3 ♖xf3+ 26 ♔e2. Score minus two for 23...♗g3.

**23...♕e3 24 ♕xh4**

|         |
|---------|
| a) 24...♖xf3+ |
| b) 24...♕xf3+ |
| c) 24...♘d3 |
| d) 24...♕d3+ |

One point for 24...♖xf3+ (a), although strangely there is no mate after 25 ♔g2. The move 24...♕xf3+ (b) also merits one point with a further bonus if you spotted 25 ♔g1 ♖f4 (threatening the white queen and ...♖g4). You score another if you judged that 26 ♕d8+ does not lead to a perpetual for White. However, it is now pay day for the defenders, who receive two bonus points for the timely 26 ♕xf4 ♕xf4 27 ♖f1.

The relentless pressure on the f2-square continues mercilessly with 24...♘d3 (c) – score five – but the alternative use of the d3-square with 24...♕d3+ (d) leads nowhere after 25 ♔g2 and scores minus one.

**24...♘d3 25 ♘d5**

|         |
|---------|
| a) 25...♕xe4 |
| b) 25...♖xf3+ |
| c) 25...♕xf3+ |
| d) 25...♕f2+ |

25...♕xe4 (a) costs you eight on account of 26 ♕xe4, while the other blunder 25...♕f2+ (d) is less costly (minus three) because of 26 ♕xf2 ♘xf2 27 ♔xf2.

25...♖xf3+ (b) appears catastrophic for White at first sight, but on closer inspection 26 ♔g2 ♕e2+ 27 ♔g1 ♘f2 28 ♕d8+ ♔g7 29 ♕e7+ ♖f7 30 ♕h4 sees White hanging on. Similarly, White does not fall off the tightrope after 26...♖f2+ 27 ♔g1. Score one point for 25...♖xf3+.

25...♕xf3+ (c) is deadly and scores three, but the smart players will be looking ahead.

**25...♕xf3+ 26 ♔g1**

|         |
|---------|
| a) 26...♕f2+ |
| b) 26...♘f2 |
| c) 26...♖e8 |
| d) 26...g5 |

26...♕f2+ (a) spoils an otherwise dramatic encounter after 27 ♕xf2 ♘xf2 28 ♖f1.

26...♘f2 (b) top scores with three points. If you just thought you were threatening 27...♘h3+ with this manoeuvre, only take two – 27...♕xh1 mate is the real issue.

Minus one for the bizarre 26...♖e8 (c), which permits White to come back from the brink with 27 ♕f6+.

26...g5 (d) has some merits in that 27 ♕xg5 allows 27...♕f2 mate. If this was your reasoning you are entitled to two points, but only one if you thought 27 ♕xg5 was a cue for 27...♖g8. If you passed over 26...g5 due to the solid 27 ♕g3, award yourself one bonus in addition to the points attached to your own move selection.

**26...♘f2 27 ♔f1**

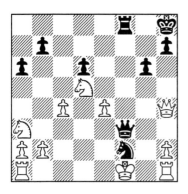

a) 27...♕xh1+
b) 27...♘xh1+
c) 27...♘xe4+
d) 27...g5

27...♕xh1+ (a) scores four as it can't be bad to pocket a pair of rooks. If you saw that this was on the cards before White's 27th move, then add two to your total.

Two points for 27...♘xh1+ (b), which leads to much the same after 28 ♔g1 ♘f2 29 ♔f1 ♕h1+. Have a bonus if you realised this. 28 ♔e1 ♕f1+ also gives the same result.

Nothing for 27...♘xe4+ (c) 28 ♔g1 because if you try and repeat with 28...♘f2, you have opened yourself up to 29 ♕d4+. Why permit White any chance at all?

Finally, one point for 27...g5 (d) if you foresaw 28 ♕xg5 ♘xe4+, with two further bonuses for analysing 28 ♕g3 ♕xh1+ 29 ♕g1 ♘h3+ as hopeless for White.

**27...♕xh1+ 28 ♔e2**

a) 28...♕xe4+
b) 28...♘xe4
c) 28...♕xa1
d) 28...♕d1+

28...♕xe4+ (a) fails to finish White off and scores minus two, while capturing with 28...♘xe4 (b) is even worse after 29 ♖xh1 (minus ten for this). The impetuous 28...♕d1+ (d) may be final after 29 ♔e3 ♕d3 mate, but is final for you after 29 ♖xd1 so drop your total by ten.

28...♕xa1 (c) earns two for successfully mopping up

**28...♕xa1 0-1**

It is time to give up the fight as 29 ♘e3 ♕xb2+ 30 ♘ac2 ♕e5 leaves White helpless.

It only remains to compare your total with the comments below.

Less than 14: I wonder whether your score would shoot up if you were permitted to take off your lowest two scores.

14-24: A stable result but searching deeper into the variations will help you.

25-35: A commendable performance. You must have spotted some important lines.

36-47: This is a fine score for a highly complex encounter. Your tactics are spot on.

48+: Even with the multiple choice format, this is a true grandmaster achievement..

## Game 4
# N.Pert-Hebden
Hastings 2001/02

**1 d4 ♘f6 2 ♘f3 g6 3 c4 ♗g7 4 ♘c3 0-0 5 ♗g5 c5 6 d5 d6 7 e4 a6 8 ♘d2 h6 9 ♗h4 e5**

With the last move, Hebden has steered the game into a more typical kind of King's Indian, an opening at which he excels.

**10 ♗e2 ♕e8 11 a3 h5**

The centre is blocked and so the play should concentrate on the wings. Black is absolutely correct in attempting to mount a kingside offensive.

**12 b4 ♘bd7 13 f3 ♘h7 14 ♗f2 b6 15 ♖b1 ♗h6 16 bxc5 bxc5 17 ♕a4**

White continues to try and infiltrate via the queenside.

**17...♕e7 18 ♘b3 h4 19 ♘a5 ♕g5 20 0-0**

Note that 20 ♕c6 runs into 20...♕d2+.

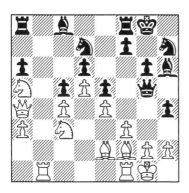

Both players have been attempting to further their ambitions. Now it is time to see if you can.

> a) 20...h3
> b) 20...♘hf6
> c) 20...♘df6
> d) 20...f5

20...h3 (a) is worth one, although after 21

g3 Black must still face the threat of 22 ♕c6.

20...♘hf6 (b) drops one point but, perhaps more vitally, 21 ♕c6 ♖a7 22 ♕xd6 causes the base of Black's pawn chain to disintegrate.

20...♘df6 (c) scores three and cleverly intends to meet 21 ♕c6 with 21...♗h3, after which Black's rooks are connected and a kingside attack is underway.

20...f5 (d) may be a typical pawn break in the King's Indian, but again 21 ♕c6 would be difficult to meet so no score.

**20...♘df6 21 ♔h1**

> a) 21...h3
> b) 21...♘h5
> c) 21...♕d2
> d) 21...♗d7

Hebden has been perfecting these lines for many years and is adept at placing his knights on their most effective 'circuits'. 21...♘h5 (b) takes the honours with three points, with an additional bonus if you analysed 22 ♕c6 ♘g3+. If White wants to avoid losing an exchange by capturing the knight, then unstoppable mate occurs with, for example, 23 hxg3 hxg3 24 ♗xg3 ♕xg3 25 ♕xa8 ♗e3. If you had no trouble executing this thematic attack, then maybe you should consider taking up the energetic King's Indian Defence if you haven't done so already. Of course, you should also give yourself another bonus.

21...h3 (a) is reasonable and scores one point, although Black would prefer to keep the option of plonking a piece on g3 or f4 later. This possibility would be virtually ruled out after 21...h3 22 g3.

Also worth one point is 21...♗d7 (d),

which certainly keeps the white queen out of c6 but it has the drawback of leaving the b7-square unattended after 22 ♘c6.

Deduct one for 21...♕d2 (c) as 22 ♖fd1 pushes you back – 22...♕xc3 23 ♖d3 traps her majesty.

**21...♘h5 22 ♖fd1**

> a) 22...f5
> b) 22...♗d7
> c) 22...♘g3+
> d) 22...♘7f6

Starting at the lowest, 22...♗d7 (b) drops three due to the simple 23 ♕xd7. Next up comes 22...f5 (a), which loses two on account of the strength of 23 ♕c6 ♖a7 24 ♕xd6 ♖f6 25 ♕xc5. Still in negative territory, but less damaging, is 22...♘7f6 (d) for minus one. It should be clear by now that 23 ♕c6 is waiting to happen if Black does not distract White on the kingside.

22...♘g3+ (c) pushes forward and scores three, again with the theme of 23 hxg3 hxg3 24 ♗e1 ♕h4+ 25 ♔g1 ♕h2+ 26 ♔f1 ♕h1 mate. Take a bonus point for seeing that out to the finale.

**22...♘g3+ 23 ♔g1**

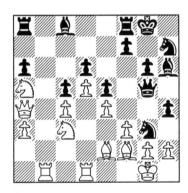

> a) 23...♗h3
> b) 23...h3
> c) 23...♘xe2+
> d) 23...♘h5

Here Hebden missed the powerful

23...♗h3! (a), after which 24 hxg3? hxg3 25 ♗e1 ♕h4 gives Black a devastating attack. Take five points if you saw this, plus a bonus of three for spotting the superior defence 24 ♗xg3 hxg3 25 gxh3 ♕e3+ 26 ♔h1, although Black is still doing well after 26...♕f2 27 hxg3 ♕xg3 28 ♗f1 ♕xf3+ 29 ♗g2 ♕xc3.

23...♘xe2+ (c) was Hebden's preference as he seeks to eliminate an important enemy defender. Take two points for this.

23...h3 (b) proves to be too ambitious after 24 hxg3 and costs you three points.

Maintaining the knight with 23...♘h5 (d) scores nothing unless you realised that you have 24 ♕c6 covered on the strength of 24...♘f4 etc., in which case your score increases by one.

**23...♘xe2+ 24 ♘xe2**

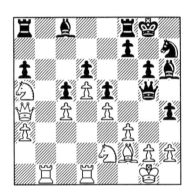

> a) 24...♖a7
> b) 24...♗h3
> c) 24...h3
> d) 24...♖d8

It is incredible how Black can continue to create threats to forestall the white invasion. 24...♗h3 (b) is no exception and scores three points.

One point for 24...♖a7 (a), although 25 ♖b8 leaves Black struggling to hold his queenside together. 24...h3 (c) is also sufficient for one, but nothing for 24...♖d8 (d) which invites 25 ♘c6 and ♖b8.

**24...♗h3 25 g3**

> a) 25...hxg3
> b) 25...♘f6
> c) 25...♖ab8
> d) 25...f5

25...♖ab8 (c) is a timely challenge of the b-file and scores two points. You score an extra one if you reasoned that you have prevented ♖b6 by White. Further justification for Black's last can be found in the following variations, with bonuses given in brackets:

1) 26 ♖xb8 ♖xb8 27 ♘c6 ♖b2 (one point) 28 ♘c1 ♕e3 (one point) 29 ♗xe3 ♗xe3+ 30 ♔h1 ♗g2 mate (one point).

2) 26 ♘c6 ♖xb1 27 ♖xb1 ♕d2 (one point), threatening the knight and further progress with ...♗e3 (one point for both) and ...♘g5 (one point).

3) 26 ♘b7 ♕h5 (one point), threatening f3, ...♘g5 and a potential pin on the b7-knight should White play 27 ♖d3 (one point for everything).

One point for 25...hxg3 (a), but the h4-pawn can prove to be a useful asset in some variations. No score for 25...♘f6 (b) allowing 26 ♘b7 and, if necessary, ♖b6.

25...f5 (d) comes into strong consideration and scores a point, but for those who felt that 26 ♕d7 would be too constrictive and therefore passed over this move, take a well deserved bonus.

**25...♖ab8 26 ♖b3**

> a) 26...♖xb3
> b) 26...hxg3
> c) 26...♗g4
> d) 26...♖be8

26...♖xb3 (a) scores two, while delaying a decision with 26...hxg3 (b) is okay for one.

26...♗g4 (c) 27 fxg4 is as ridiculous and loses three and, finally, giving up the b-file so easily with 26...♖be8 (d) leaves your score static for the time being.

**26...♖xb3 27 ♕xb3**

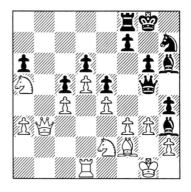

> a) 27...hxg3
> b) 27...f5
> c) 27...♕d8
> d) 27...♔h8

You must have notched up a few points by now if you have been playing ...hxg3. I will again give one for (a), but really there is no need to release the tension.

Hebden prefers to get on with the thematic thrust 27...f5 (b), which scores four points. If you exchanged rooks on move 26, consciously saving your f8-rook to lend weight to ...f7-f5, take a bonus. You either have great foresight or have been studying classic masterpieces of the King's Indian, of which Kasparov is also a great adherent.

One point for 27...♕d8 (c), although instinct alone should rule out such a backward move in this game.

27...♔h8 (d) does nothing to improve Black's position, so nothing for you.

**27...f5 28 exf5**

> a) 28...♖xf5
> b) 28...gxf5
> c) 28...♕xf5
> d) 28...hxg3

Everyone's a winner here, but to different degrees.

One for 28...♖xf5 (a), two for 28...gxf5 (b), and three for 28...♕xf5 (c). However, this time Black has decided that it is high time to open the h-file with 28...hxg3 (d), which scores four. One extra is credited to you if you realised that white must recapture on g3 first before doing anything else.

**28...hxg3 29 hxg3**

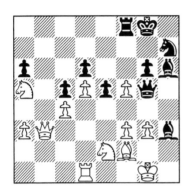

> a) 29...♖xf5
> b) 29...gxf5
> c) 29...♕xf5
> d) 29...♗xf5

Again 29...♖xf5 (a) scores one, 29...gxf5 scores two, and 29...♕xf5 (c) scores three. With 29...♕xf5 you can add one to your total if you realised that f3 is under attack.

29...♗xf5 (d) does not score as it is a backward move that releases some pressure around the white king.

**29...♕xf5 30 ♕d3**

> a) 30...♕xd3
> b) 30...♕xf3
> c) 30...♕d7
> d) 30...e4

Nothing for 30...♕xd3 (a) as 31 ♖xd3 ♘g5 32 f4 is not so clear. The answer is also not found in 30...♕d7 (c) 31 ♕xg6+, which sets you back one.

You can be forgiven for assuming that 30...♕xf3 (b) is a logical conclusion to a carefully controlled build up by Black as he pockets his reward of a pawn. It pockets you three points, especially as White is obliged to exchange queens due to the mate

threat on g2. There is nothing fundamentally wrong with 30...♕xf3, but Hebden wants more...

30...e4 (d) is the star performer for five, with 31 fxe4 out of the equation due to 31...♕xf2+. You score a bonus if you saw that.

**30...e4 31 ♕xe4**

> a) 31...♕xf3
> b) 31...♕xe4
> c) 31...♘f6
> d) 31...♘g5

31...♕xf3 (a) is obviously a worse version of the previous 30...♕xf3, so only one point there.

31...♕xe4 (b) scores four. If you have not worked out what Hebden is up to, then all will be revealed following 31...♕xe4.

Neither 31...♘f6 (c) nor 31...♘g5 (d) are likely to impress the crowds that Hebden thrives on drawing (I don't mean in a sketch book!), so zero for these.

**31...♕xe4 32 fxe4**

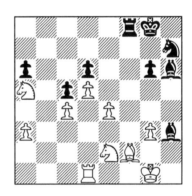

> a) 32...♘g5
> b) 32...♘f6
> c) 32...♗g4
> d) 32...♖e8

32...♘g5 (a) and 32...♘f6 (b) are reasonably active for one and two points respectively. 32...♖e8 (d) is satisfactory for one, but by no means the stunning culmination of Black's recent play.

It is 32...♗g4 (c) that illustrates what Black's play was all about and scores four points. Award yourself two bonuses if you planned this when selecting 30...e4, while you score one if you cottoned on when choosing 31...♕xe4. Look now at how the bishop pair is working in harmony.

**32...♗g4 33 ♘b7**

A bonus point is awarded for those who intended to meet 33 ♖e1 with 33...♗d2.

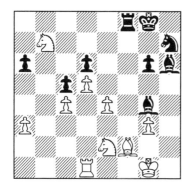

a) 33...♗xe2
b) 33...♘f6
c) 33...♖f6
d) 33...♘g5

33...♘f6 (b) 34 ♘xd6 and 33...♖f6 (c) 34 e5 dxe5 35 d6 give White a glimmer of hope and therefore temporarily stagnate your total.

Don't be hard on yourself if you made the assumption that 33...♗xe2 (a) was a foregone conclusion, and award yourself two points for this. However, 33...♘g5 (d) is most punishing and scores four. 34 ♘xd6 is now met by ...♘h3+ (one point) with disastrous consequences for White.

**33...♘g5 34 ♘f4**

a) 34...♗xd1
b) 34...♘f7
c) 34...♘h3+
d) 34...♘xe4

The hard graft is over and Black need look no further than 34...♗xd1 (a) for three points.

Zilch for 34...♘f7 (b) 35 ♖b1 and minus two for 34...♘h3+ (c) 35 ♘xh3 ♗xh3 36 ♘xd6. I'm sure you will be disappointed for overlooking (a) if you opted for 34...♘xe4 (d), but you can have one point in consolation.

**34...♗xd1 35 ♘xd6**

a) 35...♖d8
b) 35...♖b8
c) 35...♘f7
d) 35...♗b3

35...♖d8 (a) is sufficient is for one point – 36 ♗xc5 ♗f8 could follow. Both 35...♘f7 (c) and 35...♗b3 (d) also score one, although I hope you analysed the capturing sequences 35...♘f7 36 ♘xf7 ♔xf7 37 ♗xc5 ♖c8 and 35...♗b3 36 ♘xg6 ♘h3+ 37 ♔g2 ♘xf2 38 ♘xf8 ♗xf8 39 ♔xf2 ♗xd6.

Typically, the King's Indian stalwart prefers to play actively for mate. 35...♖b8 (b) scores three points.

**35...♖b8 36 ♗xc5**

a) 36...♖b1
b) 36...♖b2
c) 36...♗f8
d) 36...♔h7

Four points for 36...♖b2 (b), which confines the white monarch to the back rank, thus aiding the task of setting up a mate.

36...♖b1 (a) scores one and indirectly defends the g-pawn (37 ♘xg6 ♗h5+). 36...♔h7 (d) is sensible and also scores one, but nothing for 36...♗f8 (c).

**36...♖b2 37 ♗e3**

a) 37...♘f3+
b) 37...♘h3+
c) 37...♗f8
d) 37...♗f3

37...♗f3 (d) restricts the opponent's movements and scores four points. Suddenly there are back rank threats appearing such as 38 e5 ♘h3+ 39 ♔f1 ♖b1+ 40 ♗c1 ♖xc1 mate and 39 ♘xh3 ♗xe3+ 40 ♔f1 ♖b1 mate. Up to two bonus points are available if you were able to back up your decision with either or both of the variations given.

37...♗f8 (c) scores two, with the main lines running 38 e5 ♘f3+ and 38 c5 ♗xd6 39 cxd6 ♗a4, which leaves White's lifeline only temporarily connected.

37...♘f3+ (a) is tempting for one point, especially if you think it's a 50-50 shot at 38 ♔h1 ♖h2 mate! Finally, 37...♘h3+ (b) also nets one, as long as you realised that 38 ♘xh3 is well met by 38...♗xe3+. Nothing for those not aware of any tactics here.

**37...♗f3 38 ♗d4**

> a) 38...♘h3+
> b) 38...♖b1+
> c) 38...♘xe4
> d) 38...♖d2

Liquidating with 38...♘xe4 (c) is worth two points, but this is conditional on you having calculated both 39 ♘xe4 ♖b1+ 40 ♔f2 ♗xe4 and 39 ♗xb2 ♘xd6 40 c5 ♗xf4 41 gxf4 ♘c4 to a satisfactory conclusion. No points here if you did not make any calculations.

Take two for 38...♖b1+ (b) 39 ♔f2 ♘xe4+, although it is the quiet but deadly 38...♖d2 (d) which is worth double that at four points.

This time 38...♘h3+ (a) 39 ♘xh3 holds no regrets for White, so reduce your total by three.

**38...♖d2 39 ♗b6**

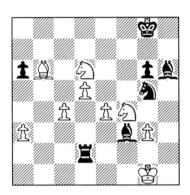

> a) 39...♗g4
> b) 39...♘xe4
> c) 39...♗xe4
> d) 39...♗f8

39...♗g4 (a) entices White to resign and scores four. A bonus point is scored if you have already set your sights on 40...♘f3+ 41 ♔f1 ♗xf4 42 gxf4 ♗h3 mate, which White is hard pushed to delay, let alone prevent.

The materialistic 39...♘xe4 (b) and 39...♗xe4 (c) are both worthy of three, while 39...♗f8 (d) scores two points.

**39...♗g4 40 a4**

White either lost on time or played his move here and was left looking at a hopeless position and so therefore resigned.

It only remains for you to see how you did.

Less than 18: I would have set the minimum target at 18 for all serious chess players so I hope you were not too far short. I bet it is still those blunders that are costing you.

18-31: A proficient performance. Nothing wrong with your chess understanding but do you lack the killer instinct to hunt for the most devastating continuation?

32-45: A strong, solid result. You have come through the maze of calculations with your head held high. An average club player should expect to score in this range.

46-59: You can be delighted with this score as it must have been made up of best or second best moves. The King's Indian Defence must suit your style too.

60+: Amazing precision. Not many players can maintain such control over a position.

# CHAPTER TWO

## Attack is the Best form of Defence

There's nothing like a good old fashioned quote to create a chapter heading!

In this chapter we look at some attacks being defended or repelled. In the first encounter we see our very own British home-grown Grandmaster Michael Adams in action, admittedly swamped in the rest of the chapter by a hoard of Eastern Europeans. This game, along with Game 7, witnesses the player with the black pieces keeping the position tight and sound so that White cannot break down his defences. Later in these games, and in their own way, the tables are turned and Black goes on to win.

Naturally there is a time and a place to defend, but it is pleasing and can often be rewarding if one can distract an opponent from his threats by creating a more powerful one, or a series of menaces, of your own.

In Game 6 and, more particularly, in Game 8, White launches his attack first, only to have to defend against a fiercer attack in return.

It is also certainly true in some endings, that constant passivity will lead downhill to disaster and it's the sudden counterattack that could save the day. The final game of the chapter displays some complications that spill over in to the ending. For much of this game it is not at all obvious which player stands better, as they both do their fair share of attacking. The final result of a draw illustrates that not all games are decisive.

Again I hope you enjoy the variety of openings and remember that sensible moves will be rewarded, as will refuting some of the suggestions given.

## Game 5
## Shirov-Adams
### European Team Championship, Leon 2001

**1 e4 e5 2 ♘f3 ♘f6**

The Petroff is regarded as one of the most solid defences to 1 e4.

**3 ♘xe5 d6 4 ♘f3 ♘xe4 5 ♗d3**

The drawback for the ambitious player of the black pieces is that White can extinguish any life from the position with 5 ♕e2 ♕e7 6 d3 ♘f6 7 ♕xe7+ etc.

**5...♘f6 6 0-0 ♗e7 7 h3 0-0 8 c3 ♖e8 9 ♗c2 b6 10 d4 ♗b7**

Adams finds a nice diagonal for his fianchettoed bishop.

**11 ♗g5 h6 12 ♗h4 ♘e4 13 ♗xe7 ♖xe7 14 ♘bd2**

The symmetrical nature of the pawns makes it hard for either side to achieve any imbalance in the position. Now choose how you think the English Grandmaster continued.

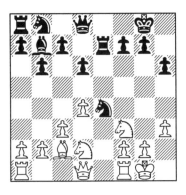

a) 14...♘xd2
b) 14...f5
c) 14...♘f6
d) 14...d5

14...♘xd2 (a) scores two points. Either recapture by White will probably leave Shirov with no alternative but to mentally discard this line from future use as White can hardly claim any opening advantage.

14...f5 (b), 14...♘f6 (c) and 14...d5 (d) are all playable and score one point.

**14...♘xd2 15 ♕xd2**

a) 15...♗e4
b) 15...♗xf3
c) 15...♘d7
d) 15...d5

15...♘d7 (c) scores two as an important developing move, but 15...♗xf3 (b) gets top marks of three points. One has to feel a bit sorry for Shirov because if he had got away with doubling his pawns in such a manner he would have been praised for such a concept. However, since he went on to lose an otherwise equal game up to this point, people wondered what he was playing at to allow his pawn structure to be shattered in such a fashion.

It feels odd to shut in the bishop with 15...d5 (d) for no reason. 16 ♕d3 g6 17 ♖fe1 is clearly extremely comfortable for White, so no points.

The attempt at exchanging bishops with 15...♗e4 (a) 16 ♗xe4 ♖xe4 17 ♖fe1 can have one, but moving the bishop like this loses time for Black.

**15...♗xf3 16 gxf3**

a) 16...♘c6
b) 16...♘d7
c) 16...♕d7
d) 16...♕c8

One point for everything here with the exception of 16...♘d7 (b), which scores two – the knight is heading to lend support to the kingside. If you sensed that this was where the knight belonged or worked out that you may need it to cover the h7-square, award yourself a bonus point.

**16...♘d7 17 ♔h2**

> a) 17...♘f6
> b) 17...♕f8
> c) 17...♖e6
> d) 17...d5

If you have realised that White is intending 18 ♖g1, when he will be threatening to capture on h6 with his queen, have a bonus point. If you are regretting the fact that you opened up the g-file to allow this 'attack', however, take it off again. If you are to progress, you have to learn how to weather the odd storm. Think of your beautiful pawn formation in the long term!

No points for 17...♘f6 (a) which doesn't prove seaworthy after 18 ♖g1 ♔h8 19 ♖g3 19...♕d7 20 ♖ag1 ♖g8 21 ♖xg7 ♖xg7 22 ♕xh6+ ♖h7 23 ♕xf6+ ♖g7 24 ♕xg7 mate. Also potent is 19 ♖xg7 ♔xg7 20 ♖g1+ ♔f8 21 ♕xh6+ ♔e8 22 ♗a4+ ♖d7 23 ♖e1+ ♕e7 24 ♕h8+ ♘g8 25 ♕xg8 mate. 17...d5 (d) also asks for trouble after 18 ♖g1 ♔h8 19 ♖xg7 ♔xg7 20 ♖g1+ ♔f8 21 ♕xh6+ ♔e8 22 ♖g8+ ♘f8 23 ♗a4+ ♖d7 24 ♕xf8 mate. I am not saying these lines are forced but they are very dangerous and best avoided. If you passed over (a) and (d) due to these sacrificial possibilities, you deserve two bonuses.

17...♕f8 (b) nets one point since 18 ♖g1 ♔h8 covers all the sacrifices on g7, but 17...♖e6 (c) gets you three. You score an extra one as long as you appreciated that the f6-square will be a major pivot, from which Black will both defend and attack.

**17...♖e6 18 ♖g1**

> a) 18...♔h8
> b) 18...♕h4
> c) 18...♖e8
> d) 18...♕f6

18...♔h8 (a) defends satisfactorily for two points, but none for 18...♕h4 (b),

which invites White to gain time with ♖g4.

18...♖e8 (c) puts your position in disarray with 19 ♕xh6 and drops two points.

18...♕f6 (d) was the preferred option by Adams and scores three.

**18...♕f6 19 ♖g3**

> a) 19...g6
> b) 19...♔h8
> c) 19...♖ae8
> d) 19...g5

19...g6 (a) could well have been in the picture if the black pawn was still on h7, but given that it is strongly met by 20 ♕xh6, deduct one from your total.

It shows a certain amount of experience to want to get your king off the semi-open g-file with 19...♔h8 (b) – score two for this.

19...♖ae8 (c) must come into consideration. Score two for this, and there is a bonus available if you realised that the black rooks can be held at bay with 20 ♗d3.

Finally, let us consider 19...g5 (d). One should try not to do this to one's king protection as a general rule, but with the specific analysis of 20 f4 backing up that theory here, lose two points.

**19...♔h8 20 ♖ag1**

> a) 20...c5
> b) 20...♖ae8
> c) 20...♖g8
> d) 20...h5

One of the hardest types of judgements in chess is whether two rooks or a queen are likely to be stronger. So, the critical question here is whether 21 ♖xg7 ♕xg7 22 ♖xg7 ♔xg7 is a threat or not. Adams certainly made the effort to prevent it, so three points for 20...♖g8 (c). Both 20...c5 (a) and 20...♖ae8 (b) both fail to score, while 20...h5 (d) loses one point on account of 21 ♖xg7 ♕xg7 22 ♖xg7 ♔xg7 23 ♗f5 ♖e7 24 ♕g5+.

**20...♖g8 21 f4**

> a) 21...♖e7
> b) 21...♕e7
> c) 21...a5
> d) 21...g5

With 21...♖e7 (a) Black is still strengthening his position and ruling out any future attacks on his rook. Score two points for this and one apiece for 21...♕e7 (b) and 21...a5 (c).

21...g5 (d) is still out of the question, not least because of 22 fxg5 hxg5 23 ♖xg5 ♖xg5 24 ♖xg5. Deduct two if you chose this.

**21...♖e7 22 ♕d3**

> a) 22...♕xf4
> b) 22...g5
> c) 22...♘f8
> d) 22...g6

I am reminded of Monopoly when you are sent to jail and cannot collect the £200. Your punishment for 22...♕xf4 (a) or 22...g5 (b), both falling for 23 ♕h7 mate, is to return to zero. If you had not moved into positive territory anyway, count yourself lucky. If you are actually sniggering because you are on a minus score and expect now to promote yourself to zero, deduct a further five and set your new overall target at zero.

Two points' credit goes to 22...♘f8 (c) as Black's position is as safe as houses. Adams will now turn his attention to chipping away at his opponent's weaknesses.

I'm afraid that 22...g6 (d) shouldn't score.

It invites White to play for f4-f5 and is unfair to Adams' carefully constructed defence – he has been so diligent at avoiding any weakening pawn moves on his kingside. However, if you are still with me, to ease my feelings of perhaps being too harsh, I will award one point for preventing the mate on h7.

**22...♘f8 23 ♕f3**

> a) 23...c5
> b) 23...d5
> c) 23...♘e6
> d) 23...♘g6

Two points for 23...c5 (a), which sees the start of Black's counterplay. Now Shirov has to decide whether to limit the scope of the black knight (and his own bishop!) with d4-d5, or to exchange on c5, allowing knight use of the e6-square.

23...d5 (b) and 23...♘e6 (c) are reasonable for one point. However, you needed to have calculated that 23...d5 24 ♕xd5 allows Black to regain the pawn with 24...♕xf4.

23...♘g6 (d) is the only mistake on offer here. The sequence 24 ♗xg6 fxg6 25 ♖xg6 costs you one point.

**23...c5 24 d5**

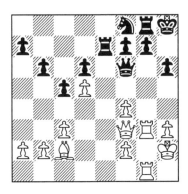

> a) 24...c4
> b) 24...b5
> c) 24...a6
> d) 24...♘h7

Expanding on the queenside with 24...b5 (b) is worth two points. The alternatives score one, although I am not sure where you are heading with 24...♘h7 (d).

**24...b5 25 ♖1g2**

a) 25...a6
b) 25...♘d7
c) 25...♖e1
d) 25...♖b7

25...a6 (a) is safe for one point. Also take one for 25...♘d7 (b), as long as you realised that 26 ♕d3 is still on the cards.

25...♖e1 (c) scores one as it asks White what he is up to, but nothing for vacating the open e-file with 25...♖b7 (d).

**25...♖e1 26 ♖g1**

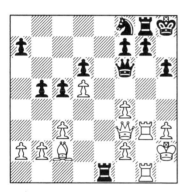

a) 26...♖xg1
b) 26...♕e7
c) 26...♖e7
d) 26...♖e8

It is quite normal for grandmasters to allow one repetition and then try something else. 26...♖e7 (c) adds two to your score, while the other three options gain a respectable one.

**26...♖e7 27 a3**

a) 27...♖e8
b) 27...c4
c) 27...a6
d) 27...♕h4

Three points for 27...c4 (b), a move which cleverly takes the possibility of ♕d3 out of the equation, thus releasing the knight from his duties at f8.

Protecting the potentially loose b-pawn with 27...a6 (c) is okay for one, as is 27...♕h4 (d).

Black is not short of a plan and therefore does not have to resort to waiting with 27...♖e8 (a) – no points for this.

**27...c4 28 ♕g4**

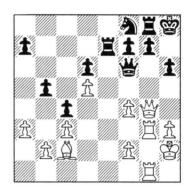

a) 28...h5
b) 28...g6
c) 28...♘d7
d) 28...♖c7

I hope no one chose 28...h5 (a). If you did, go back to zero. This choice was really put in to highlight the pretty mate after 29 ♕xh5+ ♕h6 30 ♕xh6+ gxh6 31 ♖xg8 mate.

28...♘d7 (c) raises your credit by two, but nothing for 28...♖c7 (d). I still mistrust 28...g6 (b) on account of 29 f5, so no score there.

**28...♘d7 29 a4**

a) 29...bxa4
b) 29...a6
c) 29...♖b8
d) 29...♘e5

There is no reason (and therefore no points awarded) to exchange pawns here with 29...bxa4 (a) 30 ♗xa4, which deprives the black c-pawn of back up. 29...a6 (b) is the most logical response to keep the pawn chain intact – score two for this.

Lose one for 29...♖b8 (c). This may be designed to save the b-pawn but unfortunately deserts the g7-pawn. I am not accusing you of simply chucking a piece with 29...♘e5 (d), but after 30 fxe5 ♕xf2+ 31 ♖1g2 that is what it amounts to (lose two points).

**29...a6 30 a5**

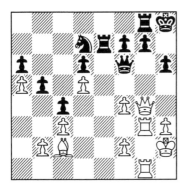

a) 30...♘c5
b) 30...g6
c) 30...♖ee8
d) 30...♖ge8

I don't like repeating myself too much, but as it is the first time this saying has surfaced during this encounter, please forgive me for pointing out that 'the pawns tell the pieces where to go'. If that black knight could speak, don't you think he would be asking his master for a great view on c5? Take two points for 30...♘c5 (a).

30...g6 (b) can have one point since White will not be so tempted by 31 f5 if the black knight is immediately going to jump into e5.

30...♖ee8 (c) and 30...♖ge8 (d) both slip up in their own way and drop two points. Make sure you work out why before moving on.

**30...♘c5 31 ♖e3**

a) 31...♖xe3
b) 31...♖ge8
c) 31...♘b3
d) 31...♘b7

31...♘b3 (c) automatically nets two as the text move, although the next few steps do indicate that it may not have been best. Both 31...♖xe3 (a) and 31...♘b7 (d) are worth one.

Although 31...♖ge8 (b) is perhaps a natural response, you lose five for not pursuing every check and capture to the end of the variations. If you had, you would have discovered that 31...♖ge8 32 ♖xe7 ♖xe7 33 ♕c8+ is highly embarrassing, as is 32...♕xe7 33 ♕xg7 mate.

**31...♘b3 32 ♖ge1**

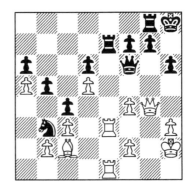

a) 32...♖xe3
b) 32...♖c7
c) 32...♖b7
d) 32...b4

Only one move is going to move you in the right direction here and that is 32...♖xe3 (a). Take two points for this.

Scrambling around with 32...♖c7 (b) and 32...♖b7 (c) 33 ♖e8 ♘xa5 34 ♖xg8+ ♔xg8 35 ♕c8+ is asking for trouble. Black cannot afford to give up the e-file for nothing. No points for 32...♖c7 and lose one for 32...♖b7.

Don't forget to give some respect to your opponent's previous move and at least ask yourself if he is up to anything. In this case he is after your rook on e7 so diminish your running total by five if you went for 32...b4 (d).

**32...&xe3 33 fxe3**

White has successfully rid himself of the doubled pawns but it is a bit draughty around his king.

> a) 33...&e8
> b) 33...&xa5
> c) 33...&c5
> d) 33...g6

One point for 33...&e8 (a), but if you rejected it because you did not relish facing 34 &d7, take a bonus.

33...&xa5 (b) is logical and scores one, but again award yourself a bonus if you are looking ahead and saw that in response White has 34 e4 (with the idea of a later e4-e5) or indeed the immediate 34 &a1, when Black will be hard pushed to hang onto his a6-pawn.

Retreating with 33...&c5 (c) maximises Black's position and your score by two.

33...g6 (d) keeps you static as 34 &xb3 cxb3 35 &d1 is fine for White.

**33...&c5 34 h4**

> a) 34...&b7
> b) 34...&b3
> c) 34...&d3
> d) 34...&e8

34...&b7 (a), in order to threaten the a-pawn which Adams has just rejected, does not score. Neither does returning the knight to b3.

34...&d3 (c) shows a willingness to try and push forward but must lose a point on the basis of 35 &xd3 cxd3 36 &d1.

Now that White cannot infiltrate with &d7, it is time to activate the rest of the forces with 34...&e8 (d) – score two points for this.

**34...&e8 35 &g1**

I would not be surprised if you suspected this of being a typing error. Take a bonus point if you then worked out that the e3-pawn is indirectly defended by 35...&xe3 36 &c8+. If you had already decided on 35...&xe3, deduct five but have another go too.

> a) 35...&d3
> b) 35...&xe3
> c) 35...&b7
> d) 35...&d8

This time the knight springboards from its post at c5 to 35...&d3 (a) for two points.

35...&xe3 (b) 36 &c8+ leading to mate means no more points from now on as this trick has been pointed out enough if you were to read the notes.

We know that the game is not revolving round the a5-pawn, so no points for 35...&b7 (c) 36 e4 &xa5 37 &a1. Eyeing up the a5-pawn with 35...&d8 (d) is far more regrettable, however, due to 36 &xg7 mate. Take off five.

**35...&d3 36 &xd3**

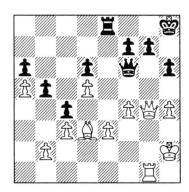

> a) 36...cxd3
> b) 36...&xe3

One point for 36...cxd3, but we all know what happens after the move 36...&xe3 (b) by now.

**36...cxd3 37 &g3**

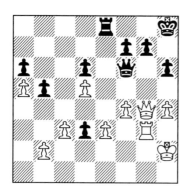

a) 37...d2
b) 37...♔g8
c) 37...♖e4
d) 37...b4

37...d2 (a) is a major consideration but the position is not without drawing chances for White after 38 ♕d1 ♕xh4+ 39 ♔g2 (score two points). Both 37...♔g8 (b) and 37...♖e4 (c) score one.

Incredibly, it is this inoffensive looking 37...b4 (b) which proved to be the breaking point for White. Take three points for starters and get ready to see your calculations in action.

**37...b4 38 cxb4**

a) 38...d2
b) 38...♕xb2+
c) 38...♖c8
d) 38...♖b8

Take two points for 38...♕xb2+ (b). This is clearly the reason for prising open the diagonal.

38...d2 (a) earns one, but the simplifying line 39 ♕d1 ♕xb2 40 ♖g2 ♖xe3 41 ♕xd2 ♕xd2 42 ♖xd2 ♖b3 43 ♖d4 should be (and was) avoided by Adams.

It may be the only open file on the board but without a rook to occupy it... Unfortunately, 38...♖c8 (c) loses five points to 39 ♕xc8+.

Finally, take one point for 38...♖b8 (d).

**38...♕xb2+ 39 ♖g2**

a) 39...♕xb4
b) 39...♕c1
c) 39...♕c3
d) 39...d2

It may be time to go routing the white pawns but the enemy queen has been waiting to perform her 'kiss of death'. If you fell for 39...♕xb4 (a) 40 ♕xg7 mate, divide your score by two, and if you are left with something and a half, then round up to the nearest digit. 39...♕c1 (b) 40 ♕xg7 mate suffers the same fate as in (a), but here you have to round it down to the nearest whole number.

39...♕c3 (c) increases your score by two and 39...d2 (d), by one. If you dismissed 39...d2 because you suspected 40 ♕e2 ♕xb4 41 ♕xd2 ♕xd2 42 ♖xd2 ♖xe3 43 ♖c2 to be drawish you deserve an extra point.

**39...♕c3 40 ♕d7**

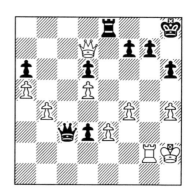

a) 40...♖xe3
b) 40...d2
c) 40...♖g8
d) 40...♖c8

Score one for 40...♖xe3 (a), but if you realised that White would get some counterplay with 41 ♕xf7 you can have a bonus. Indeed, the potential checks on f8, f5 and c8, and the mate threat on g7, all of which keep Black fully occupied, should in fact have led you to search for a different variation to aid Black to victory.

40...d2 (b) 41 ♕xe8+ just goes to show that you must stay alert. That costs you five points.

It is poignant that in the early stages of the game Black bolstered his defences with ...♖g8. A repeat with 40...♖g8 (c) notches up three here.

Finally, 40...♖c8 (d) earns one for being relatively harmless.

**40...♖g8 41 ♕g4**

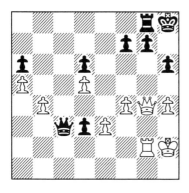

> a) 41...d2
> b) 41...♕xb4
> c) 41...♕c4
> d) 41...♕e1

41...d2 (a) 42 ♕e2 rounds up the pawn in favourable circumstances for White, so no score there.

41...♕xb4 (b) no doubt leaves Black bet-ter after, for example, 42 ♕f5 d2 43 ♕d3 ♕xa5 44 ♕xd2 – you net two points for this move.

41...♕c4 (c) is sufficient for one point, although 42 ♕f5 is annoyingly resilient here.

41...♕e1 (d) is the star move for three. Note how the queen hits b4, e3, h4 and supports d2 with her powerful web.

**41...♕e1 42 f5**

> a) 42...f6
> b) 42...g6
> c) 42...♕xe3
> d) 42...d2

No score for the insipid 42...f6 (a), when White can breathe a sigh of relief with 43 ♕d4. Also not good is 42...g6 (b) as the diagonal is opened for 43 ♕d4+. Drop two for this.

42...♕xe3 (c) 43 f6 g6 is okay for two points, but 42...d2 (d) forced resignation and is worth three points. Take a bonus if you had 43 f6 under control and planned the response 43...g6. Those who planned to push on after 43 f6 with 43...d1♕, allowing 44 fxg7+ ♔h7 45 ♕f5 mate, had better deduct one.

Last but not least, go to the position after 42...d2 43 f6 g6 44 ♖g1 and there is a final point for those who found 44...♖e8 as the most decisive continuation. 45 ♕d7 ♕xg1+ 46 ♔xg1 d1♕+ makes for an amusing finish.

**42...d2 0-1**

You can read the comments below to complete this game.

Less than 20: Watch out for those pitfalls!

20-34: Not bad, but have a go at analysing a bit deeper for a few of those bonus points.

35-49: You saw deep into the position to get this highly respectable score. A formidable club player.

50-59: You handled the variations superbly. A realistic score for a strong county or regional player.

60+: Your national chess team could be your next port of call, unless you achieved this result with the aid of any electronic friend.

## Game 6
## **Ki.Georgiev-Smirin**
### Elenite 1994

**1 d4 ♘f6 2 c4 g6 3 ♘c3 ♗g7 4 e4 d6 5 f3 ♘c6 6 ♘ge2 a6 7 ♗g5 ♖b8 8 ♖c1 ♗d7 9 ♕d2 h5**

Black takes the sting out of ♗h6. Also seen in tournament practice is 9...h6 10 ♗e3 h5 11 d5 ♘e5 12 ♘d4 c5 13 dxc6 bxc6 14 ♗e2 with a slight opening edge to White.

**10 h4 0-0 11 ♘d5 b5 12 c5 ♖e8 13 g3**

White goes for a kingside fianchetto because the normal ♘g3 leaves d4 too loose.

**13...a5 14 cxd6 cxd6 15 ♘xf6+ exf6 16 ♗e3**

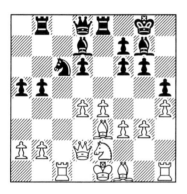

Now take over the black pieces and choose your next move...

a) 16...d5
b) 16...f5
c) 16...♖c8
d) 16...a4

Three points for 16...f5 (b), which allows the black bishop on g7 to see the light of day again and is also a thematic challenge on the centre.

16...d5 (a) is an effective strike in the centre for two points. Although White goes a pawn ahead after 17 exd5, Black can round it up with 17...♘e7 18 ♘c3 b4 or 18 ♘f4

♗f5 etc. White is better off, however, just completing his development with 17 ♗g2.

16...♖c8 (c) and 16...a4 (d) both score one as sensible alternatives.

**16...f5 17 ♗g2**

a) 17...d5
b) 17...fxe4
c) 17...♕f6
d) 17...♗e6

17...fxe4 (b) breaks up the continuity of the white pawn structure and scores two points. You can have one for 17...d5 (a), but it allows White to keep his formidable centre with 18 e5 f6 19 f4. The final two options, however, are outright blunders. Drop three for 17...♕f6 (c), due to 18 ♗g5 ♕e6 19 d5, and four for the even more obvious 17...♗e6 (d) 18 d5. Award yourself a bonus point for rejecting each of these for the tactical reasons given.

**17...fxe4 18 fxe4**

a) 18...♖c8
b) 18...f5
c) 18...♗g4
d) 18...♕b6

18...f5 (b) was the move chosen by Smirin, who has great understanding of the King's Indian. He is still stubbornly chipping away at the white centre. You must feel pretty smug if you have been playing like the grandmaster and you can increase your score by two.

You are totally forgiven for rejecting 18...f5 due to 19 exf5, which appears to win material due to the loose knight on c6. These are the type of ideas that stand a grandmaster in a class above the rest. Rest assured that all will be revealed...

18...♖c8 (a) is likely to prove useful so take two points for good judgement. The variation 19 0-0 f5 20 ♘c3, however, is slightly better for White.

Two more points are at stake if you noticed that the last two choices are blunders (one for each reason you spotted). 18...♗g4 (c) falls foul of 19 ♖xc6 and loses three points from your score as well as over the board. Likewise, 18...♕b6 (d) 19 d5 ♕b7 20 dxc6 ♗xc6 drops two.

**18...f5 19 exf5**

a) 19...♗xf5
b) 19...gxf5
c) 19...♖c8
d) 19...d5

Only one move scores above zero here. Don't worry if you found the answer by process of elimination – players have to resort to that over the chess board on occasion.

If you recaptured the pawn with 19...♗xf5 (a), diminish your score by four as I have already alerted you to 20 ♖xc6. The other recapture, 19...gxf5 (b), also sets you back by four on account of 20 ♗xc6. The move 19...d5 (d) is even worse than the rest, so five off for not working out 20 ♗xd5+ ♔h8 21 ♗xc6.

19...♖c8 (c) is the way forward and earns two points. Take a bonus point if you realised that Black has pressure down the e-file.

**19...♖c8 20 0-0**

You could say that Smirin was bluffing to some extent as it is not clear if Black has enough compensation after 20 fxg6 ♘b4 21 0-0 ♕e7 22 ♖xc8 ♗xc8 23 ♔f2. It's always difficult to judge over the board, however.

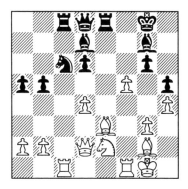

a) 20...♗xf5
b) 20...gxf5
c) 20...♕e7
d) 20...♖xe3

Black has been relying on his initiative and 20...♕e7 (c) keeps it going – score three points for this.

You must still watch your knight on c6, so it's minus three if you went for 20...♗xf5 (a).

It doesn't look pleasant to have a pawn structure like the one after 20...gxf5 (b), but you can have one point as it balances material.

Take off two for 20...♖xe3 (d), which is a bit drastic and leads nowhere after 21 ♕xe3 gxf5 22 ♔h1.

**20...♕e7 21 ♗d5 +**

a) 21...♔f8
b) 21...♔h8
c) 21...♔h7
d) 21...♗e6

21...♔h8 (b) is the safest move and is worth one point.

On basic principles, one doesn't want to

have a king lined up against an enemy rook, so 21...♔f8 (a) drops four. On analysis, it also looks decidedly risky after 22 fxg6+ ♗f6 23 ♗h6+.

21...♔h7 (c) should be rejected as it allows White to capture on g6 with check. This time lose two.

21...♗e6 (d) drop six points (that assumes you have that many in the bag; if not, go into negative numbers) and is a particularly strange way to get out of check. This should only be used if you are trying to completely confuse your opponent during a blitz or lightning game of chess. Even then, White's reaction would quickly turn into one of joy. 22 ♗xe6+ is not that hard to find.

**21...♔h8 22 ♖f3**

For those wanting deep answers to this complicated game, this is a critical stage of the game and where White misses an opportunity with 22 ♔f2.

> a) 22...♗xf5
> b) 22...♘b4
> c) 22...gxf5
> d) 22...♗h6

There is a problem with 22...♗xf5 (a), which scores minus three. You may have planned to meet 23 ♗xc6 with 23...♖xc6 24 ♖xc6 ♗e4, in which case you can have one point back. The solution for White is 23 ♖xc6. You can have another point if you saw that but did not know what to do about it. You lose one more if you did not realise that your knight was a write off here.

22...♗h6 (d) earns one if you intended to meet 23 ♗xh6 with 23...♕xe2 and 23 f6 with 23...♗xe3+. Having said that, if you felt uneasy about giving up your dark-squared bishop award yourself a bonus point (sorry, that does not include those who opted for 22...♗h6 because you clearly did not feel uneasy enough!) and take two more if you saw that 23 ♗xh6 ♕xe2 24 ♕g5 verges on the suicidal for the defence-

less black king.

22...gxf5 (c) scores one for the materialist, but it is the active 22...♘b4 (b) that scores maximum marks of three.

**22...♘b4 23 ♖xc8**

> a) 23...♗xc8
> b) 23...♖xc8
> c) 23...♗xd4
> d) 23...♘xd5

23...♗xc8 (a) is the most natural way to recapture and scores two points. Two also for 23...♖xc8 (b), which takes some pressure off the e-file but creates some play down the c-file. There is a bonus point available for those avid readers who analysed 23...♖xc8 24 ♗g5 ♖c2 25 ♕xc2 ♘xc2 26 ♗xe7 and then decided that 23...♗xc8 was preferable.

There is no doubt that Black must recapture the rook so the superfluous 23...♗xd4 (c) drops five and the less damaging 23...♘xd5 (d) 24 ♖xe8+ ♕xe8 drops two from your score.

**23...♗xc8 24 ♘f4**

Or 24 f6 ♗xf6 25 ♘f4 ♕g7 26 a3 ♘xd5 27 ♘xd5 ♗d8 and Black's position holds together well.

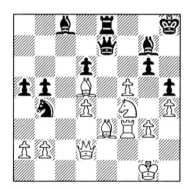

> a) 24...♘xd5
> b) 24...♘xa2
> c) 24...gxf5
> d) 24...♗xf5

The real key here was to be aware that White is not only defending the bishop on d5 with his last move but it also hits g6 and threatens to fork the black king and queen. Therefore the first three moves that do nothing to combat the threat lose material and points in different degrees.

24...♘xd5 (a) loses three points on account of 25 ♘xg6+ ♚h7 26 ♘xe7 ♖xe7.

It is certainly not the time to go pawn grabbing with 24...♘xa2 (b), especially when the bishop on d5 is protecting that one. This brings a whole new meaning to the phrase 'double blunder'. Lose eight for this.

24...gxf5 (c) 25 ♘g6+ drops six, leaving 24...♗xf5 (d) as the star move that increases your score by one. Perhaps not a fantastic reward for having avoided all the pitfalls, but I bet you have been dying to get that pawn back for the last five moves.

**24...♗xf5 25 ♗e6**

Now we see White being flashy. 25 ♗f2 is more stable.

> a) 25...♗xe6
> b) 25...♕xe6
> c) 25...♕b7
> d) 25...♕f6

The bishop is immune from capture, so minus four if you thought 25...♗xe6 (a) 26 ♘xg6+ ♚g8 27 ♘xe7+ ♖xe7 was the answer. It is best to smell a rat and be suspicious if your opponent offers a free piece, especially if they are ranked so high in the world.

White's 25th move was not so powerful that Black has to give up his queen here with the line 25...♕xe6 (b) 26 ♘xe6 ♗xe6, so drop three if you resorted to this defence.

25...♕b7 (c) makes excellent use of the diagonal which has just been vacated by the white bishop and scores three.

Drop one point for 25...♕f6 (d) on account of 26 ♘xg6+!.

**25...♕b7 26 ♕g2**

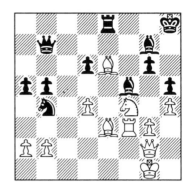

> a) 26...♗xe6
> b) 26...♖xe6
> c) 26...♗g4
> d) 26...♗e4

There is a tempting array here for Black. 26...♗xe6 (a) scores one, with two bonus points dependant on you having calculated the variation 27 ♘xe6 ♖xe6 28 ♖f8+ ♗xf8 29 ♕xb7 ♖xe3 and judging that Black is okay in the final position.

26...♖xe6 (b) collects one point, but only if you intended to answer 27 ♘xe6 with 27...♗e4! (27...♗xe6 28 ♖f8+ ♗xf8 29 ♕xb7 drops one since in this line Black collects a lot less material for the queen).

26...♗g4 (c) is worth two, and the forcing variation 27 ♗xg4 hxg4 28 ♖f1 ♕xg2+ 29 ♘xg2 ♖xe3 30 ♘xe3 ♗xd4 31 ♚f2 ♘c2 reveals that Black is better here. Take two bonus points if you saw this line to the end, whether or not you chose to go with 26...♗g4.

Top marks of three points go to 26...♗e4 (d), which was favoured by the grandmaster.

**26...♗e4 27 ♚f2**

> a) 27...♖xe6
> b) 27...d5
> c) 27...♘d3+
> d) 27...♗xf3

27...♖xe6 (a) scores one. Then 28 ♘xe6 ♗xf3 29 ♕xf3 ♘d3+ (score one more if you saw this) 30 ♔e2 ♕xf3+ 31 ♔xf3 ♘xb2 leaves Black a pawn ahead, but with the white king actively placed it is not a trivial win.

27...d5 (b) scores one, although it rather lets White off the hook and invites counter-play with 28 g4.

27...♘d3+ (c) is likely to transpose to the notes to (d) and scores two points.

27...♗xf3 (d) 28 ♕xf3 ♘d3+ 29 ♘xd3 ♕xf3+ 30 ♔xf3 ♖xe6 liquidates efficiently for two points.

**27...♘d3+ 28 ♘xd3**

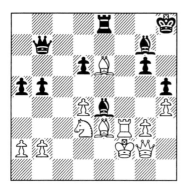

a) 28...♗xd3
b) 28...♗xf3
c) 28...♖xe6
d) 28...♖f8

28...♗xd3 (a) enables White to breathe a sigh of relief with 29 ♕h3, but you can have one point for this. Award yourself a bonus point if you checked out 29 ♖f8+ with the idea of seizing the queen on b7, only to realise that that 29...♖xf8+ is the embarrassing consequence.

Smirin now simplifies into the ending an exchange (rook for minor piece) ahead as in the note to choice 'd' of Black's 27th moves. If you chose 28...♗xf3 (b) or 28...♖xe6 (c) to be the most precise form of action, then you can increase your score by three.

28...♖f8 (d) drops three as White escapes

with 29 ♖xf8+ ♗xf8 30 ♕f1.

**28...♗xf3 29 ♕xf3**

a) 29...♕xf3+
b) 29...♖f8
c) 29...♕e7
d) 29...♖xe6

I have indicated enough times that Black is heading for the ending so there's no reason not to exchange queens with the obvious 29...♕xf3+ (a) to score one point.

29...♖f8 (b) does not win the queen due to 30 ♘f4, so lose three if you thought it did. The same penalty is apportioned for 29...♕e7 (c) which is well countered by 30 ♘f4. The move 29...♖xe6 (d), on the other hand, is punished more severely with minus seven since 30 ♕xb7 will take the tension out of the position.

**29...♕xf3+ 30 ♔xf3**

a) 30...♖f8+
b) 30...♖xe6
c) 30...♖c8
d) 30...♗f6

While the reader may have to ponder over four respectable-looking moves on occasions and make a difficult decision, this should not be one of them. Only 30...♖xe6 (b) scores one point. The others will be ignored.

**30...♖xe6 31 ♘f4**

a) 31...♖e7
b) 31...♖e8
c) 31...♖f6
d) 31...♖xe3+

Again, this selection should not be tempting beyond 31...♖f6 (c) since the g-pawn needs defending. Score one point for this move. However, rather than ignoring the rest, this time they deflate your score in proportion with the harm they inflict on your position. 31...♖e7 (a) drops six due to 32 ♘xg6+, 31...♖e8 (b) 32 ♘xg6+ drops just one, and finally 31...♖xe3+ (d) 32 ♔xe3 loses two.

**31...♖f6 32 ♔e4**

> a) 32...♗h6
> b) 32...♔h7
> c) 32...♔g8
> d) 32...♖f8

Black needs to activate his king in the ending as a priority. 32...♔h7 (b) scores one, but it is 32...♔g8 (c) which takes the king in the right direction and nets two points.

32...♗h6 (a) can have two points as it ties White down, as long as you planned to then bring your king out. If you did not think ahead, then just add one to your score.

It would be a shame not to keep you on your toes, so 32...♖f8 (d) 33 ♘xg6+ is the blunder to avoid. Those who stumbled on that one, take off three.

**32...♔g8 33 b3**

> a) 33...♔f8
> b) 33...♔f7
> c) 33...♗h6
> d) 33...a4

Both 33...♔f8 (a) and 33...♔f7 (b) score one, although it is clear that White has some activity with 34 ♔d5. Score one bonus if you are already calculating any king and pawn endings in case pieces are exchanged.

33...♗h6 (c) is a classic case of how the minor pieces might come off the board. Take two for this manoeuvre and one if you predicted that 34 ♘d5 is met by 34...♖e6+. Meanwhile, take one point for the more docile 33...a4 (d).

**33...♗h6 34 a4**

> a) 34...b4
> b) 34...bxa4
> c) 34...♗xf4
> d) 34...♖f8

34...b4 (a) scores one point, but Smirin preferred to create an extra open file for his rook with 34...bxa4 (b) – take two for this.

It is unnecessary to allow White the best positioning of his pieces with 34...♗xf4 (c) 35 ♗xf4 bxa4 36 bxa4 ♔f7 37 ♔d5 and this option scores zero.

34...♖f8 (d) is possible if you are tired of having your most valuable piece stuck in a defensive role. Since you presumably calculated that 35 ♘xg6 fails to 35...♖e8+ and 35 axb5 ♖b8 is also fine for Black you can have one point. If you rejected this on the other hand because of 35 ♔d5 with the idea of ♗d2, then present yourself with two bonus points. I suspect that I might be studying a book of yours in my old age...

**35...bxa4 35 bxa4**

> a) 35...♗xf4
> b) 35...♔f7
> c) 35...♔g7
> d) 35...g5

Who said that there was less analysing to do in endings? It is not true.

35...♔f7 (b) is both natural and sound here for three points. White can threaten to round up a pawn with 36 ♗d2 ♖f5 37 d5, but after 37...♖e5+ (this is worth a bonus point if seen in conjunction with 35...♔f7) 38 ♔d4 ♗xf4 39 ♗xf4 (39 gxf4 ♖e2 40 ♗xa5 ♖a2 also regains the pawn) 39...♖e1 40 ♗xd6 (or 40 ♔c4 ♔e7 41 ♔b5 ♖d1 keeps the pawns level) Black's rook is able to stamp its authority over the bishop and snaffle one back with 40...♖a1, leaving a relatively trivial ending.

Other options are less good. 35...♗xf4 (a) receives the same lack of points and enthusiasm as in the last round of comments. 35...♔g7 (c) is unnaturally slow and could fall foul of a bishop check or even a knight check (nil points). 35...g5 (d) runs into 36 ♘d5 ♖e6+ 37 ♔f5 so again no points.

**35...♔f7 36 d5**

a) 36...♔e7
b) 36...♗xf4
c) 36...♖f5
d) 36...g5

Smirin decided it was time to relieve the pressure on the g6-pawn with 36...♗xf4 (b). It can't be bad to agree with a grandmaster so add three to your score.

36...♖f5 (c) is fine for one point, but 36...♔e7 (a) 37 ♗d4 is not easy to meet and therefore fails to score, while 36...g5 (d) drops one on account of 37 ♘xh5.

**36...♗xf4 37 ♗xf4**

a) 37...♔e7
b) 37...♔e8
c) 37...♔g7
d) 37...♖f5

The move 37...♔g7 (c) is heading in the wrong direction and does nothing to meet a white invasion commencing with 38 ♔d4 to c4 to b5. You score nothing here. Even in time trouble there is no excuse for 37...♔e7 (a), which drops two points due to the reply 38 ♗g5 pinning the rook. 37...♔e8 (b) is the correct route for the monarch to take and scores three.

37...♖f5 (d) is has no point and does not score either.

**37...♔e8 38 ♔d4**

a) 38...♔d8
b) 38...♔e7
c) 38...♔d7
d) 38...♖f7

Again Black's king should be careful

when treading on black squares and so alarm bells should ring at 38...♔d8 (a), which costs you five hard earned points and the game after 39 ♗g5 ♔e7 40 ♔c4 ♔f7 41 ♗xf6 ♔xf6 42 ♔b5 ♔f5 43 ♔xa5 etc. Note that White wins even more quickly after 42...♔e5 43 ♔c6, but please take care to avoid 42...♔f5 43 ♔c6 ♔e5, which is instructive on how to go wrong.

If you chose 38...♔e7 (b) you must dock four points as this mistake was highlighted in the previous notes. I may be slightly unfair as I believe the king and pawn ending after 39 ♗g5 ♔f7 40 ♗xf6 ♔xf6 41 ♔e4 g5 or 41 ♔c4 ♔e5 is still better for Black, but that is down to good fortune. If you opted for 38...♔e7 and claim to have worked out the king and pawn ending to a win for Black in all lines, then sorry, I don't believe you.

It is often difficult to adjust from a wild opening and middlegame to a delicate ending but you are doing a good job if you went for 38...♔d7 (c) and plan to meet 39 ♗d2 with 39...♖f3. Take two points for this.

The careless 38...♖f7 (d) costs you one point on account of 39 ♗xd6.

**38...♔d7 39 ♔c4**

a) 39...♔c7
b) 39...♔c8
c) 39...♖f8
d) 39...♖f5

While White has his eye on the a5-pawn,

you have done well if you intend to pick off the d5-pawn in return. There are several ways to go about it, however.

39...♔c7 (a) 40 ♔b5 ♖f5 is worth one point, as is 39...♔c8 (b) 40 ♔b5 ♔c7 41 ♔xa5 ♖f5. It must be a relief to finally bring the rook swinging round to the queenside, so two points if you opted for 39...♖f8 (c) with the intention of 40 ♔b5 ♖c8 41 ♔xa5 ♖c5+. Just the one point is awarded if there was no plan in mind.

Finally, 39...♖f5 (d) is the most accurate for three points as it ties White down. Again, 40 ♗d2 ♖f3 41 ♗xa5 ♖xg3 is the end of the road for White.

**39...♖f5 40 ♔d4**

> a) 40...♔c7
> b) 40...♔c8
> c) 40...♖f8
> d) 40...♖f6

White is running out of decent moves here.

Take one point for 40...♔c7 (a) and one for the slightly repetitive 40...♖f6 (d), but 40...♔c8 (b) is a relapse that drops the d-pawn and a point.

It is 40...♖f8 (c) that is crying out to be played – take three points for this. Finally the extra material is about to make a difference in a more obvious manner.

**40...♖f8 41 ♔d3**

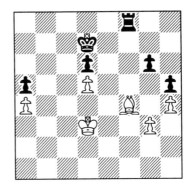

> a) 41...♖f5
> b) 41...♖e8
> c) 41...♖b8
> d) 41...♔e7

All moves are destined to score here. 41...♖f5 (a) earns one point as I'm sure you are just toying with your opponent rather than repeating the position. 41...♖e8 (b) also gets one, as does 41...♔e7 (d).

41...♖b8 (c) really clinches the game and three points. The resignation is in no way premature since the threat is 42...♖b4, and 42 ♗d2 is met by 42...♖b3+ 43 ♗c3 ♖a3. Take one extra bonus point if you had this worked out to the end.

**41...♖b8 0-1**

Now compare your total with the descriptions below, which I hope are of some use.

Less than 14: You would probably prefer a quieter style of game.

15-29: I guess this game was a bit frustrating. Only attempt to get your head round a tactical battle if you have the time to check out the complications. Otherwise, it is easy to come unstuck.

30-44: You must have intermingled many sound ideas with a few mistakes. Avoid the blunders and you will improve drastically.

45-59: You can be pleased with this result. You are a real player so I hope a club has the benefit of your talent.

60-69: Excellent score for a complicated encounter.

70+: You missed nothing. Perhaps I could recommend you to write the next book?

---

**Game 7**
# Grischuk-M.Gurevich
Esbjerg 2000

---

**1 e4 e6 2 d4 d5 3 e5 c5 4 c3 ♘c6 5 ♘f3 ♗d7 6 ♗e2**

If you are new to the French Advanced it is worth pointing out here that if the white bishop rushes to its natural square d3, the d4-pawn comes under too much fire. There is the Milner-Barry Gambit where White places his bishop on d3 and then sacrifices the d4-pawn, but that is another story that actually featured in Games 8 and 10 of *Multiple Choice Chess*.

**6...♘ge7 7 ♘a3 cxd4 8 cxd4 ♘f5 9 ♘c2 ♛b6 10 0-0**

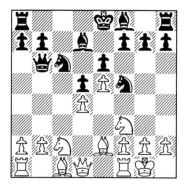

Now choose how you would like to continue in this standard French Advanced position.

a) 10...a5
b) 10...♗e7
c) 10...0-0-0
d) 10...h5

All moves have some merit here.

10...a5 (a) scores two as it serves to generally expand on the queenside and, more specifically, it prevents White from executing the standard manoeuvre 11 ♗d3 ♘cxd4 12 ♘fxd4 ♘xd4 13 ♗e3 ♗c5 as 14 b4 is

not effective.

10...♗e7 (b) illustrates sound development for two points. Note that 11 g4 can be met by 11...♘h4.

We are taught that it is always the sign of a mature player if one castles. While 10...0-0-0 (c) has certainly been tried and tested here, tournament practice has shown that it is rather risky after 11 ♖b1, when White is ready to launch an attack. Take one point if you chose this.

10...h5 (d) seeks to secure the knight on its f5-square and scores one, its drawback being that it is rather committal.

**10...a5 11 ♔h1**

a) 11...♖c8
b) 11...a4
c) 11...♘b4
d) 11...♖d8

As it occupies the only open file around, 11...♖c8 (a) is sensible and scores two points. Take one for 11...a4 (b), but nothing for the obscure 11...♖d8 (d). Finally, 11...♘b4 (c) earns two points as Black seeks to exchange pieces to relieve his slight lack of space.

**11...♘b4 12 ♘e3**

a) 12...♘xe3
b) 12...♗e7
c) 12...f6
d) 12...♖c8

Black is posed with a difficult question here. Does he capture on e3, giving White the possibility of 13 fxe3 and pressure down the f-file, or wait for White to exchange knights on f5, thus breaking up his central pawn chain? It is largely a matter of taste, so 12...♘xe3 (a), 12...♗e7 (b) and Gurevich's choice 12...♖c8 (d) all score two points.

Nothing for 12...f6 (c) as Black is casually prising open the position on both wings with his king still in the centre. At the very least, 13 ♘xf5 exf5 14 a3 ♘a6 (the pawn structure becomes very ugly for Black after 14...♘c6 15 exf6 gxf6) 15 exf6 ♕xf6 gives White the e5-square for his knight to occupy.

**12...♖c8 13 ♘xf5**

> **a) 13...exf5**
> **b) 13...♘c2**

13...exf5 (a) is the only real consideration and scores one point. If you tried to be clever with 13...♘c2 (b), then deduct two from your score since 14 ♘e3 ♘xa1 15 ♗d2 ♕xb2 16 ♕xa1 is better for White.

**13...exf5 14 ♗d2**

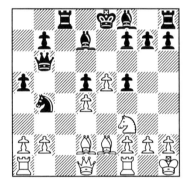

> **a) 14...♗b5**
> **b) 14...♖c2**
> **c) 14...♘c2**
> **d) 14...♗e7**

It is often thematic for Black to swap off light-squared bishops as his own minor piece is deemed 'bad' because its activity is stemmed by its own pawns. For this reason 14...♗b5 (a) scores one point. However, in this actual situation award yourself a bonus if you thought that the overriding factor is that you need your bishop to settle on e6 in order to bolster your pawns and blockade

any later e5-e6 thrust by White.

14...♖c2 (b) drops three points as White is able to immediately gain material with 15 a3 or 15 ♗xb4.

One point for 14...♘c2 (c), although this is somewhat pointless as long as White defends correctly with 15 ♖b1 (not 15 ♖c1 ♕xb2). Now we can see the point of the prophylactic 11 ♔h1 as 15...♘xd4 hangs a piece to 16 ♗e3. If the white king were still on g1, 16...♘xf3+ or 16...♘xe2+ would allow Black to escape with the booty. If you intended to grab the d-pawn, thus falling into White's trap, lose one instead of the original gain.

Gurevich's choice of 14...♗e7 (d) earns you two points.

**14...♗e7 15 a3**

> **a) 15...♗a4**
> **b) 15...♘c6**
> **c) 15...♘c2**
> **d) 15...♘a6**

The knight has done its job and so 15...♘c6 (b) makes sense and is worth two points. On the other hand, 15...♘c2 (c) again runs into trouble after 16 ♖b1 0-0 (again 16...♘xd4 17 ♗e3 rounds up the knight) 17 ♗c3 ♗a4 18 ♗d3, so deduct two from you total.

If you went for 15...♘a6 (d) purely to avoid returning your knight to the square from whence it came (after all, there is a lot of psychology in chess, particularly at the top level, and we can't have our opponent thinking we are eating humble pie), deduct two for having an ego that will ultimately handicap your ability. If, however, you believed that this knight would have a brighter future on a6, for example to e6 via c7, score zero. The knight does a superb job on c6, constantly watching the weak d4-pawn.

15...♗a4 (a) stubbornly eyes up the c2-square, but 16 ♕xa4+ puts paid to that one and costs you three points.

**15...♘c6 16 ♗c3**

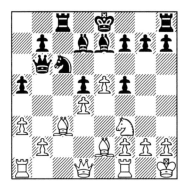

a) 16...g5
b) 16...0-0
c) 16...h6
d) 16...♗e6

16...g5 (a), 16...h6 (c) and 16...♗e6 (d) are all respectable and earn one point. Black may have ideas of setting a kingside offensive in motion (for which you score a point if you thought about it), particularly with the first of these choices. Black's priority, however, should be to look after his own king and so completing development with 16...0-0 (b) maximises your score with an additional three.

**16...0-0 17 ♕d2**

a) 17...♖a8
b) 17...♗e6
c) 17...h6
d) 17...♘b4

The flexible 17...♖a8 (a) shows that Gurevich has no problems with his ego and scores one point. Black is making space to swing his other rook over to the queenside and bolstering his a-pawn.

17...♗e6 (b) is fine for one point, while again 17...h6 (c) is a common method for Black to try and gain activity with ...g7-g5 and even ...f5-f4 (score one for this).

17...♘b4 (d) is too flash to merit a score but I do appreciate that 18 axb4 axb4 traps the bishop on c3. My main question is what

are you hoping to achieve with 17...♘b4 if White doesn't oblige and does not capture?

**17...♖a8 18 ♘e1**

First of all have a bonus if you aware that now 18...g5 is less palatable due to the positional response 19 f4 when Black will not be able to get in the freeing move ...f4 himself.

a) 18...a4
b) 18...♖a7
c) 18...♖fb8
d) 18...♔h8

Score two points for 18...a4 (a), which sets up a clamp on White's queenside and allows Black the option of regrouping his knight to a5 and b3.

Both 18...♖a7 (b) and 18...♔h8 (d) represent overkill in the waiting department and score no points. There is, however, a skill to remaining flexible and awaiting your opponent's next step, and 18...♖fb8 (c) appears to be one example (score two points). In the long term Gurevich appears to be contemplating ...♕d8 followed by pushing his b-pawn to embarrass the white bishop perched on c3.

**18...♖fb8 19 ♘c2**

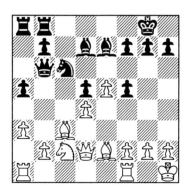

a) 19...♗f8
b) 19...g6
c) 19...♕d8
d) 19...h6

Award yourself a bonus if you asked

what White is up to with ♘c2. Take a further one if you came up with the conclusion that 20 ♘e3 ♗e6 21 f4, followed by g2-g4, is in the air.

19...♗f8 (in case you need the e7-square for the knight), 19...♕d8 (c) and 19...h6 (d) are all worth one point, but a generous two is awarded for the text move 19...g6 (b).

**19...g6 20 ♘e3**

> a) 20...♗e6
> b) 20...♕d8
> c) 20...♕b3
> d) 20...♘b4

20...♗e6 (a) is the natural way to defend the d5-pawn and scores two points.

Other moves are not good. Lose one for the careless 20...♕d8 (b) 21 ♘xd5. The move 20...♕b3 (c) tries to prove that 20...♗e6 is not the only way to defend the d5-pawn, but after 21 ♗d1 ♕c4 22 b3 ♕b5 23 a4 ♕a6 24 ♘xd5 the pawn drops off – lose two. Okay, so 20...♘b4 (d) also defends the d5-pawn, but 21 axb4 (why not?) 21...axb4 22 ♘xd5 wins easily for White.

**20...♗e6 21 f4**

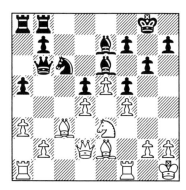

> a) 21...♕d8
> b) 21...h5
> c) 21...♗b4
> d) 21...♗f8

21...♕d8 (a) scores two, with another if you analysed that 22 g4 fxg4 23 f5 gxf5 24

♘xf5 ♗g5 is perfectly playable by Black. Two points also for 21...h5 (b), which prevents White from launching his attack with g2-g4 (you score another if you realised that). Attempting to exchange bishops with 21...♗b4 (c) may be safe tactically due to 22 axb4 axb4, but does not score on anti-positional grounds. Black's dark-squared bishop is a superior piece to its white counterpart and it is needed to protect the weakened dark squares around its monarch.

Finally, the resilient 21...♗f8 (d) is worth one point.

**21...h5 22 ♕d1**

> a) 22...h4
> b) 22...♔g7
> c) 22...♕d8
> d) 22...♘xe5

22...♘xe5 (d) may be okay if White were to recapture 23 dxe5, when 23...♕xe3 24 ♗d4 ♕e4 25 ♕d2 ♖c8 26 ♖ac1 g5 just about regains the piece with a live queen, but 23 fxe5 really makes the whole concept a non-starter and sets you back two points.

22...♕d8 (c) drops one point for overlooking White's intention of 23 ♗xh5 gxh5 24 ♕xh5 ♔g7 25 ♖f3. I refer to the acronym SPORT (Safe, Protect, Open, React, Take) throughout this book. First, this move is safe. Everything on the board (both black and white) is protected from being captured for free. One also notices that, following the queen move, the bishop on c3 has an open diagonal on which to move. However, a bishop move loses the safe d4-pawn due to lack of protection. Black is therefore left to react to White's last move. The move ♕a4 does not look scary and, as we know that ...♘b4 or ...♗b4 are not threats, then ♗xh5 may well be. In many cases it comes down to spotting something to take.

22...h4 (a) is interesting and worth one point, while 22...♔g7! (b) covers any threats of sacrificing on h5 and earns two points.

**22...⌾g7 23 ⌾xh5**

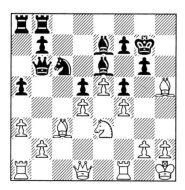

a) 23...⌾f8
b) 23...gxh5
c) 23...⌶h8
d) 23...g5

White has just taken a pawn so the only logical response is to capture the bishop on h5 with 23...gxh5 (b) – this scores three points. If you thought it too risky to allow 23...gxh5 24 ♕xh5, then you can have one point for the best of a bad job with 23...⌶h8 (c), but nothing for 23...⌾f8 (a) or 23...g5 (d).

**23...gxh5 24 ♕xh5**

a) 24...⌶f8
b) 24...⌾f8
c) 24...⌶h8
d) 24...♘xd4

Utilising the f8-square spells disaster in either case. Knock three off your score for 24...⌶f8 (a) on account of 25 ⌶f3. Even worse is 24...⌾f8 (b) 25 ♕h8 mate (lose six for this).

Deduct one for the dubious 24...♘xd4 (d). For those of you who rejected this because of 25 ♗xd4 ♕xd4 26 ⌶f3, award yourself a bonus.

The best move here is 24...⌶h8 (c), which keeps White at bay and scores three points.

**24...⌶h8 25 ♘xf5 +**

a) 25...⌾g8
b) 25...⌾f8
c) 25...♗xf5

Any king move is lethal here, so take off five for 25...⌾g8 (a) 26 ♕g4+ ⌾f8 27 ♕g7+ and six for 25...⌾f8 (b) 26 ♕xh8 mate. If you calculated these and realised that the only feasible way out of check was 25...♗xf5 (c), then score two. If you found yourself tossing up between (a) and (c), only add one to your score.

**25...♗xf5 26 ♕xf5**

a) 26...⌾f8
b) 26...♘xe5
c) 26...♘xd4
d) 26...⌶h6

26...⌾f8 (a) invites e5-e6, so no points here, while 26...♘xe5 (b) 27 fxe5 puts White firmly on top, so reduce your total by two. I am sorry if you spotted a fantastic variation against 27 dxe5 or 27 ♕xe5+; you must consider every possibility for your plans to bear fruit.

26...♘xd4 (c) is now ripe for picking and is worth three, and 26...⌶h6 (d) is safe enough for one point.

**26...♘xd4 27 ♕d3**

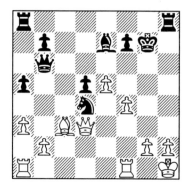

All credit to you (well, actually two points for each of the following lines) if you considered:

1) 27 e6 fxe6 28 ♗xd4+ ♕xd4 29 ♕xe6

♖ae8 and

2) 27 ♕g4+ ♔f8 28 f5 ♖h4 as winning for Black.

> a) 27...♗c5
> b) 27...♘e6
> c) 27...♖xh2+
> d) 27...♕h6

27...♗c5 (a) enables White to create randomness with 28 b4, 28 ♖ad1 or 28 e6 – no points for this.

27...♘e6 (b) positively encourages the advance 28 f5 ♘c7 29 f6+, so deduct one.

27...♖xh2+ (c) is the star performer for six, but nothing for 27...♕h6 (d), which temporarily threatens mate but ultimately fails to 28 ♕g3+ and then ♗xd4.

**27...♖xh2+ 28 ♔xh2**

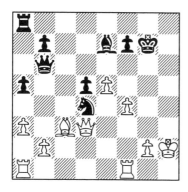

> a) 28...♖h8+
> b) 28...♕h6+
> c) 28...♘f3+
> d) 28...♘b3

28...♖h8+ (a) brings the rook into the equation, forces the monarch forward into dangerous territory and scores four points. Take a well deserved bonus point if you have already dismissed 29 ♔g1 on account of 29...♘f3 mate (or indeed 29...♘e2 mate).

No score for 28...♕h6+ (b) 29 ♔g1 or for 28...♘b3 (d) 29 ♕g3+ ♔h7 30 ♖ad1, which runs the risk of shutting out the black rook from participating.

Finally, remove three points for 28...♘f3+ (c) 29 ♖xf3 ♖h8+ 30 ♖h3, which sees Black getting his move order mixed up.

**28...♖h8+ 29 ♔g3**

> a) 29...♕g6+
> b) 29...♗h4+
> c) 29...♕e6
> d) 29...♕h6

29...♗h4+ (b) is the real blow to White and scores three points. Look how all the black pieces are harmonising to their fullest potential.

Allowing queens to be exchanged with 29...♕g6+ (a) 30 ♕xg6+ fxg6 31 ♗xd4 significantly wrecks Black's position and your running total by four points.

29...♕e6 (c) 30 ♗xd4 sees Black lose the thread and three points, while 29...♕h6 (d) earns a generous one point if you are going for the mate with 30...♕h4. For those who saw the relatively trivial way out for White with 31 ♗xd4, award yourself a bonus.

**29...♗h4+ 30 ♔g4**

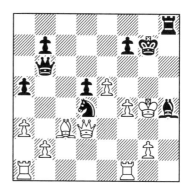

> a) 30...♕e6+
> b) 30...♖h6
> c) 30...♕h6
> d) 30...f5+

One point for 30...♕e6+ (a), as long as you realised that the almost forced reply is 31 f5, when you need to find a useful square for the queen.

30...♖h6 (b) 31 ♗xd4 is too slow for Black and sets your score back by three.

30...f5+ (d) is sufficient for one point, but 31 exf6+ ♗xf6 32 ♖h1 is clearly winning for White.

Amazingly, it is the calm 30...♕h6 (c) which causes instant resignation and nets you five points. Black has 31...♕h5+ 32 ♔h3 ♗f2 mate lined up and each attempt to prevent mate is futile. There is one bonus point up for grabs for each of the following variations you have analysed through to mate.

1) 31 f5 ♕g5+ 32 ♔h3 ♗f2 mate.

2) 31 g3 ♕h5+ 32 ♔h3 ♗e7+ 33 ♔g2 ♕h2 mate.

3) 31 ♗xd4 ♕h5+ 32 ♔h3 ♗f2 mate.

4) 31 ♔h3 ♗f2+ 32 ♔g4 ♕h5 mate.

So that is a maximum of four there. I will let you judge yourselves, but as you will no doubt find, there are some similar alternatives that can also score.

**30...♕h6 0-1**

Did you score as well as you had hoped? Please read the comments below.

Less than 13: Eliminate those mistakes and your scores cannot fail to increase.

13-25: This score range implies that the majority of your moves were sensible, but try hard to pursue some variations during your deliberations as there are bonus points available.

26-39: You are a real player. I hope your talent is put into practice over the board.

40-49: You are both razor sharp and able to handle quieter positions. If you are not listed on the international rating system, you deserve to be.

50+: I am assuming that your score is genuine and that you enjoy the game. For further information on where to play and how to practice, you could consult the Internet.

## Game 8
## Shirov-Kamsky
Moscow 1992

**1 d4 ♘f6 2 c4 g6 3 ♘c3 d5 4 cxd5 ♘xd5 5 e4 ♘xc3 6 bxc3**

The Grünfeld allows White a dominant centre that Black plans to undermine later.

**6...♗g7 7 ♗c4 c5 8 ♘e2 ♘c6 9 ♗e3 0-0 10 ♖c1**

A very sharp continuation, which was introduced into practice by a Russian player, Lev Polugaevsky, in 1987. White avoids the more well-trodden path of 10 0-0 ♗g4 11 f3 ♘a5 etc.

**10...cxd4**

The most consistent, although 10...♕c7 is also popular.

**11 cxd4 ♕a5+ 12 ♔f1**

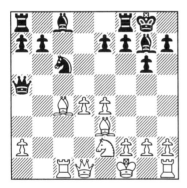

Still in this theoretical position, you are invited to imagine you are playing alongside Grandmaster Gata Kamsky, born Russian but now resident in the US. You may rightly wonder where he is these days, for at a rather young age he elected to give up his chess career at its peak and study medicine.

a) 12...♗d7
b) 12...♗g4
c) 12...♕a3
d) 12...♖d8

Completing the development of your minor pieces with 12...♗d7 (a) is spot on for three points. Almost equally viable for one point is 12...♗g4 (d) 13 f3 ♗d7, although the inclusion of f2-f3 tends to be a support for the white centre rather than a weakness.

12...♕a3 (c), intending 13...♗g4 as f2-f3 is now an inadequate reply (a bonus if you realised that), has now been accepted as the most accurate continuation and scores three points here. 12...♕a3 13 ♖c3 ♕d6 14 e5 ♘xe5 15 dxe5 ♕xd1 mate is a nice touch.

Take one point for 12...♖d8 (d), but 13 ♕b3 e6 14 d5 can be calculated as strong for White.

**12...♗d7 13 h4**

a) 13...♗g4
b) 13...h5
c) 13...♖ac8
d) 13...♖fc8

No score for the belated 13...♗g4 (a) 14 f3, but you can have one if you held up the h4-h5 advance with 13...h5 (b).

13...♖ac8 (c) is extremely sensible and scores two. I must agree that transferring this rook to the queenside appears far more natural than the alternative choice. However, it is 13...♖fc8 (d) which comes up trumps for three points. Without explanation this move looks decidedly odd, so the reasoning behind such a manoeuvre is in order to meet 14 ♕b3 with 14...♘d8, thus defending the f7-square and ensuring that the black rooks are connected. It is often a tricky decision to know which rook to put where, especially when there is only one open file. If it is any consolation, 13...♖fc8 proves to be no exception.

**13...罝fc8 14 h5**

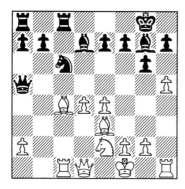

---

a) 14...gxh5
b) 14...b5
c) 14...勾d8
d) 14...e5

---

Rupturing one's kingside pawn formation with 14...gxh5 (a) is rarely appropriate, so deduct two points. However, if you really chose such a daring plan, anticipating that White would fall into the trap 15 勾f4 勾xd4 16 象xd4 罝xc4 17 罝xc4 象b5, you can have your two points back. If you rejected 14...gxh5 on the grounds of general ugliness have a bonus, but if you saw the tactic and realised that White could exercise safety first with 15 象b3 before embarking on 16 勾f4, you deserve an extra two bonus points.

It is not obvious to predict that Kamsky would willingly retreat his knight with 14...勾d8 (c) before being forced to, for example, to bolster f7. All the more reason to be proud of the two points obtained here, for piece coordination is the key and Black is preparing to create queenside activity to counteract White's attack.

14...b5 (b) is worth one point, as is staking a claim in the centre with the move 14...e5 (d).

**14...勾d8 15 f3**

Shirov is not new to this situation and has already had success with this idea. The monarch now has some breathing space.

---

a) 15...象b5
b) 15...b5
c) 15...象a4
d) 15...象e6

---

No losers here, and since a number of international players have gone for 15...象b5 (a) 16 象xb5 豐xb5 17 含f2, it is worth two points. One point for 15...b5 (b), with an extra if you planned to meet 16 象d5 with 16...罝xc1 17 豐xc1 罝c8, thus gaining control of the c-file.

15...象a4 (c) is what Kamsky had up his sleeve (take four points for this). Not devastating, but now Shirov is on his own and Kamsky has no doubt spent several hours analysing various ideas and continuations which could materialise.

Finally, 15...象e6 (d) fails to score as 16 d5 sends the black bishop straight back to d7.

**15...象a4 16 豐d3**

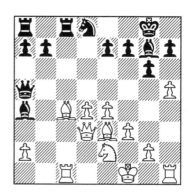

---

a) 16...a6
b) 16...b5
c) 16...gxh5
d) 16...罝xc4

---

The somewhat slow 16...a6 (a) scores one, but the immediate and energetic 16...b5 (b) improves your total by three.

Again 16...gxh5 (c) saddles Black with unnecessary weaknesses and drops two points, while the same fate befalls the dubious sacrifice 16...♖xc4 (d) 17 ♕xc4 ♗b5 18 ♕c2.

**16...b5 17 ♗d5**

> a) 17...♖ab8
> b) 17...♖xc1+
> c) 17...b4
> d) 17...♘c6

There are only two serious contenders here: 17...♖ab8 (a) scores one, and 17...♖xc1+ (b) scores three.

The blunder 17...b4 (c) 18 ♗xa8 ♖xa8 sets you back two, while 17...♘c6 (d) 18 ♖xc6 is even more costly at minus three.

**17...♖xc1+ 18 ♗xc1**

> a) 18...♖b8
> b) 18...♖c8
> c) 18...♕c7
> d) 18...e6

One point for 18...♖b8 (a), but commanding the open file with 18...♖c8 (b) merits the maximum three.

18...♕c7 (c) either overlooks that the black rook on a8 is under fire or that the white bishop on c1 is protected, so remove five points from your total. Likewise, if you chose 18...e6 (d), dock five points. Don't worry about sliding below zero because there are plenty of opportunities to redeem yourself.

**18...♖c8 19 hxg6**

> a) 19...♘e6
> b) 19...e6
> c) 19...hxg6
> d) 19...fxg6

You are on a tightrope here with only one decent reply.

19...♘e6 (a) loses five as your position falls apart on 20 gxf7+ ♔xf7 21 ♘f4. Things are also far from ideal after 19...e6 (b) 20 gxh7+ ♔h8 21 ♗b3, so diminish your current total by three.

19...fxg6 (d) is downright illegal so feel embarrassed. I won't penalise you because it

is one of those lucky occasions when you would have touched your opponent's pawn on g6 but, as you can't recapture 19...fxg6, you would have been forced to play the text move 19...hxg6.

If you genuinely went for 19...hxg6 (c), then score one.

**19...hxg6 20 ♗h6**

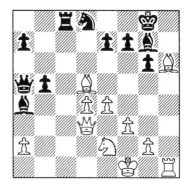

> a) 20...♗xh6
> b) 20...♗h8
> c) 20...♗f6
> d) 20...e6

The accurate 20...♗xh6 (a) scores three points because Black doesn't want the white queen quickly joining in the attack with ♕e3. At least with the rook recapturing on h6, an infiltration square has been temporarily blocked.

Retreating the bishop with 20...♗h8 (b) is a theme found in similar set-ups, so take one point.

20...♗f6 (c) walks into 21 e5 ♗h8 22 ♕xg6+ ♗g7 23 ♕xg7 mate, so lose three. A bonus for anyone who spotted that, with the advance of the e-pawn, there's the mighty threat of ♕xg6 as the f-pawn is pinned by the white bishop on d5.

Attempting to reduce the power of the said bishop with 20...e6 (d) scores one, but a further bonus is available for those who rejected 20...e6 due to the strength of 21 ♗xg7, when 21...exd5 22 ♗f6 wins.

**20...♗xh6 21 ♖xh6**

a) 21...♔g7
b) 21...e6
c) 21...♗c2
d) 21...b4

21...♔g7 (a) is logical for three points and is also what Shirov half expected. If you at first thought that 22 ♕e3 would be hard to meet, but persisted and found 22...♖c2 with the idea of 23 ♖h4 ♕d2 (to prevent 24 ♕h6+), award yourself three bonuses. White can actually push on with 23 ♕g5!, however, which is highly complicated.

Minus one for 21...♗c2 (c), which drives the white queen to exactly the spot she wants to go (the e3-square), while 21...b4 (d) is too slow and scores no points.

21...e6 (b) was Kamsky's preferred mode of defence and scores four points.

**21...e6 22 f4**

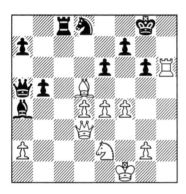

Later Shirov was to criticise this move as being too ambitious. The game was still very much balanced after both 22 ♗b3 and 22 ♕e3. With the latter, Black is unwise to capture with 22...exd5 due to 23 ♕g5 when White has a strong attack. Instead, Black should maximise his position with 22...♗d1.

a) 22...exd5
b) 22...♔f8
c) 22...♖c2
d) 22...♔g7

22...exd5 (a) walks into White's mating net after 23 ♕h3 ♕c7 24 ♖h8+ ♔g7 25 e5 etc. and lets you down by four points.

22...♔f8 (b) attempts to run and is worth one point, but if you appreciated the strength of 23 f5! exd5 24 f6 ♔e8 25 ♕h3 ♘e6 26 exd5 or 23...gxf5 24 exf5 exd5 25 ♕e3, you are entitled to two bonus points.

22...♖c2 (c) is perhaps the star move of the encounter and scores four. Shirov certainly missed it coming. If this one didn't feature in your thinking, it will be worth you spending some time on this position to understand what motive lies behind this move if you want to benefit from later scores.

Lastly, the rather tame 22...♔g7 (d) invites 23 ♕h3, so no points.

**22...♖c2 23 ♕h3**

a) 23...exd5
b) 23...♕d2
c) 23...♔f8
d) 23...♖xe2

You need to be clear how to contend with the threat of 24 ♖h8+ ♔g7 25 e5 followed by 26 ♕h6 mate. If you were fully aware that this was the immediate threat, take a bonus.

23...exd5 (a) does nothing to meet the aforementioned threat, so take five points off your total.

23...♕d2 (b) falls foul of another forced mate, so minus four for failing to analyse 24 ♖h8+ ♔g7 25 ♕h6+ ♔f6 26 e5+ ♔e7 29 ♕f8+ ♔d7 30 ♕xd8 mate. There are two bonus points if you did have this covered.

23...♖xe2 (d) avoids the mate in variation (b) because the black queen will be defending the knight on d8 in the final position. However, the theme is similar and this time it costs you three points for allowing 24 ♖h8+ ♔g7 25 ♕h6+ ♔f6 26 e5+ ♔e7 (or 26...♔f5 27 ♕g5 mate) 27 ♕f8+ ♔d7 28 ♕d6+ ♔c8 29 ♕c6+ ♔b8 30 ♕b7 mate. 29...♕c7 is no better due to 30 ♕a8+ ♔d7 31 ♗c6+ ♔e7 32 ♖e8 mate, while also mating are 31...♕xc6 32 ♕xd8 and 31...♘xc6 32 ♕e8. A bonus point for each line you calculated ending in mate. The length of these variations may have bamboozled you, but forcing lines are the easiest to calculate and an important method for improving.

The only escape route is found in 23...♔f8 (c), which is worth three points. A bonus is available if you plan to meet 24 ♕h4 by running for your life with 24...♔e8 25 ♖h8+ ♔d7 etc.

**23...♔f8 24 e5**

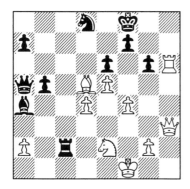

| a) 24...exd5 |
|---|
| b) 24...♕d2 |
| c) 24...b4 |
| d) 24...♔e7 |

24...exd5 (a) is playable and scores three, although it's not without complications following 25 f5.

24...♕d2 (b) again lands Black in the soup after 25 ♖h8+ ♔e7 26 ♕h4+, so deduct five for this.

24...b4 (c) earns one point, although I fear White is back in the game after 25 ♗f3. If you wanted to keep open the a5-e1 diagonal in case the black queen gets a chance to swing to d2, award yourself a bonus for excellent judgement.

In anticipation Kamsky moves out of danger with 24...♔e7 (d) – this scores five. It is noticeable that, in contrast, the white monarch is now more exposed.

**24...♔e7 25 ♖xg6**

| a) 25...fxg6 |
|---|
| b) 25...exd5 |
| c) 25...♔d7 |
| d) 25...♕d2 |

Two points for 25...fxg6 (a), which runs the risk of allowing perpetual check. If Black blocks 26 ♕h7+ with 26...♘f7, then White has the cheeky 27 ♗xe6 ♔xe6 28 ♕xg6+ ♔e7 29 f5 with counterplay. A further important line runs 26 ♕h7+ ♔e8 27 ♗e4, hitting g6.

Nothing for 25...exd5 (b) 26 ♕h4+, which allows White too much activity for too small a price.

Minus two for 25...♔d7 (c), which keeps up the trend of running away to another quarter. However, 26 ♖g7 ♕d2 27 ♗xe6+ ♘xe6 28 ♖xf7+ ♔c6 29 ♕xe6 mate stops Black in his tracks.

25...♕d2 (d) takes top honours with five points. White has two of his pieces attacked, and Black attacks a third one.

**25...♕d2 26 ♔g1**

| a) 26...♕xe2 |
|---|
| b) 26...fxg6 |
| c) 26...exd5 |
| d) 26...♕e1+ |

The burning question for Black is which piece to take.

Relatively safe and worth one point is 26...♕xe2 (a), although Black has to tread carefully after 27 ♕h4+ ♔d7 28 ♖g8 ♘c6 29 ♗f3.

Kamsky swiped the rook with 26...fxg6 (b) – take four points for this. Take a bonus if you appreciated that the difference between this and capturing the rook on move 25 lies in the fact that 27 ♕h7+ ♔e8 28 ♗e4 is met by 28...♕e3+ and the bishop finally succumbs.

The bishop is immune at the moment due to the variation 26...exd5 (c) 27 ♕h4+ ♔d7 28 ♖d6+ ♔c7 29 ♕e7+ ♔b8 30

♖xd8+ ♖c8 31 ♕d6+ ♔b7 32 ♖d7+ ♔a8 33 ♕xd5+ ♔b8 34 ♕b7 mate. Drop five if you opted for 26...exd5 and earn a bonus if you rejected the line even as early as 28 ♖d6+.

26...♕e1+ (d) scores one point as long as you carried out this check to cover ♕h4 by White.

**26...fxg6 27 ♕h7 +**

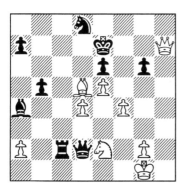

a) 27...♘f7
b) 27...♔f8
c) 27...♔e8

One point for 27...♘f7 (a), although we have previously discussed that 28 ♗xe6 ♔xe6 29 ♕xg6+ keeps Black on his toes.

27...♔f8 (b) heads in the wrong direction so direct your score down by one.

27...♔e8 (c) gives the black monarch freedom to avoid the perpetual checks and scores three points. Take a bonus if you have covered the likely eventualities following 28 ♕xg6+. For example, 28...♔d7 29 ♗xe6+ ♔c7 30 ♕h7+ ♔b8 31 ♗d5 ♕xe2, when White must admit defeat.

**27...♔e8 28 f5**

a) 28...gxf5
b) 28...exf5
c) 28...exd5
d) 28...♕xe2

One has to admire Shirov's resilience as he fights to the death. I hope you have

taken time to find your way through the complications here because even now Black must be accurate. You have been warned that only two of the multiple choice answers here score above zero!

Deduct one point for 28...gxf5 (a), which allows White the use of the h5-square after 29 ♗f3 b4 30 ♗h5+ ♔f8 31 ♕h8+ ♔e7 32 ♕g7+ ♘f7 33 ♕xf7+. Black should not have to go through those contortions to avoid perpetual check.

28...exf5 (b) is even worse after 29 e6, so that gives you a deficit of four points.

Capturing the knight with 28...♕xe2 (d) is safe enough for two points, but only if you intended to meet 29 fxe6 with 29...♕d1+ 30 ♔h2 ♕h5+, exchanging queens. There are two bonuses for anyone who saw the opportunity of mate that would arise after 28...♕xe2 29 ♕xg6+ ♔d7 30 fxe6+ ♔c8 31 e7 ♕e1+ 32 ♔h2 ♕h4+ 33 ♔g1 ♖c1 mate.

Kamsky, however, decided it was time to eliminate the centralised bishop with 28...exd5 (c). Take four points for this.

**28...exd5 29 f6**

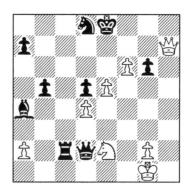

a) 29...♕xe2
b) 29...♕e3+
c) 29...♘c6
d) 29...♕b4

29...♕xe2 (a) misses the point behind 29 f6 and it wasn't particularly subtle either, so lose six for allowing 30 ♕e7 mate.

It is vital to look at every check but 29...♕e3+ (b) is a case where it doesn't help after 30 ♔h2, so deduct two for this.

Take one point for 29...♘c6 (c), which certainly has the merit of stopping mate in one. However, it is 29...♕b4 (d) which secures three points and concentrates on reducing any counterplay White's combination of queen and pawns can rustle up.

**29...♕b4 30 ♕xg6 +**

> a) 30...♘f7
> b) 30...♔f8
> c) 30...♔d7

30...♘f7 (a) 31 e6 ♕f8 32 ♘f4 gives White pressure and lets the steam out of your score to a tune of minus four.

Nothing for 30...♔f8 (b) since 31 ♕g7+ ♔e8 32 ♕g6+ displays a distinct lack of progress. If you thought you were offering one repetition in order to exert power and gain time on the clock, you are again mistaken since White may prefer to deviate with 31 ♕h6+ ♔e8 32 ♘f4.

30...♔d7 (c) is the correct answer for four points.

**30...♔d7 31 e6 +**

> a) 31...♔xe6
> b) 31...♘xe6
> c) 31...♔c8
> d) 31...♔c7

Take one point for 31...♔xe6 (a), although there are an awful lot of checks after 32 ♕e8+ ♔f5 33 ♘g3+ or 32...♔xf6 33 ♕xd8+ ♕e7 34 ♕h8+.

31...♘xe6 (b) helps to ensure that the white knight will not play a part in the game via f4 and gives the black monarch room to shelter on the queenside – score three.

Score one for 31...♔c8 (c), although 32 e7 gives White a shouting chance after 32...♕e1+ 33 ♔h2 ♕h4+ 34 ♔g1 ♖xe2 35 ♕f5+ etc. Take two for 31...♔c7 (d), which sees White running out of checks more

quickly, but again, why allow White activity?

**31...♘xe6 32 ♕f7 +**

> a) 32...♔d8
> b) 32...♔c8
> c) 32...♔d6
> d) 32...♔c6

There is one superior choice over the others and that is 32...♔d8 (a) for three points.

Why let the knight drop with check with 32...♔c8? You may well still be winning after 33 ♕xe6+ ♔c7 34 ♕f7+ ♔b6 35 ♕e6+ ♔a5, but that is beside the point as we are also searching for the most precise moves. The more tactical an encounter is, the more precise we must be. Lose one point for this. 32...♔c6 (d) runs into exactly the same, including the one point penalty.

32...♔d6 (c) may be the only way to save the knight, but if you had consulted all the checks you probably would have opted not to have your king and queen skewered your with 33 ♕e7+ ♔c6 34 ♕xb4. It is not the end of the world following 34...♖xe2, but this is more by luck than judgement! Lose five points.

**32...♔d8 33 ♕xe6**

> a) 33...♖xe2
> b) 33...♕e1+
> c) 33...♕f8
> d) 33...♔c7

33...♖xe2 (a) 34 ♕xe2 ♕xd4+ 35 ♔h2 ♕xf6 is a simplifying variation that winds up White's resistance and scores three points, while 33...♕e1+ (b) is the text move and also scores three.

Nothing for going passive at this stage with 33...♕f8 (c) 34 ♘f4, but 33...♔c7 (d) is worth one since 34 f7 ♖c6 35 ♕xd5 ♖f6 36 ♕e5+ ♕d6 also keeps things simple.

**33...♕e1+ 34 ♔h2**

> a) 34...♕h4+
> b) 34...♖xe2
> c) 34...♕xe2
> d) 34...♔c7

Two points for 34...♕h4+ (a) 35 ♔g1 ♕e4 36 ♕d6+ ♔e8, but not if you planned 35...♖xe2, when 36 ♕xd5+ leads to a draw.

Hard luck if you went for 34...♖xe2 (b) because it is so easy to lose one's sense of danger as the position appears trivial. That rook on c2, however, was preventing a critical check on c5. White can now embark on a checking spree that cannot be curtailed, for example 35 ♕xd5+ ♔c7 (35...♔e8 36 ♕g8+ ♔d7 37 ♕d5+) 36 ♕c5+ ♔b7 37 ♕d5+ ♔b6 38 ♕c5+ ♔a6 39 ♕d6+ ♔a5 40 ♕c7+ ♔b4 41 ♕c5+ ♔a5 42 ♕xa7+. Award yourself two bonus points if you avoided 34...♖xe2 for this very reason.

Kamsky saw fit to round up the knight with 34...♕xe2 (c) – score three for this.

This time 34...♔c7 (d) fails to score as Black is no longer covering the f8-square, thus making 35 f7 more of a nuisance.

**34...♕xe2 35 ♕xd5+**

> a) 35...♔e8
> b) 35...♔c8
> c) 35...♔c7

35...♔e8 (a) can have a generous point, but after 36 ♕g8+ ♔d7 37 ♕d5+ you will have to try again to avoid the checks.

35...♔c8 (b) reduces your total by three since 36 f7 ♕e7 37 f8♕! ♕xf8 38 ♕a8+ is bad news for Black.

35...♔c7 (c) maintains total control and scores three points.

**35...♔c7 36 f7**

> a) 36...♕xg2+
> b) 36...♕f2
> c) 36...♕e7
> d) 36...♕e1

36...♕xg2+ (a) 37 ♕xg2 loses the plot and ten points.

36...♕f2 (b) 37 ♕e5+ gives White too much rope for checking considering his lack of pieces, so this scores one point.

36...♕e7 (c) snuffs out the checks, halts the f-pawn and threatens 37...♕h4+ 38 ♔g1 ♖c1 mate all in one go. This triple-purpose move ends the game for you with three points to the good.

Nothing for 36...♕e1 (d) which allows White to play on with 37 f8♕ ♕h4+ 38 ♔g1 ♖c1+ 39 ♕f1 ♖xf1+ 40 ♔xf1, or even 37 ♕g5.

**36...♕e7 0-1**

Now add up your score.

Less than 21: Keep practising. Twenty-five points here and I would say you are ready for a serious tournament.

21-35: Basically solid chess, but try to follow some of the more intricate analysis to widen your horizons.

36-47: A strong performance worthy of a tournament competitor.

48-59: Impressive scoring. I doubt if Shirov would have broken down your defences.

60+: This was a difficult and extremely sharp series of variations to navigate. Congratulations on holding a perfect or near-perfect course.

## Game 9
# Beliavsky-Savchenko
European Championship, Ohrid 2001

**1 d4 d5 2 c4 c6**

The Slav Defence has the drawback of allowing a weaker opponent the chance to force a rather turgid position after 3 cxd5 cxd5. However, its reputation as a solid and reliable defence in combination with its counterattacking ideas, makes it popular.

**3 ♘f3 ♘f6 4 ♘c3 dxc4 5 a4 ♗f5 6 ♘e5**

This move appears to break the opening principle of moving each minor piece exactly once unless you have a good reason not to do so.

**6...♘bd7 7 ♘xc4 ♘b6**

This is the reason. Black decides to opt for quieter waters and chases the white knight. Otherwise the automatic 6...e6 allows 7 f3 and a quick and aggressive 8 e4, which really reveals White's intentions.

**8 e3 e6 9 a5 ♘xc4 10 ♗xc4 ♗d6 11 f3 e5 12 dxe5 ♗xe5 13 e4 ♕e7 14 ♕b3**

Already some tactics have begun. 14 exf5 is met by 14...♗xc3+.

**14...0-0 15 0-0 ♗g6 16 ♘e2**

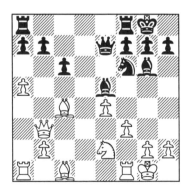

You are now taking over as Black. It does seem that your pieces are slightly congested, so take time to consider where they might settle in the near future, especially in re-

sponse to the advance f3-f4 and e4-e5.

> a) 16...♖fe8
> b) 16...♕c7
> c) 16...♗d6
> d) 16...♕c5+

16...♖fe8 (a) is sensible for one point, but I would have preferred to pre-empt any advance with 16...♗d6 – this scores two.

I had better give 16...♕c7 (b) something positive as this was played in the game, so you can have one point for this. I am happier to award a bonus if you realised that you are being provocative, even though the situation does not warrant it.

16...♕c5+ (d) is not useful, but you can have one point because it is safe.

**16...♕c7 17 f4**

> a) 17...♗d4+
> b) 17...♗xe4
> c) 17...♗d6
> d) 17...♘xe4

In complete contrast to the previous move, this time Black has only one playable option. That is found in 17...♗d6 (c) for one point. Award yourself an early bonus if you considered the continuation of the game, namely 18 e5 and have already planned your response.

17...♗d4+ (a) drops the bishop and three points, while 17...♗xe4 (b) and 17...♘xe4 (d) both smack of desperation and cost you a point.

**17...♗d6 18 e5**

> a) 18...♗e7
> b) 18...♗c5+
> c) 18...♘g4
> d) 18...b5

Again, no room for manoeuvring here. 18...♗c5+ (b) is the only move to score in positive territory with one point. The alternatives all lose material and varying degrees of points. 18...♗e7 (a) and 18...♘g4 (c) both score minus two while the slightly more plausible 18...b5 (d), minus one. Admittedly, 19 axb6 en passant puts a huge dent in its plausibility, but if you spotted that was White's best then take a bonus point.

**18...♗c5+ 19 ♗e3**

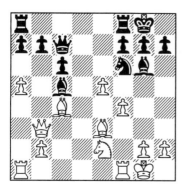

> a) 19...♗xe3+
> b) 19...♕e7
> c) 19...♘e4
> d) 19...♖fe8

One point for both 19...♗xe3+ (a) and 19...♘e4 (c), with the text move 19...♕e7 (b) scoring the highest with two. It is true that Black has danced around a bit with his queen but it is not 100% clear where the black rooks want to go, and meantime Black can hope that his opponent's act of pushing forward will create some weaknesses.

19...♖fe8 (d) works a treat if White follows up with 20 exf6 ♖xe3, but falls foul of 20 ♗xc5 so deduct three from your total.

**19...♕e7 20 ♔h1**

> a) 20...♗xe3
> b) 20...♘g4
> c) 20...♗h5
> d) 20...h6

20...♗xe3 (a) 21 exf6 is clearly not Black's best (lose one), and both 20...♗h5 (minus two) and 20...h6 (minus three) run into 21 ♗xc5 ♕xc5 22 exf6.

Those listing 20...♘g4 (b) as their preferred choice can have one point, with an extra bonus if you realised it was the only viable move.

**20...♘g4 21 ♗xc5**

> a) 21...♕h4
> b) 21...♘xh2
> c) 21...♕xc5
> d) 21...♘f2+

White has a couple of ways to prevent mate after 21...♕h4 (a), namely 22 ♗g1 and 22 h3, so score minus three there. 21...♘xh2 (b) is bizarre for minus ten and 21...♘f2+ (d) is not a whole lot better for minus six.

Again we have a lone positive scorer with 21...♕xc5 (c). This earns one point.

**21...♕xc5 22 f5**

> a) 22...♘xe5
> b) 22...♗h5
> c) 22...♕xe5
> d) 22...♘f2+

Things are hotting up so precise calculation is required...

One point for 22...♘xe5 (a), which doesn't quite work but certainly has to be considered. One extra point if your analysis ran 22...♘xe5 23 fxg6 ♕xc4. If you judged that 23 ♖ac1 ♘xc4 or 23 ♖fc1 ♘xc4 is best, then add one. The question of which rook can be answered when seeing further ahead. You are very alert if you noted 24 fxg6 ♘d2 (one point), when 25 ♕h3 deserves another bonus.

22...♗h5 (b) scores one, but how do you plan to meet 23 ♘g3 or 23 ♘f4? I am generous and I will give you one extra if you intended 23...g6, even though 24 ♘xh5 gxh5 is positional suicide. If however, you foresaw 23...♕xe5 and the potential mate on h2, then you may add three to your score.

22...♛xe5 (c) nets three points, with a bonus if you have 23...♛xh2 mate in your sights.

22...♞f2+ (d) earns one point for maintaining the material balance, but it should be avoided since two minor pieces are generally stronger than a rook and a pawn in this type of position (see Chapter 4).

**22...♛xe5 23 ♞g3**

> a) 23...♞xh2
> b) 23...♞e3
> c) 23...♝xf5
> d) 23...♝h5

Another tightrope to walk here.

23...♞xh2 (a), 23...♞e3 (b) 24 ♜fe1 and 23...♝xf5 (c) all lose two points as they weakly relinquish the tension and material as a by-product.

23...♝h5 (d) is the key move for two points, with no further bonuses as we have already discussed the mate threat on h2 in the previous notes.

**23...♝h5 24 ♜ae1**

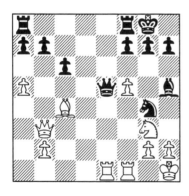

> a) 24...♛c7
> b) 24...♛d6
> c) 24...♛f6
> d) 24...♞f2+

You can be forgiven for placing 24...♛c7 (a) and 24...♛d6 (b) in the same bracket but

they are in fact quite different. 24...♛c7 (minus one) 25 ♝e2 ties Black up and threatens 26 ♝xg4 ♝xg4 27 h3. The move 24...♛d6 (three points), on the other hand, stays on the important b8-h2 diagonal for now, but allows the black queen to swing over to h6 if necessary, thus lending defence to the stranded bishop.

Lose three point if you chose 24...♛f6 (c), which succumbs to 25 ♞xh5.

24...♞f2+ (d) is flash because the knight cannot be immediately captured but its glory is certainly cut short after 25 ♚g1, as is your score by three.

**24...♛d6 25 ♝e2**

> a) 25...g6
> b) 25...♛h6
> c) 25...♞f6
> d) 25...♜ae8

I can see why you want to play 25...g6 (a), which scores one, but Black would not have entered this line if that was his intention. For example, 26 ♝xg4 ♝xg4 27 ♞e4 leads to a powerful initiative for White. Take a bonus if you rejected 25...g6 for this reason.

25...♛h6 (b) 26 ♞xh5 ♛xh5 27 h3 reduces your total by two as your knight has bitten the dust, but 25...♞f6 (c) is no better and scores minus three.

25...♜ae8 (d) is the text choice for two points, with a bonus if you plan to meet 26 h3 with 26...♜e3.

**25...♜ae8 26 ♝xg4**

> a) 26...♝xg4
> b) 26...♜xe1

One point for 26...♝xg4 (a), but nothing for 26...♜xe1 (b), which concedes the e-file.

**26...♝xg4 27 h3**

> a) 27...♛xg3
> b) 27...♜xe1
> c) 27...h5
> d) 27...♛h6

27...♛xg3 (a) is presumably an oversight,

which costs you six points. Again 27...♖xe1 (b) fails to score, while 27...h5 (c) fails to extricate the bishop and drops two.

27...♕h6 (d) is shown to be the vital tool here and scores two points.

**27...♕h6 28 ♔g1**

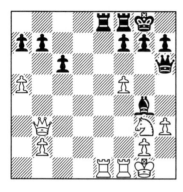

a) 28...♗h5
b) 28...♖xe1
c) 28...♗xh3
d) 28...♕h4

28...♗h5 (a) saves the bishop in the short term, so take one point. The persevering 29 ♘e4, with the idea of g4, leaves Black struggling.

28...♖xe1 (b) is still worthless, and 28...♕h4 (d) 29 hxg4 loses two.

28...♗xh3 (c) reveals Black's plot and scores two points. If you are fully aware that 29 gxh3 ♕xh3 leaves Black with three pawns for the piece, have a bonus point.

**28...♗xh3 29 gxh3**

a) 29...♖e3
b) 29...♕g5
c) 29...♕xh3
d) 29...♖xe1

29...♖xe1 (d) doesn't change your total score, but 29...♖e3 (a) drops five and 29...♕g5 (b), minus one for obvious reasons.

29...♕xh3 (c) is surely the only way forward and scores two.

**29...♕xh3 30 ♖e3**

a) 30...♕g4
b) 30...♖d8
c) 30...g5
d) 30...h5

One point for 30...♕g4 (a) and one also for 30...♖d8 (b), which threatens to infiltrate with ...♖d2.

Lose one for 30...g5 (c), which is unnecessarily weakening and it allows White to strengthen with the natural 31 ♖fe1.

The pushing of the passed pawn as an attacking aid with 30...h5 (d) takes top honours of two points. It stops 31 ♖fe1 due to 31...h4 and it avoids Black being back-rank mated.

**30...h5 31 ♖f4**

a) 31...h4
b) 31...g5
c) 31...♖b8
d) 31...♖xe3

Lose four for 31...h4 (a), after which 32 ♘e4 incredibly traps the black queen. A bonus point for those who saw that and therefore presumably chose a different course of action. It is not the time to go passive with 31...♖b8 (c), especially as 32 ♘e4 is again on the cards. Lose five for this.

Lose three for 31...g5 (b), which appears flawed for a couple of reasons, but again 32 ♘e4 should suffice. The knight and queen will combine well after 33...♕xe3+ 34 ♕xe3 gxf4 35 ♕xf4.

31...♖xe3 (d) is the one to merit two points and stop the potential threats against her majesty.

**31...♖xe3 32 ♕xe3**

> a) 32...♖a8
> b) 32...♖d8
> c) 32...h4
> d) 32...a6

I cannot quite bring myself to recognise 32...♖a8 (a) as a serious choice. It is so rare to have to use rooks in such a defensive role. Also, White is not even threatening to pilfer the a7-pawn since that would leave the knight on g3 unguarded, so no points there.

Taking the open file with 32...♖d8 (b) is more like it for three points.

Minus one for 32...h4 (c), which is indeed a move to consider. However, after 33 ♘f1 ♕xe3 34 ♘xe3 the h-pawn is in mortal danger.

Finally, the non-committal 32...a6 (d) scores one.

**32...♖d8 33 ♘f1**

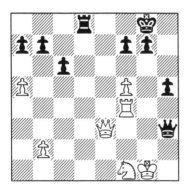

> a) 33...♖d3
> b) 33...♕xe3+
> c) 33...♖d1
> d) 33...g5

33...♖d3 (a) is fine for one point, while the text move 33...♕xe3+ (b) scores two.

On to the blunders. 33...♖d1 (c) diminishes your hard work by nine and 33...g5, by minus four.

**33...♕xe3+ 34 ♘xe3**

> a) 34...♖d3
> b) 34...♖d2
> c) 34...♖d1+
> d) 34...♖d7

Imagine that this was a case of touch move on the rook. Perhaps you would have preferred to move something else for Black. Out of the choices, 34...♖d3 (a), 34...♖d2 (b) and 34...♖d7 (d) all score one.

Whoops! Minus five for 34...♖d1+ (c).

**34...♖d2 35 ♖b4**

A useful trick to remember. White defends and attacks simultaneously with this move.

> a) 35...♖e2
> b) 35...b5
> c) 35...♖d7
> d) 35...g6

35...♖d7 (c) defends b7 and is worth two points.

35...♖e2 (a) 36 ♘c4 allows White to use ♘d6 if necessary, and I cannot see how Black stops White crashing in via the queenside. For this move, though, Black hangs on to all his pawns and so I will let you hang on to all your points. However, 35...b5 (b), allowing en passant, and 35...g6 (d) both score minus one.

**35...♖d7 36 ♔f2**

I reckon White got this one wrong. Here the king begins to erroneously rush towards the centre files. However, there is much more action about to take place on the g- and h-files where Black is pushing his pawns! Therefore, somewhere on the g- or h- files is ideal for the white king. Leaving on g1 allows 36 ♘c4, for example 36...g5 37 fxg6 fxg6 38 ♘e5 ♖e7 39 ♘d3 and ♘c5, winning a pawn.

a) 36...g5
b) 36...g6
c) 36...c5
d) 36...h4

Three points for setting the pawns in motion with 36...g5 (a). The move 36...g6 (b) is exactly the same as long as White plays 37 fxg6. If not, Black is a move behind the game and you are a point behind anyone choosing (a).

36...c5 (c) scores one, but only just – ♖b5 and ♘d5 are annoying for Black.

36...h4 (d) doesn't score because the white king can easily chase after black's h-pawn via the f3- and g4 squares. You may take a bonus if you realised that 37 ♖xh4 allows Black to grab the b-pawn with 37...♖d2+ and 38...♖xb2.

**36...g5 37 ♔e2**

White is consistent but the plan is wayward.

a) 37...♔f8
b) 37...♔g7
c) 37...g4
d) 37...h4

As discussed already, bringing the king into the action is extremely healthy. 37...♔f8 (a) scores one point and 37...♔g7 (b) scores three.

Advancing the pawns with 37...g4 (c) and 37...h4 (d) also merits one point. Once

again, I can reiterate that it would be only too easy for the white king to tackle the pawns.

**37...♔g7 38 ♖e4**

a) 38...♔h6
b) 38...♔f6
c) 38...g4
d) 38...h4

There's nothing wrong with 38...♔h6 (a) for one point, but keeping an eye on the f5-pawn with 38...♔f6 (b) takes top marks of two.

Again, 38...g4 (c) and 38...h4 (d) are worth one each.

**38...♔f6 39 ♖e8**

a) 39...g4
b) 39...h4
c) 39...♖d4
d) 39...♖e7

This time Black needs to consider how to make progress and in this case how to infiltrate with his king. 39...g4 (a) vacates the g5-square for the black monarch to march forward and for this reason it scores a creditable three points. 39...h4 (b) is far less effective and this time fails to score.

Take two for 39...♖d4 (c), but only if you intend to meet 40 ♖b8 with 40...♖b4, rather than retreating with 40...♖d7.

Last, but not least, 39...♖e7 (d) is plausible for one point, although 40 ♖h8 h4 41

♔f3 should cause Black to stumble.

**39...g4 40 ♖a8**

> a) 40...b6
> b) 40...b5
> c) 40...a6
> d) 40...♔g5

One point for each of 40...b6 (a) and 40...b5 (b), although you must be aware that White has the possibility of a5-a6 followed by ♖b8 and ♖b7. If you didn't fancy allowing White this option, then take a bonus point.

40...♔g5 (d) is rather optimistic since after 41 ♖xa7 followed by a6, it is White who looks set to queen a pawn.

It is 40...a6 (c) which cuts out White's counterplay for three points.

**40...a6 41 b3**

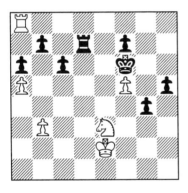

> a) 41...♔g5
> b) 41...♔e5
> c) 41...♖e7
> d) 41...g3

In decreasing order, 41...♔g5 (a) witnesses the black monarch lending support to his passed pawns for three points, while 41...♔e5 (b) also dominates the position and scores two.

41...♖e7 (c) is harmless for one point, but 41...g3 (d) fails to score as White can round up a pawn with 42 ♖g8 h4 43 ♖g4 etc.

**41...♔g5 42 ♖e8**

> a) 42...h4
> b) 42...g3
> c) 42...♔f4
> d) 42...♖d4

Minus one for 42...h4 (a), when 43 ♖g8+ wins the g4-pawn. No points for 42...g3 (b). This makes life too easy for White with 43 ♔f3, when it is hard for Black to progress.

42...♔f4 (c) restricts White's movements and scores two points, but nought for 42...♖d4 (d), which gives White something to bite on with 43 ♖e7.

**42...♔f4 43 f6**

Be warned that only one move scores higher than zero here.

> a) 43...♔g5
> b) 43...♖d6
> c) 43...♖d4
> d) 43...h4

Although Black may have a clear plan, one must always react ('R' of SPORT) to the last move. White is threatening 44 ♖e7 so Black needs to face the immediate problem. Neither 43...♔g5 (a) nor 43...h4 (d) satisfactorily meet 44 ♖e7, so minus one for both.

One point for the interesting 43...♖d4 (c), but only if you are planning to answer 44 ♖e7 with 44...♖e4. After 45 ♔d3 White is pressing to create a passed pawn. It would be a shame for Black to lose control just when it looked like he had the better of it.

It is 43...♖d6 (b) which ensures that the white f-pawn has no future and scores two points.

**43...♖d6 44 ♖e7**

| |
|---|
| a) 44...♖xf6 |
| b) 44...b5 |
| c) 44...♖e6 |
| d) 44...h4 |

With 44...♖xf6 (a) you take two points, while Savchenko has the asset of three passed pawns on the kingside.

44...b5 (b), allowing 45 axb6 en passant, is presumably not part of the plan so lose four, while 44...♖e6 (c) 45 ♖xe6 fxe6 46 f7 is even more disastrous for minus eight. It is also unwise to allow White to retain his f6-pawn, so minus one for 44...h4 (d) 45 ♖xf7.

**44...♖xf6 45 ♖xb7**

| |
|---|
| a) 45...h4 |
| b) 45...♔g3 |
| c) 45...g3 |
| d) 45...♖e6 |

A bonus point if you spotted what is wrong with 45...h4 (a). The answer is 46 ♖b4+ (lose one point if you chose 45...h4). We saw that trick from a different angle earlier!

45...♔g3 (b) cheekily saunters further into the enemy camp for two points, while White seeks to create a distraction on the other side of the board.

One point for 45...g3 (c), but minus one for 45...♖e6 (d), which fails to have the desired effect after 46 ♖xf7+.

**45...♔g3 46 ♖a7**

| |
|---|
| a) 46...c5 |
| b) 46...h4 |
| c) 46...♔h2 |
| d) 46...♖f2+ |

a) 46...c5 holds White up for one point although 47 ♖c7 or even 47 ♖b7-b6 is not the end of the road by any means.

The question is whether the straight race with 46...h4 (no points) is sufficient for Black. If you analysed that White has time to take on a6 and then play ♖a8-h8, take two bonus points. An excellent example of rooks belonging behind passed pawns.

The alternative race with 46...♔h2 (c) also needs to be calculated, but this fails to score on the evidence of 47 ♖a8 g3 48 ♖h8. Two bonuses if you worked out this preventative measure.

46...♖f2+ (d) is the text move and scores two points. If the white king retreats to the first rank, Black's pawns will promote with check in the not-too-distant future, while 47 ♔d3 occurs in the game.

**46...♖f2+ 47 ♔d3**

| |
|---|
| a) 47...f5 |
| b) 47...h4 |
| c) 47...♖f3 |
| d) 47...♖b2 |

Nothing for 47...f5 (a), which gives White the opportunity to try 48 ♖xa6, when the a-pawn is quick to the finishing line.

47...h4 (b) is also too slow to merit a score, as White can take on a6, c6 and then play ♖h6.

Three points for 47...♖f3 (c), which keeps up the pressure on White as Savchenko seeks to win the knight with 48...♔f2.

47...♖b2 (d) is not exactly where the action lies, but is sensible enough for one.

**47...⧅f3 48 ⧄e2**

a) 48...f5
b) 48...⧄f4
c) 48...⧅f2+
d) 48...h4

Nothing for 48...f5 (a), which is ineffective. If you realised that 49 ⧅xa6 f4 50 ⧅f5+ stops Black in his tracks, award yourself a bonus.

Minus one for 48...⧄f4 (b), which has lost a tempo on earlier comments when the rook was on f6. The position is critical and one lost move could very well result in the difference between success and complete failure.

48...⧅f2+ (c) scores three points. If the winning attempts do not lead to victory, Black is right to repeat.

Take one point for 48...h4 (d), with a bo-

nus available if you calculated that White's defence lies in 49 ⧅xa6 followed by rook behind the h-pawn.

**48...⧅f2+ 49 ⧄d3**

a) 49...f5
b) 49...h4
c) 49...⧅f3
d) 49...⧅b2

These are the same moves as in the previous position but with slightly different scoring as now it is clear that a repetition is on the cards. Nothing for 49...f5 (a), but one point for the alternatives.

It is worth mentioning that Beliavsky has been one of the world's leading grandmasters for many years. This perhaps affected the decision of Black not to push too hard as a draw with the black pieces against such a respected player is not to be gambled away in a random finish.

**49...⧅f3 50 ⧄e2 ½-½**

It would be extremely risky, at the least, for either of the players to break the deadlock and do something different in this position. White is happy with a draw because he clearly worsens his position by not repeating. Black is happy with a draw because he has scrambled from behind to slightly in front, but it is not clear in which direction he can look in order to search for a win. Remember, one ought to assume that the opponent is going to play the best moves that they can find.

Not every game in chess is decisive. I hope you did not try too hard to win and therefore perhaps ruin your score. Please see below.

Less than 30: You failed to always choose safe, sensible moves.
31-39: You saw your way reasonably well through all the action.
40-49: A commendable result for a regular tournament player.
50-59: A high score for even an international player.
60+: Excellent. Sound judgement in both a complicated middlegame and difficult ending.

# CHAPTER THREE

## A Crossfire of Bishops

In the vast majority of cases, when one is taught how to play chess, one is normally told that the bishop assumes a value of three points. This, however, given all the different types of positions, is just an average value for the bishop. In this chapter we see examples of 'good' bishops that tear the board in half as well as 'bad' bishops that sometimes take the role of a big pawn.

In Games 10-12 we see some bishops that all have their moments. In each of these games, the bishops have their turn to strike. The notes to the games often mention how the game could have turned out badly for the bishop. Perhaps the most striking kind of idea is best explained with the following game when I was on the receiving end.

**Buckley-Lalic**
London 1999
*Bird's Opening*

**1 f4 d5 2 e3 g6 3 ♘f3 ♗g7 4 ♗e2 c5 5 0-0 ♘f6 6 d3 ♘c6 7 a4 b6 8 ♘e5 ♗b7 9 ♘d2 0-0 10 c3 ♕c7 11 d4 ♘e8 12 ♗d3 ♘d6 13 ♕f3 e6 14 ♖b1 f6 15 ♘g4 f5 16 ♘e5 ♘e4 17 ♕e2 g5 18 g3 gxf4 19 gxf4 ♗xe5 20 fxe5 ♔h8 21 ♘f3 ♖g8+ 22 ♔h1 ♕g7 23 ♗d2 ♕h6 24**

**♗xe4 dxe4 25 ♘e1 cxd4 26 cxd4**

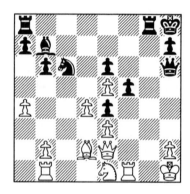

**26...♘xd4 27 exd4 e3+ 28 ♘f3 exd2 29 ♖bd1 ♖g3 30 ♖xd2 ♗d5 31 ♖d3 ♖ag8 32 a5 ♕h3 0-1**

Often children at school ask which is more powerful, a knight or a bishop? They can be satisfied at a young age that each piece is worth three points, but then differences emerge in the pieces that imply that one must be preferable to the other. In Game 14 (just as in the first game of this book), the knight turns out to be superior to the bishop. This is partly because the bishop has little scope because it's blocked.

It can be necessary to go into lengthy explanations that it depends on the position and the structure of the pawns as to which minor piece is better. Whether the diagonals are blocked etc. is also important. Some of the pupils have heard rumours from America, or their dads, that bishops are worth 3.1 or even 4 (against knights, which are worth 3).

The bishop pair on an open board can often be a 'tour de force' and so it proves in Games 10 and 13. In the former, a pair of bishops takes on a knight, bishop and pawn. In this way it is possible for one to assume that each bishop is worth closer to 3.5 points. Indeed, in extreme circumstances, like Game 13, it is not uncommon for play-ers to prefer a pair of bishops to a pair of rooks! Whether in unison, raking down a couple of adjacent diagonals or in crossfire formation, this chapter should illustrate how strong a bishop pair can be.

The fact that it is possible to mate with two bishops and a king versus a king and it is not possible to mate with two knights and a king versus a king (with correct play) is another point to bear in mind when comparing bishops and knights.

It only remains for me to remind you to try and avoid any blunders to maximise your scores in this chapter. Enjoy the high-class games.

## Game 10
## **Ivanchuk-Anand**
Shenyang 2000

**1 e4 c5 2 ♘f3 d6 3 d4**

For those readers interested in but not familiar with nomenclature, this is an Open Sicilian, which Black chooses to meet with the Najdorf Variation on move five, only to transpose into a Scheveningen Variation on move 6.

**3...cxd4 4 ♘xd4 ♘f6 5 ♘c3 a6 6 ♗e2 e6 7 0-0 ♗e7 8 f4 0-0 9 ♔h1 ♕c7 10 a4 ♘c6 11 ♗e3 ♖e8 12 ♗f3 ♖b8**

The last two rook moves are sort of waiting moves. There is no immediate threat by White and so Black wants to see how White intends to play the position. The thrust g2-g4-g5 is not uncommon here.

**13 ♕d2 ♗d7 14 ♘b3**

The reader is now invited to take control of the black position after the diagram.

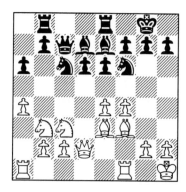

a) 14...♖bc8
b) 14...♘b4
c) 14...b6
d) 14...♘a5

It is essential to answer the basic question of why White retreated on his previous move. First off, he wanted to avoid the exchange of knights, when Black can follow

up with ...♗c6. Secondly, White is threatening a4-a5 which would really cramp Black. This is important from the point of view of completing this exercise successfully. Therefore, Black scores three points for 14...b6 (c) or, if you must, then 14...♘a5 (d) scores one point. With the latter you are a bit stretched and you have allowed 14...♘a5 15 ♘xa5 ♕xa5 16 e5 dxe5 17 fxe5 ♕xe5 (17...♘d5 18 ♘xd5 ♕xd2 19 ♘xe7+ ♖xe7 20 ♗xd2 is a worse way of playing it for Black) 18 ♗f4 ♕a5 19 ♗xb8 ♖xb8. That was a lengthy variation for just a one-point material advantage, but if you spotted it then you can add two points to your score.

If you chose 14...♖bc8 (a) or 14...♘b4 (b), then you can also have one point to get you off the mark, but be warned, the game has started!

**14...b6 15 ♖ae1**

a) 15...e5
b) 15...d5
c) 15...♗f8
d) 15...♗c8

Now that Black has played ...b7-b6, it makes more sense to switch the bishop round to b7. Additionally, by vacating the d7-square, the knight from f6 may have somewhere to retreat if it is required. For those players not acquainted with the Scheveningen, this may look as though Black has wasted time in the opening. However, Black's play is correct since he could not have played ...b6 earlier than he did because ♘d4xc6 and e4-e5, if appropriate, would have dealt Black a devastating blow. I hope this fully explains why 15...♗c8 (d) scores three points whereas 15...♗f8 (c) scores just two points. With the latter, it seems that ....♗c8 is inevitable so Black should not delay. For example, 15...♗f8 16 ♗f2 (or 16 g4) 16...♗c8 17 ♗g3.

One point for 15...e5 (a), which leaves Black in a tight squeeze after 16 f5. Deduct one for 15...d5 (b), when White is spoilt for choice between 16 exd5, which wins a pawn, and 16 e5 ♘e4 17 ♘xe4 dxe4 18 ♗xe4, which also nets a pawn.

**15...♗c8 16 e5**

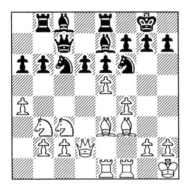

> a) 16...♘d7
> b) 16...dxe5
> c) 16...♘xe5
> d) 16...d5

It is obviously not wise to give away material at this stage by just playing 16...♘xe5 (c), which loses two points, or 16...d5 (d), which also loses two points in view of 17 exf6.

16...♘d7 (a) is safe and earns one point, while 16...dxe5 (b) scores two.

**16...dxe5 17 ♗xc6**

> a) 17...♘d7
> b) 17...exf4
> c) 17...♕xc6
> d) 17...♖d8

It is too late to start working out the consequences. It surely has to be 17...♕xc6 (c) for one point. 17...♘d7 (a) is a straightforward blunder and loses three points, and 17...exf4 (b) loses five from your total because of 17...exf4 18 ♗xf4 ♕xc6 19

cause of 17...exf4 18 ♗xf4 ♕xc6 19 ♗xb8. The move 17...♖d8 (d) does not work either and loses four points because of 18 ♕f2 ♕xc6 19 fxe5 ♘d7 20 ♕xf7+ ♔h8 21 ♕xe7. If you rejected (d) and saw that White can get through to f7 like this, then give yourself an extra point.

Alert readers amongst us can take an extra point for noticing that White could have tried 17 fxe5 on his previous turn. The idea that earns you another bonus is that after 17...♘xe5 White has 18 ♗f4, which is somewhat awkward for Black. There could have followed 18...♘xf3 19 ♖xf3 ♕a7 20 ♗xb8 ♕xb8, when White is a point up but Black has two bishops that are sometimes valued at seven points when they are on an open board.

**17...♕xc6 18 fxe5**

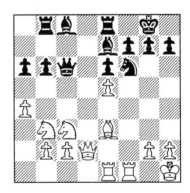

> a) 18...♘d5
> b) 18...♘d7
> c) 18...♘e4
> d) 18...♘g4

Three points for the most active response, 18...♘d5 (a), although it looks like White may be able to win a pawn.

18...♘d7 (b) is passive but scores one because White looks ready to bring his knights into the attack after 19 ♕f2 ♖f8 20 ♕g3 (threatening ♗h6) 20...♔h8. The move 18...♘e4 (c) scores one too, although White's minor pieces look better after 19

♘xe4 ♕xe4 20 ♗xb6 (or 20 ♗g5 ♕b7) 20...♕xa4 21 ♕f2 ♖f8 22 ♗a7 ♖a8 (or 22...♖b4 23 ♖e3) 23 ♗c5.

18...♘g4 (d) is the only serious mistake on the list because the knight is left out on a limb after 19 ♗f4 ♗b7 20 h3 – please deduct one from your score.

## 18...♘d5 19 ♕f2

> **a) 19...♖f8**
> **b) 19...♗f8**
> **c) 19...♗b4**
> **d) 19...♘xe3**

It had to be 19...♖f8 (a) in order to meet White's threat (score two points for this). Deduct one point if you did not notice that White was threatening f7. Deduct two points if you chose 19...♗b4 (c) and one if you chose 19...♘xe3 (d), which fails to 19...♘xe3 20 ♕xf7+ ♔h8 21 ♖xe3.

If you chose 19...♗f8 (b), then you lose all the points you have gained so far but count yourself lucky! The crucial line that you have missed is 19...♗f8 20 ♕xf7+ ♔h8 21 ♕xf8+ ♖xf8 22 ♖xf8 mate. Other readers score a bonus for noticing this mate.

## 19...♖f8 20 ♘xd5

> **a) 20...♕xd5**
> **b) 20...exd5**

It is a fifty-fifty shot this time. 20...♕xd5 (a) scores two points, while 20...exd5 (b) scores one. As well as not looking right, White has a fantastic idea in 20...exd5 21 ♘d4 ♕xa4 22 ♕g3 ♔h8 23 ♖xf7 ♖xf7 24 e6. If you saw this position when analysing, where both Black rooks are attacked, then give yourself a bonus. The advantage for White following 24...♗xe6 25 ♕xb8+ ♖f8 26 ♕xb6 is slight.

## 20...♕xd5 21 ♗xb6

> **a) 21...♖xb6**
> **b) 21...♗b7**
> **c) 21...♗h4**
> **d) 21...♗b4**

21...♗b7 (b) is the most natural and scores three points for developing Black's last piece, while 21...♖xb6 (a) loses two points because of 22 ♕xb6.

Other moves might comes in handy later although neither of them work very well right now. For example, 21...♗h4 (c) scores only one point because after 21...♗h4 22 ♕xh4 ♖xb6 23 ♕g3 White is a pawn up. The move 21...♗b4 (d) scores two points because 22 ♖d1 ♕xe5 23 ♗d4 ♕g5 (23...♕h5 24 ♕g3 is one way that things can go wrong for Black) 24 ♖d3 gives White the chance to play for some tricks even though Black has got his pawn back. If White wants to be more accurate, then he should find 22 ♖e2 a5 23 ♗a7 ♖a8 24 ♗c5 in order to hang onto the pawn, but these moves strike me as tricky to find.

## 21...♗b7 22 ♗c5

The alert reader may have noticed that White can hang onto the pawn with 22 ♖g1, but after 22...f6 he is completely passive. By the way, and another point if you noticed it, White was defending against 22...♕xg2+ 23 ♕xg2 ♗xg2+ 24 ♔xg2 ♖xb6.

> **a) 22...♗xc5**
> **b) 22...♗h4**
> **c) 22...♖fe8**
> **d) 22...♖be8**

Now is the time for 22...♗h4 (b), which scores three points.

22...♗xc5 (a) is safe enough for one point, but it does drive the White knight onto a good square with 23 ♘xc5.

22...♖fe8 (c) loses one point unless you noticed the mischievous trap 22...♖fe8 23 ♕xf7+ ♔h8. Now suddenly White finds himself without a good move and has to play 24 ♕f2 ♗h4 25 ♕g1 ♗xe1 26 ♖xe1, in which case you can add two to your score for choosing this option. Unfortunately for you, if you were banking on that, White can play simply with 23 ♗xe7 ♖xe7 24 ♘c5 and Black's position is not great.

22...♖be8 (d) scores one point because it safe, but again play should continue 22...♖be8 23 ♗xe7 ♖xe7.

**22...♗h4 23 ♕e2**

23 ♕g1 ♗xe1 24 ♗xf8 ♖c8 25 ♗c5 ♗h4 is also useful for Black.

> a) 23...♗xe1
> b) 23...♖fd8
> c) 23...♖fc8
> d) 23...a5

Black fails to make any impression with either 23...♗xe1 (a) 24 ♗xf8 ♖xf8 25 ♖xe1 or 23...♖fd8 (b) 24 ♗d6 ♗xe1 25 ♗xb8 ♖xb8 26 ♖xe1, both of which score one point. That leaves 23...♖fc8 (c) to top score with four points because Black has both rooks very nicely positioned.

23...a5 (d) is irrelevant and loses three due to 24 ♗xf8 ♗xe1 25 ♗d6, which means that, albeit in vain, Black should try 24...♖xf8 once 23...a5 has been played.

**23...♖fc8 24 ♖d1**

> a) 24...♕xg2+
> b) 24...♕e4
> c) 24...♕c6
> d) 24...♖xc5

24...♕xg2+ (a) is a straightforward way to lose two points. Black should not rely on the bad ending following 25 ♕xg2 ♗xg2+ 26 ♔xg2 ♖xb3 27 cxb3 ♖xc5.

24...♖xc5 (d) loses five points, not just

because Black is giving away the queen but because he is in for a nasty shock with 24...♖xc5 25 ♖xd5 ♖xd5 26 ♕h5.

24...♕e4 (b) is best and scores a maximum three points. Notice how Black is not afraid to exchange queens even though he is a pawn down. First off, he has a lot going for him with his rooks. Secondly, the bishop pair often triumphs against bishop plus knight in such an open position. Having pawns on both sides of the board will also suit Black more than White here.

That only leaves us to comment on 24...♕c6 (c), which loses one point. As a matter of fact, it leaves White with an interesting choice. He could try 25 ♗d6 ♖a8 26 ♘c5 with a formidable position, and it is even worse if Black tries 25...♕xc2 26 ♖d2 ♕xb3 27 ♗xb8 ♖xb8 because of the ingenious 28 ♕h5 ♕b4 29 ♖d4 ♕xd4 30 ♕xf7+ ♔h8 31 ♕f8+ ♖xf8 32 ♖xf8 mate. I suppose if White did not see that then 25 ♖d4 would also be sufficient for a large advantage.

**24...♕e4 25 ♕xe4**

> a) 25...♗xe4
> b) 25...♗g5

One point for 25...♗xe4 (a). If you really did suggest 25...♗g5 (b), then as a punishment you must complete this game and only include minuses in your score from here.

**25...♗xe4 26 ♗d6**

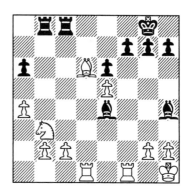

a) 26...♖b6
b) 26...♖b7
c) 26...♖xc2
d) 26...♗xc2

26...♖b6 (a) is okay for one point. Black can hang on to all his pieces after 27 ♖d4 ♗xc2 28 ♘a1 ♗d8 29 ♖c1 ♖bc6. The move 26...♖b7 (b) is much worse because White has 27 ♖d4 ♗xc2 28 ♘c5, so lose three points.

That leaves two interesting captures on c2. With 26...♖xc2 (c), which only scores two points, White has 27 ♗xb8 ♖xg2 28 ♘c5 ♗a8 29 ♖d7 ♖xb2+ 30 ♔g1 ♖g2+ 31 ♔h1, and Black is forced to take a draw from a slightly better endgame position because 31...♖g6+ 32 ♘b7 wins for White! If you saw White's 28th and 29th, then you can have two points for each. It is also rather messy for Black to allow White to complicate with 27 ♘d2 ♖bxb2 28 ♘xe4 ♖xg2 29 ♖f3 ♖xh2+ 30 ♔g1 ♖bg2+ 31 ♔f1 ♖a2 32 ♗c5. Once again, take two points each for spotting White's 27th and 32nd moves.

It remains to say that 26...♗xc2 (d) is best, scores four and keeps some winning chances alive.

**26...♗xc2 27 ♗xb8**

a) 27...♗xd1
b) 27...♖xb8
c) 27...♗xb3
d) 27...♖c4

You have to check your calculation, but it is often good advice in a situation like this to take the piece that is worth the most. Therefore, 27...♗xd1 (a) top scores with three points. The other moves all fail to the same thing in that White then moves and saves his rook from capture by attacking one of Black's pieces. 27...♖xb8 (b) and 27...♗xb3 (c) each lose two points and, more seriously, 27...♖c4 (d) loses four due to 28 ♖d4 ♗xb3 29 ♖xc4 ♗xc4 30 ♖f4.

**27...♗xd1 28 ♖xd1**

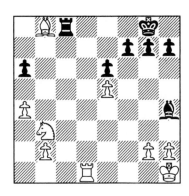

a) 28...♖xb8
b) 28...♖c2

Another fifty-fifty, but it had to be 28...♖xb8 (a) for one point. Lose three if you chose 28...♖c2 (b).

**28...♖xb8 29 ♘a5**

29 ♘c5 tries to get the important black a-pawn but then Black plays 29...a5 and the ending with rook plus bishop versus rook plus knight still favours Black. Notice how Black has exchanged advantages in that he once had the bishop pair and now he has a bishop versus knight ending, still with a rook each and with pawns on both sides of the board.

a) 29...♖xb2
b) 29...♖b4
c) 29...♗d8
d) 29...♖c8

Hopefully this was a simple move to find. Give yourself a point for 29...♖xb2 (a), whether or not you noticed that White cannot 'bank rank' mate you due to your bishop being on h4. You have been warned.

29...♖b4 (b) allows 30 b3 and 29...♖c8 (d) allows 30 b4, when White is able to keep his b-pawn (no points for these). More serious at a cost of three points was 29...♗d8 (c) 30 ♘c6.

**29...♖xb2 30 g3**

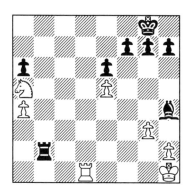

a) 30...♗g5
b) 30...♗e7
c) 30...♖a2
d) 30...♖e2

One for 30...♗g5 (a) and two for 30...♗e7 (b). It is better for Black if White cannot play h2-h4 with a tempo on the bishop.

It is misguided to try and win some pawns with the rook as in 30...♖a2 (c) and 30...♖e2 (d), which both lose two points. When it comes to it, Black cannot even take the pawns because of the back rank mate, for example 30...♖a2 31 gxh4 ♖xa4 32 ♖d8 mate.

**30...♗e7 31 ♘c6**

a) 31...♔f8
b) 31...♗c5
c) 31...♗f8
d) 31...♖b7

The text move 31...♗f8 (c) is worth two points. One point for 31...♔f8 (a) because after 32 ♖d7 ♗g5 33 h4 Black has the easy-to-miss saving resource 33...♔e8.

As for 31...♖b7 (d), take off three points for missing the simple 32 ♘xe7+, when you would have to play 32...♔f8 to avoid mate. As for 31...♗c5 (b), that's a really bad slip that will cost you ten points now and for every move where you blunder anything from now on. After all, you have allowed

yourself to be mated via 31...♗c5 32 ♖d8+ ♗f8 33 ♘e7+ ♔h8 34 ♖xf8 mate.

**31...♗f8 32 ♖d8**

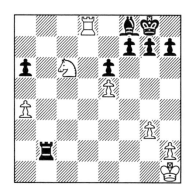

a) 32...h6
b) 32...g6
c) 32...g5
d) 32...♖b7

32...h6 (a) does not really help your cause and you lose four points because of 33 ♘e7+ ♔h7 34 ♖xf8.

32...♖b7 (d) loses just one point due to 33 ♖a8. (That has cost you a pawn and ten points if you got mated on the previous move.)

32...g6 (b) is appropriate and scores you two points. An improvement on this, however, is 32...g5 (c) for three points. If in addition you noticed 32...g5 33 ♖a8 g4, when the immediate 34 ♖xa6 ♗c5 35 a5 leads to mate with 35...♖b1+ 36 ♔g2 ♖g1 mate, then take a point for 33...g4 and another one for noting some checkmating lines. The reality is that White must bail out with 35 h4 gxh3, which suits Black very nicely. Well done.

**32...g5 33 h4**

a) 33...h6
b) 33...gxh4
c) 33...g4
d) 33...♖c2

33...b4 (c) is the wrong application of the

checkmating idea given in the note to Black's previous move. It is not mate now because White has played h4 and given himself the escape square h2, should Black try ...♗c5 and ...♖g1.

You lose one point because of 33...g4 34 ♖a8. If you realised that White was threatening ♖a8, then give yourself a bonus. 33...h6 (a) has the same problem and also loses one point. 33...♖c2 (d) will also run Black into trouble but this time via 33...♖c2 34 ♘b8, so lose a point from your total if you chose this option.

33...gxh4 (b) makes most sense and scores three points.

**33...gxh4 34 gxh4**

> a) 34...♖a2
> b) 34...♖c2
> c) 34...♖e2
> d) 34...♔g7

34...♖a2 (a) earns one point and is safe for the very next move, but how can Black meet the threat to the a-pawn that follows ♖a8? A likely continuation is then the move 35 a5.

34...♖e2 (c) loses one because White can continue 35 ♖a8 immediately. 34...♖c2 (b) earns three and is best, but as we shall see, Black's task is still not easy.

'What about 34...♔g7?' I hear you cry. Yes, you should try and activate your king in the ending, and yes, ...♔g8-g7 is where it wants to go. However, the white rook and knight are combining together fiendishly well after 35 ♖a8 ♖b6 36 ♘b8. It looks like the a-pawn will vanish but then 36...a5 is suddenly a defence. If you spotted that, give yourself two points. A likely continuation is 37 ♘d7 ♖b1+ (forced) 38 ♔g2 ♗b4 (forced if you want to defend the a-pawn) 39 ♔f3. White's king is also active now and you can give yourself another two points if you spotted that. This position is not at all easy for Black.

**34...♖c2 35 ♘b8**

> a) 35...♖c4
> b) 35...♖c1+
> c) 35...♔g7
> d) 35...a5

No score to 35...♖c1+ (b), which just puts off an important decision for one move after 36 ♔g2. Both 35...♖c4 (a) and 35...a5 (d) both fail to the white knight not taking the a-pawn but playing 36 ♘d7. Both lose two points.

Now it is right to play 35...♔g7 (c) for three points. Black wins more than just the a-pawn after 36 ♘xa6 ♖c4.

**35...♔g7 36 ♖d4**

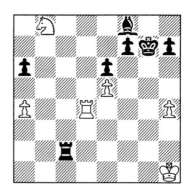

> a) 36...a5
> b) 36...♖c5
> c) 36....♗c5
> d) 36...♔g6

The a-pawn is under fire and it is best to move it. Take three points for 36...a5 (a). White has nothing dangerous after 36...a5 37 ♖g4+ ♔h6 38 ♘d7. The first stage is to stop the knight joining in (38...♗e7 39 ♖f4). Then Black has a good defence to stop any shuttle checks on his king and can play 39...♖c7 40 ♘b6 ♗b4 41 ♘c4 ♔g6. Finally, he can sort out his king before activating the rook with 42 ♔g2 h5 43 ♔f3 ♖d7.

36...♖c5 (b) allows a pair of pawns (not pieces) to be exchanged, which is exactly what White wants as he is a pawn down.

Therefore 36...♖c5 37 ♘xa6 ♖xe5 scores just one point.

36...♗c5 (c) is not a success and loses one point after 37 ♖g4+ ♔h6 38 ♘xa6.

36...♔g6 (d) is an attempt to further activate the king in the ending. Right idea, wrong application because White has 36...♔g6 37 ♘xa6 ♔f5 38 ♖d7. You lose a point from your score.

**36...a5 37 ♘d7**

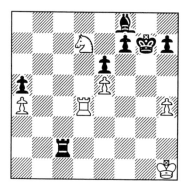

a) 37...♗e7
b) 37...♗c5
c) 37...h5
d) 37...♖c1+

This is a case of being prepared to exchange advantages. At one stage, with pawns on both sides of the board, then it would have been wise for Black to avoid exchanging minor pieces. Now, however, one can study the pawn formations and see that the rook ending is very comfortable for Black. Therefore Black need not worry about the minor piece exchange but he does have to have ♖g4+ covered. 37...h5 (c) fits

the bill nicely for three points.

37...♗e7 (a) scores one point and it can transpose into the note to 36...a5 on the previous move. Black, however, has now been given a chance to make things even easier for himself and can avoid 37...♗e7 38 ♖g4+ ♔h6.

37...♗c5 (b) is certainly not best and scores nothing because it lets the knight cause some havoc around the black king with 38 ♖g4+ ♔h6 39 ♘f6 ♗e7 40 ♘g8+ ♔h5 41 ♖g7.

37...♖c1+ (d) is silly and only helps the white king, so lose a point.

**37...h5 38 ♘xf8**

a) 38...♔xf8
b) 38...♖c1+
c) 38...♔g8
d) 38...♔h8

There is only one serious move here and it is 38...♔xf8 (a) for one point. No score for anything else.

**38...♔xf8 39 ♖d8 +**

a) 39...♔e7
b) 39...♔g7

39...♔e7 (a) is a slip and only scores one point because White can go hunting after a pawn with 39...♔e7 40 ♖h8.

39...♔g7 (b) scores three points and, with a methodical approach, Black should win easily after 40 ♖a8 ♖c5 or 40 ♖d4 ♖e2, when Black is free to advance his king and can win another pawn.

**39...♔g7 0-1**

White resigns. At this level, this position is hopeless for White.

Now add up your points and see if you played like one of the world's elite.

Less than 15: Sorry, not up to scratch today.
15-28: I hope you can see what you need to do to improve.
29-49: The middle ground indicates sensible play with few lapses.
50-70: Well done! This is getting to be a really serious score.
71+: Fantastic! Challenge Anand and the winner plays...

---

# Game 11
## Motylev-Adams
European Club Cup, Neum 2000

---

**1 e4 e5 2 ♘f3 ♘c6 3 d4**

The Scotch experienced a revival when Kasparov included it in his opening arsenal just over a decade ago.

**3...exd4 4 ♘xd4 ♘f6 5 ♘xc6 bxc6 6 e5 ♕e7 7 ♕e2 ♘d5 8 c4 ♘b6 9 ♘d2 ♕e6 10 ♕e4 ♗a6**

A useful post for the bishop. Of particular importance is whether the bishop can become active along the a6-f1 diagonal. If not, it can be too time-consuming for Black to play ...d7-d6, ...♗c8 and then develop.

**11 a3 ♗e7 12 ♗d3**

The time has arrived for the reader to take over. Remember, you are playing from Black's point of view. I would advise turning your chess set around if you have not already done so and then you can look at the game from the black perspective.

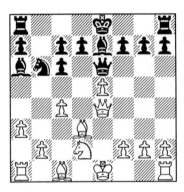

a) 12...0-0
b) 12...0-0-0
c) 12...d5
d) 12...♗g5

12...d5 (c) is a good strike for two points. I hinted that Black should be playing to free the bishop and so 12...d5 was a logical try.

You had the right sentiment if you wanted to castle. 12...0-0 (a) loses a nominal five points for falling for 13 ♕xh7 mate. 12...0-0-0 (b) is much more sensible and scores one point. It is interesting to note that Black can often castle on either side in this variation.

12...♗g5 (d) scores no points and encourages 13 f4, when Black loses a tempo.

**12...d5 13 exd6**

a) 13...cxd6
b) 13...♗xd6
c) 13...♕xe4+
d) 13...♕xd6

Two points for 13...cxd6 (a), which is the best way not to damage Black's pawn structure. Both 13...♗xd6 (b) 14 ♕xe6+ (lose one if you planned the illegal 14 ♕xc6+ as White is in check here!) and 13...♕xd6 (d) fail to score. The pawn islands are chronically weak. Should Black survive to an endgame, the pawns would be eaten up easily.

13...♕xe4+ (c) loses three points. If you rejected this on account of 14 ♗xe4 cxd6 15 ♗xc6+, then take a bonus point.

**13...cxd6 14 ♕xe6**

a) 14...fxe6
b) 14...0-0

No messing about this time. 14...fxe6 scores one point, while no comment and no points for 14...0-0 (b).

**14...fxe6 15 b3**

a) 15...0-0
b) 15...0-0-0
c) 15...♗f6
d) 15...♘d7

Black's moves are all safe this time.

15...0-0 (a), 15...0-0-0 (b) and 15...♘d7 (d) all allow White to develop with 16 ♗b2 and so they each get one point. 15...♗f6 (c) scores three points as it takes into account what White wants to do and prevents it.

**15...♗f6 16 ♖a2**

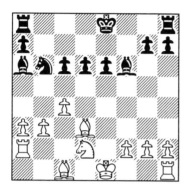

> a) 16...d5
> b) 16...♗c3
> c) 16...e5
> d) 16...♘d5

16...♘d5 (d) scores minus two if you did not even notice 17 cxd5 ♗xd3, but take off just one if you had not foreseen 18 dxc6 ♖c8 or 18 dxe6 ♔e7. If you saw all that then you can have two points, although the move is hardly a stunner because White can just play 17 ♘e4, which is a more than significant reaction to Black's move. No, 16...d5 (a) is consistent. Nothing has changed to alter Black's plan, so 16...d5 scores three points.

16...♗c3 (b) and 16...e5 (c) are both adequate for one point.

**16...d5 17 ♔e2**

> a) 17...dxc4
> b) 17...d4
> c) 17...e5
> d) 17...♗c3

17...dxc4 (a) and 17...d4 (b) each score one point but they are both too committal and give squares away to White, which will

allow him a freer game. 17...e5 (c) is much more flexible and scores two points. Notice how White's pieces have been deprived of many squares.

17...♗c3 (d) scores no points. Black is found wanting after 17...♗c3 18 cxd5 ♗xd3+ 19 ♔xd3. Whatever Black plays, the white rooks will quickly come to the c- and e-files. Even the white king is now well placed in an ending because now there are far fewer pieces on the board.

**17...e5 18 f3**

> a) 18...0-0-0
> b) 18...♖d8
> c) 18...d4
> d) 18...dxc4

Nothing has changed since I last commented on 18...d4 (c) and 18...dxc4 (d), so these both score one point.

Castling gets the rook into the action and hides the king while there remains so many pieces on the board. I know queens have been exchanged, but that is about all and so 18...0-0-0 (a) scores two points.

18...♖d8 (b) was Adams' choice, which also earns two points.

**18...♖d8 19 a4**

> a) 19...d4
> b) 19...dxc4
> c) 19...♘d7
> d) 19...0-0

I am losing patience if you suggested 19...d4 (a) or 19...dxc4 (b), so no points. There's plenty to be doing instead of these moves, namely getting your other rook into play, and so 19...0-0 (d) scores two points. Just one for 19...♘d7 (c), which is not necessary before castling.

**19...0-0 20 ♗a3**

> a) 20...♖fe8
> b) 20...♖f7
> c) 20...dxc4
> d) 20...e4

Minus one for 20...e4 (d), which is the only outright blunder because of 21 fxe4. 20...dxc4 (c) still does not score.

Whichever move you chose (except for 20...e4), you can have a point if you spotted that the bishop attacks the rook on f8. In addition, 20...♖fe8 (a) scores two points and 20...♖f7 (b) scores one point.

**20...♖fe8 21 ♗c5**

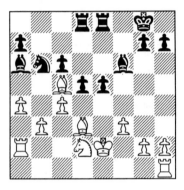

> a) 21...e4
> b) 21...♘c8
> c) 21...♘d7
> d) 21...d4

21...e4 (a) loses a pawn and a point. If you have reason to protest violently to this scoring and, if you thought of any of the following reasons, then please add on a point for each:

1) The bishop on f6 has increased scope now.

2) You can foresee that White will have split and weak pawns so it is no great shakes that he will have an extra one.

3) The position will open up considerably, which will give Black practical chances against a white's king which hasn't castled.

21...♘c8 (b) scores one point because it is safe, but White improves the positioning of his pieces 22 ♖c1.

You can have one point for 21...d4 (d), although I do not like such a committal pawn move that allows White to play into

the e4-square at will.

21...♘d7 (c) loses one, unless you spotted the idea of trapping the bishop with 22 ♗xa7 d4 (score one). This threatens ...♖a8 so it makes sense for White to play 23 a5 ♖a8 24 ♗b6, which earns you a bonus. Any subsequent counterplay that Black may find is due to the earlier part of the game and is not as a result of playing 21...♘d7.

**21...e4 22 fxe4**

> a) 22...dxe4
> b) 22...dxc4
> c) 22...d4
> d) 22...♘d7

I have already commented on the idea contained in 22...♘d7 (d), which loses one unless you applied the note to Black's 21st move and spotted 22...♘d7 23 ♗xa7 d4. A further point can be rewarded for calculating 24 a5.

You can have one point, just about, if you chose 22...d4 (c), but it blocks the position and Black is the one who should be trying to open up the board so that he can have a go at the white king.

22...dxe4 (a) captures a pawn so you can have one point for this. Another point is due if it was your instinct that told you to open up the board. Two more points (one for each) can be scored for realising that it was important to try to (1) free the bishop on a6 and (2) open the d-and e-files for the rooks. In detail, one more point for noticing 22...dxe4 23 ♗xe4 ♖xd2+ 24 ♖xd2 ♖xe4+, which is nice for Black. Another can be scored for seeing 23 ♘xe4 ♘xc4 24 bxc4 ♖xe4+ 25 ♗xe4 ♗xc4+ 26 ♔f3 ♗xa2, but after 27 ♖c1 Black has to admit that the pawn advantage will not last long. You are also tactically alert to notice 23 ♗b1 e3 24 ♘e4 ♘xc4, so you had better score another point for that.

If you saw some of these 'clever' lines but still rejected this option, then you did well and can score two more points. If you chose more favourably with 22...dxc4 (b), then add two extra to your score. There's no more for spotting 22...dxc4 23 ♘xc4 ♘xc4 24 bxc4 ♖xe4+ 25 ♗xe4 ♗xc4+ 26 ♔f3 ♗xa2 because we have already seen this, but you can have two points for seeing 23...♘d5, which contains a large number of threats.

One final addition before we move on. For one point, did you spot that 23 ♗xc4+ ♘xc4 24 bxc4 appears to be a tougher nut to crack than anything else so far? It is possible that 24...♗d4 gives a lasting positional advantage.

**22...dxc4 23 bxc4**

> a) 23...♗d4
> b) 23...♘c8
> c) 23...♘d7
> d) 23...♖d7

One point for 23...♗d4 (a), which allows 24 ♗xb6 ♗xb6 and the light-squared bishop may have trouble breaking out. One point also for 23...♘c8 (b) and for 23...♖d7 (d), which may continue 24 a5 ♘c8 and is therefore similar to (b).

23...♘d7 (c) scores two points. You can have one for noticing a sample continuation of 24 ♗xa7 c5 25 a5 ♘e5 26 ♖a3 ♗g5, when White has to tread very carefully to avoid dropping material in a major way.

**23...♘d7 24 ♗d6**

> a) 24...♘e5
> b) 24...♗e5
> c) 24...♖e6
> d) 24...♗g5

You can have one point for 24...♗g5 (d), even though it encourages 25 ♘f3. The move 24...♖e6 (c) also scores just one because White plays 25 ♗c7 and kicks the rook away from the valuable open file. A further point is awarded for spotting the crucifying trap 25 c5 ♗xd3+ 26 ♔xd3 ♘xc5+.

That leaves Black to think about what

piece he wants to put on e5 and the consequences of a possible exchange. 24...♘e5 (a) scores one point, but 24...♗e5 (b) scores three because should there be an exchange, the knight would be a monster.

**24...♗e5 25 ♗a3**

> a) 25...♗d4
> b) 25...♗c7
> c) 25...♗f6
> d) 25...♗f4

Black vacates the e5-square in order to threaten the mighty ...♘e5. 25...♗d4 (a) scores only one as the bishop blocks the potentially useful d-file. 25...♗f4 (d) also scores just one because after 25...♗f4 26 g3 the bishop cannot eye up different diagonals and possibly has to settle for h6 as the best retreat square. In contrast, 25...♗c7 (b) scores three points. Another point is scored for realising the possible usefulness of being able to play either ...♗a5 or ...♗f4 in the future.

25...♗f6 (c) scores one and just offers to repeat the position with 26 ♗d6, which I am sure White would be more than happy to go for at this stage.

**25...♗c7 26 ♖b1**

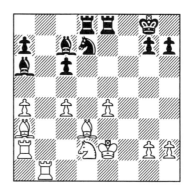

> a) 26...♗xh2
> b) 26...♗a5
> c) 26...♘e5
> d) 26...♘b6

I cannot argue with 26...♗xh2 (a), which scores two points, except to say that Black has better than this. 26...♘e5 (c) is the logical follow-up and this scores an impressive five points.

26...♗a5 (b) and 26...♘b6 (d) each score one point. The former allows White to rectify his position with 27 ♘b3 ♗c7 28 ♘c5.

**26...♘e5 27 ♖b3**

> a) 27...♖d7
> b) 27...♘xd3
> c) 27...♖xd3
> d) 27...♗a5

27...♖d7 (a) and 27...♘d3 (b) each score one point. The latter allows an exchange of pieces, which should favour White.

27...♖xd3 (c) scores one point. You can have a point for noticing 28 ♖xd3 ♘xd3 29 ♔xd3 ♗xh2. More difficult for White to meet is 28...♘xc4, which also earns a point. The following continuation is worth a point: 29 ♘xc4? ♗xc4 30 ♖c2? ♖xe4+ 31 ♔d2 ♗f4+ 32 ♔c3 ♗e5+ 33 ♔d2 ♗xd3 34 ♔xd3 ♖e3+ and Black wins a bishop.

Adams' choice of 27...♗a5 (d) top scores with five points.

**27...♗a5 28 ♔e3**

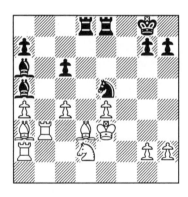

> a) 28...♗b6+
> b) 28...♗xd2+
> c) 28...♘g4+
> d) 28...♘xd3

28...♗b6+ (a) scores one point because White is more than hanging on after 29 c5 ♖xd3+ 30 ♖xd3 ♗xd3 31 cxb6 axb6.

28...♗xd2 (b) scores four points. I am assuming that if you've previously guessed the moves, then you should now try not to guess and therefore have some reason why you chose 28...♗xd2.

28...♘g4 (c) scores one point, as White can block the major threats with 29 ♔e2 ♘xh2 30 ♗b4.

If you chose 28...♘xd3 (d), then you can score one point. You are heading for a dead draw with 28...♘xd3 29 ♖xd3 ♖xd3+ 30 ♔xd3 ♗xd2 31 ♖xd2 ♖d8+ 32 ♔c3 ♖xd2 33 ♔xd2 ♗xc4 because endings with bishops of opposite colour have a tendency to be drawn and this one should not be an exception to the rule.

**28...♗xd2+ 29 ♖xd2**

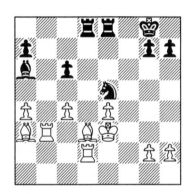

> a) 29...♗xc4
> b) 29...♘g4+
> c) 29...♘xc4+
> d) 29...♘xd3

29...♗xc4 (a) is straightforward and best for four points.

29...♘g4+ (b) scores one, but after 30 ♔f4 ♘xh2, even though Black has got the pawn back, White has an active king in the ending accompanied by the bishop pair on an open board. Black also might have to take care that the knight does not get trapped with ♖f2 and, if necessary, ♗e2 and ♔g3.

29...♘xc4 (c) scores a generous one because after 29...♘xc4+ 30 ♗xc4+ ♗xc4 31 ♖xd8 ♖xd8 32 ♖c3 White regains the pawn advantage. You can have a point if you calculated that and therefore rejected 29...♘xc4.

29...♘xd3 (d) scores one point, with another for seeing 30 ♖bxd3 ♖xd3+ 31 ♖xd3 ♗xc4, although even here White has 32 ♖d7 with a sizeable ending advantage (but not 32 ♖c3 as Black has 32...♗d5 this time).

**29...♗xc4 30 ♗c2**

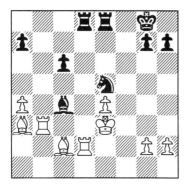

a) 30...♗xb3
b) 30...♖xd2
c) 30...♘g4+
d) 30...♗e6

30...♗xb3 (a) scores two points for capturing a safe exchange, but after 31 ♗xb3+ ♔h8 32 ♖d6 White has some practical chances of holding on. I shall score 30...♖xd2 (b) in the same way, so two

points for 30...♖xd2 31 ♔xd2 ♗xb3 32 ♗xb3+ ♔h8.

30...♘g4+ (c) scores two points, with another three for seeing that you can hold onto almost a whole rook with after 31 ♔f4 ♖xd2 (just one extra if you only saw this far) 32 ♖c3 ♗e6. I know that White can grab a pawn with 33 ♖xc6, but then Black has time to find a move to defend the threat of ♖xe6 followed by ♗b3 and ♔xg4.

It has been a fine line between White having an active king and White having a king that has been harassed, but with accurate play Adams has finally managed to punish the exposed king all too severely, especially for players at that advanced grandmaster level.

I have not forgotten 30...♗e6 (d), which scores nought. You have not even tried winning your pawn back if you selected this option and, as already mentioned, Black has a lot better than that.

**30...♘g4+ 0-1**

White resigns due to the analysis and reasons already given. I am sure, however, that many a lesser mortal would have played on at least a few more moves. Sometimes this is thought of as bad manners, particularly against stronger opposition, but a weaker player may use the excuse that he or she was trying to reach the time control before taking stock (and resigning), and in many international events this is not until move 40. This game saw a total humiliation for White, who faced Adams at his most devastating, combining positional play with vicious tactics.

All that remains now is for you to add up your points and see how you did.

Less than 17: Remember and repeat the good (but not the bad) in future.
17-31: Chess is a difficult game. Please do not rush these exercises.
32-49: Presumably you found safe moves but did you look for better moves?
50-62: Wonderful. Are you hardworking or just naturally gifted, or both?
63+: This is a really great score. Not many players score this high.

## Game 12
## **Leko-Adams**
Dortmund 1999

**1 e4 e5 2 ♘f3 ♘c6 3 ♗b5 a6 4 ♗a4 ♘f6 5 0-0 ♗e7**

Black can play 5...♘xe4 6 d4 b5 7 ♗b3 d5 8 dxe5 ♗e6, which is the Open Variation. If you do this in a game, please try not to hold onto the pawn at the expense of castling.

**6 ♖e1 b5 7 ♗b3 0-0 8 c3 d5**

The sharp Marshall Gambit is just another chess opening named after a great player from a different era. If White wants to avoid this possibility then he can consider 8 a4.

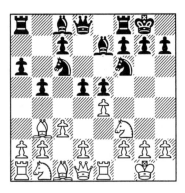

a) 9 d3
b) 9 d4
c) 9 ♗c2
d) 9 exd5

It is very passive to play 9 d3 (a), but you can have one point because White is hanging on to everything after 9...dxe4 10 dxe4 ♕xd1 11 ♗xd1 ♗b7. On the other hand, it is wrong to play 9 ♗c2 (c), which loses one point. White is pushed backwards with the simple moves 9...dxe4 10 ♗xe4 ♘xe4 11 ♖xe4 ♗f5 12 ♖e2 e4 13 ♘e1.

You can have one point for playing 9 d4

(b). However, I suspect that not many readers truly examined 9...exd4 10 exd5 or 10 e5. There are a number of different possibilities, namely 9...♘xe4 10 ♘xe5 (or 10 dxe5); or 9...♗g4 10 exd5; or even 9...dxe4 10 ♘xe5 (or 10 dxe5). If you considered all these then you can have a bonus, but it is simpler for the moment to play 9 exd5 (d) for two points.

**9 exd5 ♘xd5**

a) 10 d4
b) 10 d3
c) 10 ♘xe5
d) 10 c4

10 d4 (a) scores one point. After 10...exd4 11 ♘xd4 ♘xd4 12 ♕xd4 ♗b7 Black is nicely developed and White cannot win material with 13 ♗xd5 ♗xd5 14 ♖xe7 due to a back-rank mate at the end of the sequence.

10 d3 (b) is also safe ands earns a point. However, one feels that Black is ahead in development and so White really should take the pawn with 10 ♘xe5 (c) – take two for this.

10 c4 (d) is safe, but does not score as it does not help development. After 10...♘f4 11 ♘xe5 ♘xe5 12 ♖xe5 ♗b7 Black already stands well.

**10 ♘xe5 ♘xe5**

a) 11 ♗xd5
b) 11 ♖xe5
c) 11 d4
d) 11 ♕h5

It's asking for trouble if you did not capture back with 11 ♖xe5 (b), which scores one point. There is a bonus of one if you visualised this position when you played 9 exd5. I don't like to use the word 'obvious' because I believe that a lot of the ideas in chess are not so. However, if anything is obvious, then it is the fact that it is very important to capture as the knight on e5 is worth three points.

11 ♗xd5 (a) loses three points because of 11...♕xd5 12 d4 ♘g6. Similarly, 11 d4 (c) loses three points because of 11...♘g6. You also lose three for 11 ♕h5 (d), unless you had convinced yourself by thinking deeply, in which case you lose six. Common sense should have prevailed at some point if only to avoid something like 11 ♕h5 ♗f6 12 d4 ♗g4.

**11 ♖xe5 c6**

> a) 12 d4
> b) 12 d3
> c) 12 a4
> d) 12 ♘a3

White is a pawn up but he lags in development and therefore he should do something about that with either 12 d4 (a) or 12 d3 (b), which each earn two points.

A plan involving 12 a4 (c) is wrong and after 12...♗d6 13 ♖e1 ♕h4 14 g3 ♕h3 15 axb5 ♗g4 Black has a winning attack. White could, however, try the normal move 15 d4 in order to reach an okay position. In a similar vein, and also scoring one, is 12 ♘a3 (d) because after 12 ♘a3 ♗d6 13 ♖e1 ♕h4 14 g3 ♕h3 again White must revert to 15 d4 in order to make the position playable.

**12 d4 ♗d6**

> a) 13 ♖h5
> b) 13 ♖e2
> c) 13 ♖e1
> d) 13 ♕h5

Disastrous and losing six points is 13 ♕h5 (d) ♗xe5 14 ♕xe5 ♖e8. The last trick has previously been pointed out.

13 ♖h5 (a) loses one point because Black is comfortable after 13...g6 14 ♖h6 ♖e8.

One can play 13 ♖e2 (b) for two points,

when the rook turns out to be a useful defender along the second rank and prevents some winning sacrifices. A possible continuation is 13...♕h4 14 g3 ♕h3 15 ♘d2 ♗g4 16 f3. Probably 15...♗f5 is better from Black's point of view.

13 ♖e1 (c) is also worth two points.

**13 ♖e1 ♕h4**

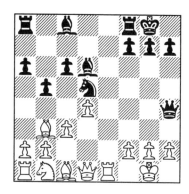

> a) 14 h3
> b) 14 g3
> c) 14 ♕f3
> d) 14 ♗xd5

The only acceptable move is 14 g3 (b), which scores three points. This move should be made with the following warning: White should only play this move if there is no satisfactory alternative because, as the position stands, the light squares around his king are a little weak. Give yourself a bonus if you foresaw this before Black played 13...♕h4.

Other moves lose. 14 h3 (a) scores one point as it stops mate, but it does allow Black to sacrifice and gain a winning attack by 14...♗xh3 15 g3 ♗xg3, or 15 gxh3 ♕xh3 16 ♗xd5 ♗h2+ 17 ♔h1 ♗g3+ 18 ♔g1 ♕h2+ 19 ♔f1 ♕xf2 mate. White's best is therefore to play 15 ♗xd5 cxd5 16 gxh3 ♕xh3 17 ♗e3 f5 18 f4 ♖f6, when he will still face mate. Give yourself a bonus if you saw the 'sac' on h3 for Black and then rejected choice (a).

14 ♕f3 (c) loses two points because Black can simply play 14...♕xh2+ 15 ♔f1 before following up with the strong 15...h5. The move 14 ♗xd5 (d) also loses two points because Black has the 'in between' move or zwischenzug 15...♕xh2+. After 15 ♔f1 cxd5 White is in a mess.

**14 g3 ♕h3**

> a) 15 ♗e3
> b) 15 ♘d2
> c) 15 ♖e4
> d) 15 ♕f3

You are on the right lines if you tried to exchange queens with 15 ♕f3 (d), so you can have one point for planning 15...♗g4 16 ♕g2 (no points if you did not see this). However, Black stands well, while White is blocked in after 16...♕h5 17 ♘d2 ♖ae8.

15 ♗e3 (a) scores two, with an extra one if you noticed that you can complete development with 15 ♗e3 ♗g4 16 ♕d3 ♖ae8 17 ♘d2. The move 15 ♖e4 (c) is also satisfactory and scores two points, but it is not a move that I would recommend unless you have played against the Marshall before.

Finally, 15 ♘d2 (b) loses three points because Black can develop sensibly and set up all kinds of threats. For example, 15...♗g4 16 f3 ♗xg3 17 hxg3 ♕xg3+ 18 ♔f1 ♘f4 (or 18 ♔h1 ♘f4) and Black wins on the spot. Black also gets exactly what he wants after 16 ♕c2 ♖ae8 17 ♖f1 ♖e6 18 ♗xd5 ♖h6 19 ♖e1 ♕xh2+ 20 ♔f1 cxd5.

**15 ♖e4 ♗b7**

> a) 16 ♖h4
> b) 16 ♕g4
> c) 16 ♗xd5
> d) 16 ♕f1

Again, you could be forgiven for trying 16 ♕g4 (b), which earns one point. However, after 16...♕xg4 17 ♖xg4 ♖fe8 18 ♔f1 c5 Black has plenty of compensation even though queens have been exchanged. 16 ♕f1 (d) also scores one, but this time Black

can keep queens on the board with 16...♕f5 17 ♗c2 c5.

Two points for 16 ♗xd5 (c), which makes some sense now that the bishop is hemmed in on b7. In general, though, I don't like the idea of exchanging a light-squared bishop for a knight with such a kingside pawn formation.

That leaves 16 ♖h4 (a) to top score with three points.

**16 ♖h4 ♕e6**

> a) 17 ♗f4
> b) 17 ♗e3
> c) 17 ♘d2
> d) 17 ♕h5

You can threaten mate with 17 ♕h5 (d) and so you can score one for spotting that idea. However, after 17...♕e1+ 18 ♔g2 ♘f6 19 ♕d1 c5+ 20 f3 ♖fe8 White finds that he lags even further behind in development than he did before, so you must deduct two from your score if you chose this option.

17 ♗f4 (a) traps the white rook on the edge, but you can have one point. Black should consider 17...♗e7 18 ♖h5 ♗f6. Worse is 17 ♗e3 (b), which loses three points because of both 17...♘xe3 18 fxe3 ♕xe3+ and 18 ♗xe6 ♘xd1.

17 ♘d2 (c) is best and it earns two points.

**17 ♘d2 f5**

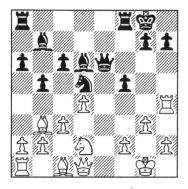

**a) 18 ♘f3**
**b) 18 ♘f1**
**c) 18 ♕h5**
**d) 18 f4**

The knight on d5 is pinned and thus ...♘f6 is not wise. Therefore, 18 ♕h5 (c) scores three points.

18 ♘f3 (a) and 18 ♘f1 (b) each get one point for developing. No score for 18 f4 (d), which allows 18...c5 and Black is building up nicely.

**18 ♕h5 h6**

**a) 19 ♘f3**
**b) 19 ♘f1**
**c) 19 ♕f3**
**d) 19 g4**

White is starting to point his pieces at Black's king with 19 ♘f3 (a), which gains three points. 19 ♘f1 (b) is fine for two points. 19 ♕f3 (c) backtracks and allows 19...c5, so just one for that. 19 g4 (d) c5 looks reckless as it leaves White bereft of kingside defences and so it does not score.

**19 ♘f3 ♗e7**

**a) 20 ♘g5**
**b) 20 ♗g5**
**c) 20 ♗xh6**
**d) 20 ♖h3**

20 ♘g5 (a) is a brave move and you can have a point if you spotted the lengthy variation 20...♕e1+ 21 ♔g2 ♗xg5 22 ♗xg5 ♕xa1 23 ♗xh6 gxh6 24 ♕g6+ ♔h8 25 ♖xh6 mate. However, your apparent 'brilliance' cannot be rewarded any more than that because you have missed 23...♖f7. And what about the simpler 20...hxg5 21 ♕h7+ ♔f7 or 21 ♗xg5 ♗xg5 22 ♕xg5? Neither give White anything to write home about so please take off three points if you chose this option.

There is no mate after 20 ♗g5 (b) ♗xg5 21 ♘xg5 hxg5 22 ♕xg5 either, so again, please deduct three points.

With 20 ♗xh6 (c) you get an extra pawn for your troubles, so just take off two points if you chose that. There's nothing for White following 20...♕xh6 21 ♕xh6 gxh6 22 ♖xh6 ♗f6.

That leaves 20 ♖h3 (d) as the only decent move, and this scores two points.

**20 ♖h3 c5**

**a) 21 ♗xh6**
**b) 21 dxc5**
**c) 21 ♗xd5**
**d) 21 ♘h4**

By a process of elimination it has to be 21 dxc5 (b), which scores two points. 21 ♗xh6 (a) ♕xh6 loses two points straightforwardly. 21 ♗xd5 (c) is generally unwise and calculation reveals 21...♕xd5 22 ♔g2 ♖f6 23 ♗e3 ♗f8 24 ♖e1 g6 (or something similar), so please deduct three points. Finally, 21 ♘h4 (d) loses a nominal five points on account of 21...c4 22 ♗c2 ♕e1+ 23 ♔g2 ♘f4 mate.

**21 dxc5 ♗xc5**

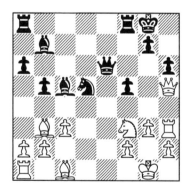

**a) 22 ♘d4**
**b) 22 ♗g5**
**c) 22 ♘g5**
**d) 22 ♗f4**

22 ♘d4 (a) is safe for one point, but there are a number of ways that Black can play which effectively uses the light-squared bishop. For example, 22...♗xd4 23 cxd4

♕e1+ 24 ♔g2 ♔h7 25 f3 ♕e2+ 26 ♔g1 ♘e3 25 ♗xe3 ♕xe3+ 26 ♔f1 ♗xf3 wins.

22 ♗g5 (b) is harder to evaluate, but I will give it two points. You score one extra for spotting 22...hxg5 23 ♕h7+ and ♘xg5+. You can also have one for seeing 23 ♘xg5 ♕h6 24 ♕f3 ♕xg5 25 ♗xd5+ ♗xd5 26 ♕xd5+ ♖f7 27 ♕xa8+. Another point is awarded for noticing the sacrifice possibility following 22...♔h7, for example 23 ♗xh6 gxh6 24 ♘g5+ wins and 23...♕xh6 24 ♖d1 ♖ad8 25 ♘g5+ ♔g8 26 ♕xh6 gxh6 27 ♘e6 ♗e7 28 ♘xd8 ♖xd8 29 ♖h5 ♔g7 30 ♖xf5 ♘f6 gives White a lead on points. If you rejected 22 ♗g5 because you noticed 22...♖ae8, then you can have a bonus.

22 ♘g5 (c) loses ten on account of 22...♕e1+ with mate in a further two moves. That leaves 22 ♗f4 (d) to score three points.

Please note the above thoughts, which are of some relevance here.

**22 ♗f4 ♖ae8**

> **a) 23 ♖e1**
> **b) 23 ♖d1**
> **c) 23 ♘e5**
> **d) 23 ♗e5**

23 ♖e1 (a) is a blunder that allows the queen sacrifice 23...♕xe1+ 24 ♘xe1 ♖xe1+ 25 ♔g2. Lose four points if you opted for 23 ♖e1, but give yourself a bonus for noticing this and another one for 25...♔h7 26 f3 ♖g1 mate. If you saw this, I am assuming that you rejected this option for White.

Hard to refute without lengthy calculations is 23 ♘e5 (c), which scores two points. 23...♔h7 24 ♘f3 ♘xf4 25 ♘g5+ ♔h8 26 ♘xe6 ♘xh5 27 ♘xf8 ♘f6 28 ♘g6+ ♔h7 29 ♘f4 leaves White an exchange up, but the rook on h3 is not worth five points in its present situation. More telling for Black is 24...♗e7 25 ♘g5+? ♗xg5 26 ♗xg5 ♕e1+! and Black mates.

23 ♗e5 (d) also scores two points, but

after 23...♖e7 White has not improved his chances and the position cries out for the a1-rook to join the game.

Although one always has to calculate variations, a common sense approach can often be useful and in this way 23 ♖d1 (b) can be found to score three points. Notice how all of White's pieces are in the game.

**23 ♖d1 ♖e7**

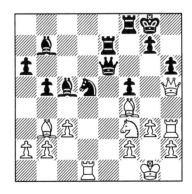

> **a) 24 ♘d4**
> **b) 24 ♘g5**
> **c) 24 ♗g5**
> **d) 24 c4**

24 ♘d4 (a) loses four points as it paves the way for a mate, for example 24 ♘d4 ♗xd4 25 ♖xd4 ♔h7 26 ♖d1 ♕e1+ 27 ♖xe1 ♖xe1+ 28 ♔g2 ♘xf4 mate is possible, although by no means forced.

24 ♘g5 (b) is a tricky move to deal with and I will give you a point. You score a point for seeing the ♖h6 idea in the variation 24...♘g5 hxg5 25 ♗xg5 ♖d7 26 ♕h7+ ♔f7 27 ♖h6. This is not at all obvious, even though it has already been mentioned. Further analysis reveals the phenomenal 27...♕e4 28 ♖f6+, which actually looks like a blunder at first sight. Additionally, 25...♖ee8 26 ♕h7+ ♔f7 27 ♖h6 ♖h8 fails this time because the knight is loose on d5 at the end of all the captures. That leaves Black to repel the attack with 24...♕e2, when a draw is likely after a lot of captures.

If you saw 24...♕e2 then take a bonus whether you chose this option or not.

24 c4 (d) scores one. One possibility is 24...♘xf4 25 gxf4 b4 26 ♘e5, when some pieces have become 'good' (or do not have obstacles in their way) and others have become 'bad' (or blocked).

24 ♗g5 (c) scores three points, with another one if you intended 24...hxg5 25 ♕h7+ ♔f7 26 ♘xg5+. Lose one if you planned 25 ♘xg5, when 25...♕h6 puts a spanner in the works. If you intended the latter and you were in a game situation, and if you were playing slowly and thoughtfully, then you would have had a chance to recover at the board by playing the right move on White's 25th.

**24 ♗g5 ♖d7**

Black appears to need his rook on the 7th rank in order to defend. Alternatively, White has a strong idea which earns you two points: 24...♖ee8 25 ♗xh6 gxh6 26 ♖xd5 ♗xd5 27 ♗xd5 ♕xd5 28 ♕g6+ ♔h8 29 ♖xh6 mate. Clearly Black would have to try 25...♕xh6 even though it puts him two points down.

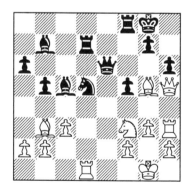

> a) 25 ♗h4
> b) 25 ♗xh6
> c) 25 ♖e1
> d) 25 ♘d4

25 ♗h4 (a) gains one point as it is safe, but 25...♕e8 is not quite adequate for White. White does win easily, however, if Black is tempted by 25...g5, when 26 ♗xg5 hxg5 27 ♕h8+ ♔f7 28 ♘xg5+ ♔e7 29 ♕xf8+ ♔xf8 30 ♘xe6+ ♔e8 31 ♘xc5 is effectively game over.

25 ♗xh6 (b) is a blunder on account of 25...♕xh6 – please deduct two. 25 ♘d4 (d) achieves the same negative marks because of 25...♗xd4 26 cxd4 hxg5.

25 ♖e1 (c) is best and earns a positive two points.

**25 ♖e1 ♕b6**

> a) 26 ♖e8
> b) 26 ♖e2
> c) 26 ♖f1
> d) 26 ♘e5

The acronym SPORT, which as I said before stands for Safe, Protect, Open, React and Take, may help you to avoid making some mistakes if you like word games. On this occasion you have to react to Black's last, which threatens f2. On first sight 26 ♖e8 (a) fails because of 26...♗xf2+ 27 ♔f1 ♖df7, but in fact White wins with 28 ♘e5! ♖c7 29 ♗d8. Take five points if you saw this.

After 26 ♖f1 (c) hxg5 there's no attack to be found for White in the variation 27 ♕h7+ ♔f7 28 ♘xg5+ ♔e8 29 ♖e1+ ♖e7 30 ♖xe7+ ♘xe7 31 ♕xg7 ♗xf2+ 32 ♔f1 ♗g1 33 ♗f7+ ♔d7. However, 27 ♘e5 wins – take three points if you saw that.

26 ♘e5 (d) is terrible and loses three points. Black's moves are relatively easy to find: 26 ♘e5 ♗xf2+ 27 ♔h1 ♔h7 28 ♖e2 ♘f4+ or 27 ♔f1 ♗xe1 28 ♔xe1 ♕g1+ are disastrous for White.

26 ♖e2 (b) scores two points and shows some necessary patience.

**26 ♖e2 ♔h7**

> a) 27 ♖h4
> b) 27 ♘e5
> c) 27 ♘h4
> d) 27 ♗c2

27 ♘e5 (b) attacks a rook and earns two points. Take a point if you noticed that Black may have a chance arrange a mate using queen and bishop by playing something like 27...♘e7 28 ♘xd7 ♛c6. However, I hope you resisted the temptation to go for this because White has 29 ♘xf8+ ♚h8 30 ♛xh6+ gxh6 31 ♖xh6+ ♛xh6 32 ♗xh6. Take another point if you saw this too. The upshot of this is that play might reasonably continue 27...♖c7 28 ♗c2.

27 ♘h4 (c) is worth one point, with another whether you chose this or not for observing the fact that ...♖d1+ is not safe unless the bishop from b3 moves away from protecting that square. Play might continue 27 ♘h4 ♘e7.

27 ♗c2 (d) scores one point, but some of the variations are complicated. For example, 27...♘f6 opens up an attack for Black and after 28 ♗xf5+ ♚g8 29 ♗xf6 ♖d1+ 30 ♖e1 Black has a number of ways to pressurise White's position to breaking point (30...♗xf3 will do). Additionally, 30 ♚g2 ♛xf6 31 ♗g4 ♖d3 is pretty neat for Black, and 31 ♗e4 ♗xe4 32 ♖xe4 ♖d2 33 ♘xd2 ♛xf2+ 34 ♚h1 ♛g1 mate or 31 g4 ♗a7 (threatening ...♖d3 but not allowing ♛xc5 after ♗xd3) 32 ♖e6 ♖d2 33 ♖xf6 ♖xf2+ 34 ♚h1 ♖f1+ 35 ♚g2 ♖g1 mate are obviously no better from White's point of view. There are other variations to spot to make a complete analysis of the position but you can have one point for spotting Black's 27th whether you chose this option or not and you can have another point for rejecting White's move if you spotted 27...♘f6.

It is possible that White's position is just about playable after 28 ♗xf6 ♛xf6 29 g4, but after 29...♗xf3 30 ♖xf3 g6 White gets driven backwards and with opposite-coloured bishops it is Black who stands comfortably because he has the attack. Alternatively, Black may jettison another pawn with 29...♗e4 30 ♗xe4 fxe4 31 ♖xe4 ♛c6, when all the various threats are too much

for White to handle.

All this goes to show that 27 ♖h4 (a) is best for three points. Sometimes in chess one must not let the opponent improve his or her position easily and now it is difficult to suggest a move for Black.

**27 ♖h4 a5**

In view of what happens, one might suggest 27...♖d6, but then 28 ♗c2 continues to allow White to have the majority of the attacking chances.

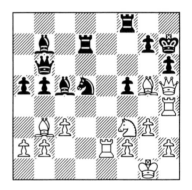

| a) 28 a4 |
| --- |
| b) 28 a3 |
| c) 28 ♗c2 |
| d) 28 ♗xh6 |

You have missed something stronger if you suggested 28 a4 (a) bxa4 29 ♗xa4 ♖d6, which scores one point, although at least you are protecting the d1-square. Even though you have been warned about this previously, 28 a3 (b), which prepares the erroneous retreat to a2 for the bishop, does not cover this important square. Maybe Black has the sharp 28...a4 29 ♗a2 ♘xc3 30 bxc3 ♖d1+ 31 ♚g2 ♖d3 32 ♖f4 ♗d6, which is difficult for White to defend.

28 ♗c2 (c) scores one point, with another if you noticed the routine 28...♘f6 29 ♗xf6 ♛xf6 followed by the trick 30 ♖e6.

28 ♗xh6 (d) is very strong, but if you are guessing, then deduct one point. If you have a follow-up, then you score three points.

**28 ♗xh6 ♕xh6**

> a) 29 ♕xh6+
> b) 29 ♘g5+
> c) 29 ♕g5
> d) 29 ♖e8

There's only one good move, which is 29 ♕g5 (c) for three points. You must have spotted this if you gained the maximum on the previous move. You can have a bonus of three points if you realised that White can unleash 28...gxh6 29 ♖e6 (just one for 29 ♘g5+ and then 30 ♖e6 or 30 ♘e6).

29 ♕xh6+ (a) loses two points because of 29...gxh6 30 ♘g5+ ♔g6 31 ♘e6 ♖c8. However, I will be generous and give you one for your calculation if you spotted White's 31st, even if you missed Black's 31st. If you saw the whole variation and rejected 29 ♕xh6+, then you can score two bonuses.

29 ♘g5+ ends up unnecessarily messy and so you lose one on account of 29...♔g8 30 ♘e6 ♕xh5 31 ♖xh5 ♖c8 32 ♖xf5.

29 ♖e8 (d) can be more easily refuted. This loses three points to 29...♕xh5 30 ♖xh5+ ♔g6.

**29 ♕g5 a4**

> a) 30 ♖xh6+
> b) 30 ♕xh6+
> c) 30 ♖e6
> d) 30 ♗c2

30 ♗c2 (d) moves the piece that is attacked and it is a common sense approach that deserves two points. Hopefully you saw 30 ♗c2 ♕xh4 31 ♕xh4+ ♔g8 32 ♘g5 ♘f6

for a bonus, when it is not straightforward to suggest what White should play in order to proceed.

30 ♖xh6+ (a) scores just two points. There are no clear cut 'wins for White' to be found after 30...gxh6 31 ♕h5 axb3 32 ♘g5+ ♔g7 33 ♘e6+ ♔h8 34 axb3 ♘f4.

You can have a point for realising that Black has a rook and two minor pieces for the queen following 31...axb3 and a further point if you analysed and then rejected 30 ♖xh6+ because you spotted at least one of the variations given in this paragraph. This option is not disastrous for White, however, because you can always head for peace with 35 ♕xh6+ ♔g8 36 ♕g5+ ♔h8 37 ♕h6+. Indeed, this is better than 32 axb3 ♘f4 33 gxf4 ♖d1+ 34 ♖e1 ♗xf3 35 ♕xf3 ♖xe1+ 36 ♔g2 (or 34 ♔g2 ♖d3), when Black has more than enough for the queen.

You have lost the thread if you selected 30 ♕xh6+ (b). Please deduct two points in view of 30...gxh6 31 ♗c2, which is worse than a chocolate fireguard for White.

Finally, and please excuse me for repeating, 'P' stands for protection and it was with 27 ♖h4 that White set up this spectacular idea which earns five points. Getting the rook to e6 was one of the ideas behind playing 25 ♖e1 some time ago and this was why it was difficult for Black to move the knight from d5. The variation 30 ♖e6 (a) ♕xh4 31 ♕xh4+ ♔g8 32 ♘g5 ♘f6 33 ♖xf6+ axb3 34 ♕h7 mate earns two more points, as does the line 32...♖fd8 33 ♕h7+ ♔f8 34 ♕h8 mate.

**30 ♖e6 1-0**

Add up your points and see how you did in this short, but fairly detailed, game.

Less than 16: There is room for improvement in your score.
16-31: You have left the higher scores for more experienced players.
32-52: Nothing humorous about your score. A sound performance.
53-73: Well done! A good, detailed performance.
74+: Excellent! A top score on a difficult game.

## Game 13
## Kotsur-Frolov
Tomsk 1997

**1 e4 e5 2 ♘f3 ♘c6 3 d4 exd4 4 ♘xd4 ♘f6 5 ♘xc6**

5 ♘c3 is far more solid, but one could argue less interesting, than the text.

**5...bxc6 6 e5 ♕e7 7 ♕e2 ♘d5 8 c4 ♗a6 9 b3 ♕h4**

Kasparov-Karpov, Tilburg 1991 continued instead with 9...g6, as Black tries to pressurise the e5-pawn. Typically Kasparov responded with the critical 10 f4 f6 11 ♗a3 ♕f7 12 ♕d2 ♘b6 13 c5 ♗xf1 14. cxb6 axb6 15 e6!!, when White stood well and went on to win in 44 moves.

A number of these moves could do with an explanation. For example, 12 ♕d2 threatens (recall CCT, or checks, captures and threats, which I have used throughout these books) to take ('T' of SPORT, or Safe, Protect, Open, React, Take) on d5 because the pawn on c4 is no longer pinned. Observe the way that the a6-f1 diagonal opens ('O' of SPORT) up with 13 c5, while White also tries to take ('T' of SPORT) on b6. The move 15 e6 is more advanced. White offers bait to the black queen because White has ♖e1 in mind at a later date.

In addition to the text, 9...0-0-0 has also been extensively tested, again with complex play guaranteed. I now give the reader the chance to continue this sharp game with White.

| a) 10 cxd5 |
| b) 10 a3 |
| c) 10 g3 |
| d) 10 ♗b2 |

10 cxd5 (a) has been taboo for some time and is particularly dire now for White due to 10...♗xe2 11 ♗xe2 ♕d4, so lose eight points. Not an auspicious start.

Incredibly, another pawn move is near-to-essential here. The threat of ...♗b4+ was proving too awkward and White will rely on the fact that he will be able to drive the enemy pieces back later, so 10 a3 (b) scores three.

10 g3 (c) drops six as 10...♕d4 11 ♗b2 ♗b4+ wins heavy material for Black. Award yourself two bonus points if you avoided this line for the reason given.

10 ♗b2 (d), to prevent 10...♕d4, is logical for two but only if you realised that 10...♗b4+ should be answered by 11 ♔d1, since 11 ♘d2 ensures Black a superior game after 11...♘c3. If you did not see that then just take one point. I don't want to bog you down with theory but the following line illustrates how Black's lead in development can be a problem for White if he is too casual: 10 ♗b2 ♗b4+ 11 ♘d2 ♘c3 12 ♕f3 ♘e4 13 ♗c1 d5 14 exd6 0-0 with an attack.

**10 a3 ♗c5**

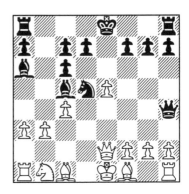

| a) 11 ♗b2 |
| b) 11 cxd5 |
| c) 11 b4 |
| d) 11 g3 |

11 ♗b2 (a) used to be the automatic choice here and scores two points, but it is not obvious how to meet 11...♘f4. If you considered 12 ♕f3 or 12 ♕c2 then that is sufficient for you to maintain your points, but if you thought 12 ♕d2 was the way forward deduct one for the tactical opportunity afforded to Black with 12...♘h3 13 gxh3 ♕e4+. If you spotted that trick and mistrusted 12 ♕d2, you may have a bonus.

11 cxd5 (b) is still out of the question, so lose ten. It is not just the queen that disappears either after 11...♗xe2 12 ♗xe2 ♕xf2+ 13 ♔d1 ♕d4+.

11 b4 (c) is too loosening and reduces your total by two. For example, 11...♗d4 12 ♗b2 ♗xc4 and White's position is on the brink of collapse.

11 g3 (d) forces Black back or invites him to embark on wild complications which White can handle, so three points here.

**11 g3 ♗xf2 +**

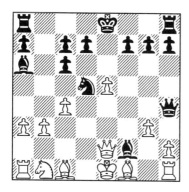

---
a) 12 ♔xf2
b) 12 ♕xf2
c) 12 gxh4
d) 12 ♔d1
---

Not 12 ♔xf2 (a) ♕d4+. Minus three if you opted for this, but a bonus point if you avoided it for the sake of your rook on a1.

12 ♕xf2 (b) is the text move and scores two points.

12 gxh4 (c) is unfortunately illegal, so no

points. Not a costly error as you would be permitted to make another move.

12 ♔d1 (d) falls for the fork 12...♕d4+, when the rook on a1 is in Black's sights, so minus five there.

**12 ♕xf2 ♕e4 +**

---
a) 13 ♗e2
b) 13 ♕e2
c) 13 ♔d1
d) 13 ♔d2
---

White would prefer that the rook does not disappear with check, so 13 ♗e2 (a) loses one.

13 ♕e2 (b) scores one because White keeps the option of castling queenside, but it is 13 ♔d1 (c) which is designed to try and cause maximum embarrassment to the black queen and the potentially loose knight on d5 – this nets three.

13 ♔d2 (d) has been seen in high-class encounters and scores two points. There followed 13...♕xh1 14 ♗g2 ♕xh2 15 cxd5 cxd5 16 ♔c2 c6 17 ♗e3 ♕h5 18 ♘c3 0-0 in M.Maric-Voiska, Subotica 1991, when Black was fine.

**13 ♔d1 ♕xh1**

---
a) 14 cxd5
b) 14 ♘d2
c) 14 ♔c2
d) 14 a4
---

14 cxd5 (a) ♗xf1 scuppers White's chances of trapping the invading queen and drops your score by three.

Three points for 14 ♘d2 (b), which now threatens to finally pick off the knight on d5 as it bolsters the bishop on f1. A bonus is due if you realised that it takes the flight square e4 away from her majesty.

14 ♔c2 (c) is worth two on the condition that you analysed 14...♕e4+ and realised that 15 ♗d3 ♕xe5 16 ♗b2 is suddenly extremely pleasant for White.

Finally, 14 a4 (d) is too nondescript and fails to score.

**14 ♘d2 ♘c3+**

> a) 15 ♔e1
> b) 15 ♔c2

White has already moved his king and so castling in the normal fashion is not allowed; White must walk his king to safety. Therefore, nothing for 15 ♔e1 (a), which is unnatural. 15 ♔c2 (b) scores one.

**15 ♔c2 ♘e4**

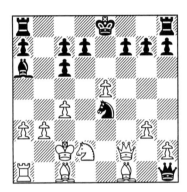

> a) 16 ♘xe4
> b) 16 ♔b2
> c) 16 ♕g2
> d) 16 ♕e2

Two points for 16 ♘xe4 (a) as it is inevitable that the knights will be exchanged.

The blunder 16 ♔b2 (b) ♘xf2 costs you nine, while the positional error of 16 ♕g2 (c), which leaves White a clear exchange (minor piece against rook) down with no compensation, fails to score.

16 ♕e2 (d) is reasonable for one point.

**16 ♘xe4 ♕xe4+**

> a) 17 ♔b2
> b) 17 ♔c3
> c) 17 ♗d3
> d) 17 ♔d1

Nothing for 17 ♔b2 (a) ♕xe5+ 18 ♔a2, which is all rather slow, although 17 ♔c3 (b) ♕xe5+ 18 ♕d4 ♕e1+ 19 ♔c2 ♕xf1 is even worse and scores minus four.

17 ♗d3 (c) is both strong and effective for two points, but 17 ♔d1 (d) sets the white position back a step and sets your score back by one too.

**17 ♗d3 ♕g4**

If you planned to meet the greedy 17...♕xe5 with 18 ♗b2 ♕g5 19 h4 and 20 ♖e1+, then award yourself a bonus as the white bishop on b2 is a huge asset.

> a) 18 ♗d2
> b) 18 b4
> c) 18 ♗f5
> d) 18 ♕f4

18 ♗d2 (a) scores one, but minus one for 18 b4 (b), allowing 18...♗xc4.

If you still have desires on the black queen with 18 ♗f5 (c), well done, for there lies your main compensation for the material deficit. Score three for this.

18 ♕f4 (d) again lets Black off the hook and scores zero as exchanging queens only relieves any pressure in the position.

**18 ♗f5 ♕h5**

> a) 19 g4
> b) 19 h4
> c) 19 ♗e3
> d) 19 ♕d4

One point for 19 g4 (a), which forces 19...♕h3 but actually snaring the queen will still prove to be a frustrating quest.

19 h4 (b) is the key for two points. A bonus point is awarded to those who appreciated that 19 h4 threatens 20 g4 and now Black must severely weaken his kingside to spare the lady her distress.

19 ♗e3 (c) is sufficient for one, but 19 ♕d4 (d) ♕xf5+ is one way to go off-key and docks you three points.

**19 h4 f6**

> a) 20 g4
> b) 20 exf6
> c) 20 ♕e3
> d) 20 e6

One point for 20 g4 (a), although it permits black the opportunity to set up a defence with 20...♕f7 21 exf6 g6.

The immediate 20 exf6 (b) exposes Black's king to devastating effect for three points. It is worth noting just how impotent the watching black bishop is on a6.

20 ♕e3 (c) again leaves the bishop hanging on f5 with check and drops four points.

Last, but no least, 20 e6 (d) scores one, with a bonus of one if you spotted that 20...d6 21 g4 rounds up the black queen. However, 20...0-0 keeps Black in the game.

**20 exf6 0-0**

> a) 21 fxg7
> b) 21 ♗xd7
> c) 21 g4
> d) 21 ♕c5

I trust everyone avoided the impetuous 21 fxg7 (a) ♖xf5, which sets you back three points.

Nothing for 21 ♗xd7 (b) ♖xf6, which allows Black's rooks to thunder into the proceedings with tempi.

Three points for 21 g4 (c), which puts Black clearly on the defensive. A bonus point if you plan to meet 21...♕f7 with 22 fxg7 followed by 23 ♗b2 with a strong initiative.

It is hard to decide how to mark 21 ♕c5 (d) for it is an 'all or nothing' category. You can certainly have one point if you have identified 21...♗c8 or 21...♖xf6, for example, as falling for your trick of 22 ♗e6+, picking up the queen on h5.

Objectively, however, after something such as 21...g6 or 21...♕e2+ Black is in the driving seat, so no points for 21 ♕c5 except the bonus mentioned.

**21 g4 ♕e8**

> a) 22 fxg7
> b) 22 ♗b2
> c) 22 g5
> d) 22 ♕d2

Nothing for 22 fxg7 (a), but two bonus points if you rejected it on the strength of 22...♕e4+, which leaves the white monarch unsure where to settle. For example, 23 ♔d1 ♕xg4+.

Four points for the text 22 ♗b2 (b), which finally prepares to activate his rook.

22 g5 (c) is interesting for one point, but no points for 22 ♕d2 (d), which is definitely barking up the wrong tree after 22...♖xf6 23 ♕xd7 ♕xd7 24 ♗xd7 ♖d8.

**22 ♗b2 gxf6**

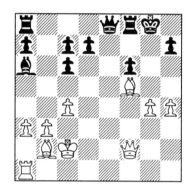

> a) 23 g5
> b) 23 ♖e1
> c) 23 ♖g1
> d) 23 ♖d1

23 g5 (a) is worth one, with an immediate bonus if you had 23...fxg5 24 ♕d4 up your sleeve. A further bonus is for those who pursued the variation to make sure that Black did not have a perpetual with 24...♕e2+ 25 ♔b1 ♕e1+ 26 ♔a2.

23 ♖e1 (b) is extremely natural for two points. It is rare that rooks don't belong on the one open file, but in this case it is a half open file with the black monarch on the end that held Kotsur's attention. Score four points for 23 ♖g1 (c).

23 ♖d1 (d) also scores one. There are so many tempting plans...

**23 ♖g1 h6**

a) 24 ♕f4
b) 24 ♕d2
c) 24 g5
d) 24 ♖g3

One point for both 24 ♕f4 (a) and 24 ♕d2 (b), as long as c7 and d7 are not your intended targets.

If you correctly judged that it is time for the final breakthrough with 24 g5 (c), then there are three points to be had, but nothing for the tame 24 ♖g3 (d).

**24 g5 fxg5**

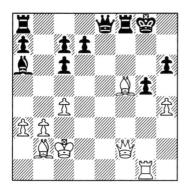

a) 25 hxg5
b) 25 ♖xg5+
c) 25 ♕f4
d) 25 ♕d4

25 hxg5 (a) is natural enough but runs into the nasty 25...♕e4+, which allows Black to create chaos – minus two for this.

There is no rhyme or reason to sacrifice a rook here as the text move is so strong, so minus four for 25 ♖xg5+ (b).

25 ♕f4 (c) indeed threatens 26 ♖xg5+ hxg5 27 ♕xg5+ leading to mate, so two points if you spotted that. Rather seriously, Black has 25...♕g6.

25 ♕d4 (d) highlights the a1-h8 diagonal in all its vulnerability for four points.

**25 ♕d4 ♕e7**

a) 26 hxg5
b) 26 ♖xg5+
c) 26 ♕h8+
d) 26 ♖e1

26 hxg5 (a) scores three, with the decisive finish that could run 26...♖xf5 27 ♕h8+ ♔f7 28 g6+ ♔e6 29 ♖e1+ ♔d6 30 ♕d4+ ♖d5 31 c5 mate. Two bonus points if you were able to follow that through to the conclusion (before seeing it in print of course!).

26 ♖xg5+ (b) also scores three and again two bonus points for having calculated 26...hxg5 27 ♕h8+ ♔f7 28 ♕h5+ ♔g8 29 ♕g6+ ♕g7 30 ♕xg7 mate.

26 ♕h8+ (c) secured resignation at the board and secures three points here. This time your two bonus points are awarded for the line 26...♔f7 27 ♕g7+ ♔e8 28 ♖e1 ♕xe1 29 ♕xd7 mate.

No score for 26 ♖e1 (d), which is inaccurate as it allows Black to fight on with 26...♕f6 27 ♕xf6 ♖xf6 28 ♗xf6 ♖f8!.

**26 ♕h8+ 1-0**

Time to match your score with the interval below.

Less than 15: Avoid those mistakes creeping in.

16-24: A sound basis on which to build.

25-35: Promising signs here.

36-44: Excellent substance here. You are obviously already an experienced player but are perhaps particularly strong with the initiative.

45+: You utilised the bishop pair to devastating effect. Congratulations on your wonderful score.

## Game 14
## Nikolic-Timman
Amsterdam 1984

**1 d4 ♘f6 2 c4 e6 3 ♘c3 ♗b4**

The Nimzo-Indian Defence has always been popular. Black challenges the centre indirectly. The e4-square is often a focal point as Black strives to maintain control of the centre stage.

**4 ♕c2 0-0 5 a3 ♗xc3+ 6 ♕xc3 b6 7 ♘f3 ♗b7 8 e3 d6 9 b4 ♘bd7 10 ♗b2**

You are Black and with the Dutchman who dominated chess in his country for many years. Remember not to let those white bishops loose...

> a) **10...a5**
> b) **10...♕e7**
> c) **10...♘e4**
> d) **10...♗xf3**

10...a5 (a) stops White having it all his own way on the queenside and scores two points. Two points also for 10...♕e7 (b), which is sensible and reasonably common in chess settings.

10...♘e4 (c) is the text move for three points as Black seeks action on the kingside. All these choices illustrate just how flexible Black's position is.

Doubling the opposition's pawns with 10...♗xf3 (d) scores one point, but the negative features are that 11 gxf3 certainly opens up the position for the white bishop pair and gives White control over the e4-square.

**10...♘e4 11 ♕c2**

> a) **11...♘df6**
> b) **11...f5**
> c) **11...d5**
> d) **11...♕h4**

11...♘df6 (a) and 11...d5 (c) both earn one as they lend support to the e4-square,

but the most natural, loaded with aggressive intentions, is 11...f5 (b) – score two for this.

If only one could launch an attack with such ease. 11...♕h4 (d) drops nine points for overlooking 12 ♘xh4. Perhaps you played out the opening moves incorrectly.

**11...f5 12 ♗e2**

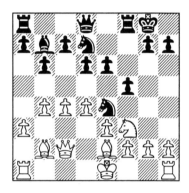

> a) **12...g5**
> b) **12...♘g5**
> c) **12...♖f6**
> d) **12...e5**

12...g5 (a) and 12...♖f6 (c) are interesting and score one, but top marks of two go to 12...♘g5 (b). Award yourself a bonus if you planned to meet 13 ♘xg5 with 13...♕xg5 rather than 13...♗xg2 14 ♖g1 ♕xg5, which walks into a nasty pin. A further bonus point is available if you are now intending to double the pawns by capturing on f3 with your knight since White will not have the luxury of the bishop pair against two knights this time.

12...e5 (d) permits White to grab a pawn with 13 dxe5 dxe5 14 ♘xe5, when the bishop on b2 comes to life too, so minus one there.

**12...♘g5 13 ♕d1**

> a) 13...♘xf3+
> b) 13...♗xf3
> c) 13...f4
> d) 13...♕e8

13...♘xf3+ (a) is Timman's choice for two points. A bonus if you quite fancied how things were panning out after 14 gxf3 ♕h4.

One point for 13...f4 (c), but nothing for 13...♗xf3 (b), which gives White a comfortable pawn formation, complemented by the bishop pair, after 14 gxf3.

As a general rule, the black queen may well come into play via the e8-square, but not here due to 13...♕e8 (d) 14 ♘xg5 – lose three points.

**13...♘xf3+ 14 ♗xf3**

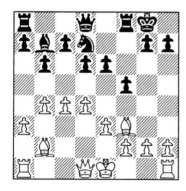

> a) 14...♗xf3
> b) 14...♕c8
> c) 14...d5
> d) 14...♗e4

14...♗xf3 (a) and 14...♕c8 (b) are both sufficient for one point and lead to roughly equal play.

14...d5 (c) now shuts the bishop on b7 out of play and leaves holes in Black's position. No score there.

14...♗e4 (d) is the text move for two points as Black wants to favourably exchange the light-squared bishops.

**14...♗e4 15 ♗xe4**

If you considered what to do if White refused to exchange the bishop with, for example, 15 0-0 and decided the way forward for Black to be 15...♕g5, when White will eventually have no choice but to exchange, you can take two bonus points.

**15...fxe4 16 d5**

> a) 16...exd5
> b) 16...♘e5
> c) 16...e5
> d) 16...♕h4

16...exd5 (a) 17 ♕xd5+ ♔h8 18 ♕xe4 should have rung alarm bells both positionally and tactically, so lose one.

16...♘e5 (b) loses one for permitting 17 ♗xe5 dxe5 18 dxe6, but there is a consolation point if you noticed 17 dxe6 ♘d3+.

Three points for 16...e5 (c), which is a necessity as Black really wants to keep the white bishop on b2 shut out.

16...♕h4 (d) scores one, with a bonus if you intended 17 0-0 e5. On the other hand, if you avoided 16...♕h4 due to the rather messy 17 g3 ♕h3 18 ♕c2 ♕g2 19 ♖f1, have a bonus for excellent judgement.

**16...e5 17 ♕g4**

> a) 17...♕f6
> b) 17...♘f6
> c) 17...a5
> d) 17...c5

One point for 17...♕f6 (a), as long as you realised that White has 18 ♕xd7, when 18...♕xf2+ 19 ♔d1 ♕xb2 completely justifies Black's play. An extra bonus if you expected 18 0-0 and assessed that 18...♕f5 is fine for Black.

17...♘f6 (b), crucially defending the e4-pawn, gains maximum points of two.

17...a5 (c) 18 ♕xe4 drops one, while 17...c5 (d) must head the list of least favourable options as White is spoilt for choice with 18 dxc6 or 18 ♕xe4 (lose two points).

**17...♘f6 18 ♕e6+**

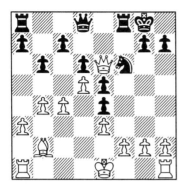

---

**a) 18...♔h8**
**b) 18...♖f7**

---

18...♔h8 (a) is natural enough for one point, but it is 18...♖f7 (b) which sees the start of a strong plan as Black seeks to utilise his pieces to greatest effect. This notches up three points.

**18...♖f7 19 0-0**

---

**a) 19...♛d7**
**b) 19...♛e7**
**c) 19...♔h8**
**d) 19...♛f8**

---

One point for 19...♛d7 (a) and 19...♛e7 (b), but minus five for the careless 19...♔h8 (c) 20 ♛xf7.

19...♛f8 (d) is the text move for two points. It is clear that Black is gradually building up his position. Take a bonus point if you planned 20...♖e8 21 ♛h3 g5.

**19...♛f8 20 f4**

It is not that surprising that White tries to stir things up in the centre.

---

**a) 20...♖e8**
**b) 20...♔h8**
**c) 20...exf3 (en passant)**
**d) 20...exf4**

---

One point for 20...♖e8 (a) 21 ♛h3 exf4 22 ♖xf4, although Black has just conceded any opening advantage. The same score and comment goes for 20...exf4 (d) 21 ♖xf4.

Minus one for 20...♔h8 (b), which fares worse after 21 fxe5. A bonus is available if you calculated 21...♖e8 (or 21...♖e7) 22 exf6, which leads to a huge position for White due to the threat of fxg7+.

If Black wishes to capture on f3 en passant, he must do it now. This is indeed how the encounter continued, so 20...exf3 (c) scores two.

**20...exf3 21 ♖xf3**

It is worth explaining here that Timman had the interesting plan of 21 gxf3 b5 22 cxb5 ♖e8 23 ♛h3 ♘xd5, which ensures him the better chances if White invites this alternative.

---

**a) 21...♛e7**
**b) 21...♛c8**
**c) 21...♖e8**
**d) 21...e4**

---

Now that the e4-square is vacant for possession Black is keen to exchange queens, when his knight will dominate the bishop in the ending. One point for 21...♛e7 (a), although White can avoid the exchange with 22 ♛h3.

21...♛c8 (b) scores two, plus one if you realised that you wanted to force the exchange of queens due to the significance of the e4-square. Don't worry if you didn't appreciate this, it is highly advanced stuff that only the top players in the world would take for granted. Now that the e4-square has been highlighted, see if you can put the theory into action during the rest of the game.

21...♖e8 (c) is also reasonable for one point, but I cannot condone 21...e4 (d), which gives a wake-up call to the otherwise sleeping bishop on b2 (no points for this).

**21...♛c8 22 ♛xc8+ ♖xc8 23 ♖c1**

---

**a) 23...♘e4**
**b) 23...c6**
**c) 23...c5**
**d) 23...a6**

---

One point for 23...♘e4 (a), which is slightly premature as White can dissolve any pressure with the forcing variation 24 ♖xf7 ♔xf7 25 c5 bxc5 26 bxc5 ♘xc5 27 ♗xe5 ♘d3 28 ♖f1+.

23...c6 (b) is worthy of consideration and scores two, but 23...c5 (c) puts a stop to c4-c5 and any counterplay that White may have had in mind – score three for this.

23...a6 (d) rather misses the mark and misses out on any points.

**23...c5 24 b5**

a) 24...♖a8
b) 24...a5
c) 24...e4
d) 24...a6

a) 26...♖xa6
b) 26...♖b8
c) 26...b5
d) 26...♘g4

Activating a rook with 24...♖a8 (a), followed by ...a7-a6 is highly tempting (score two points).

24...a5 (b) is safe and scores one point, but this only leaves the f-file for later operations.

24...e4 (c) is still anti-positional and fails to score.

24...a6 (d) is most precise (three points), as Black now applies pressure on the queenside.

**24...a6 25 bxa6**

a) 25...♖a8
b) 25...♖a7
c) 25...b5
d) 25...♘e4

Rounding the pawn up with 25...♖a8 (a) is worth two, while the text move 25...♖a7 (b) takes three. This is a thematic way to prise open a file if you haven't seen the idea before.

25...b5 (c) is overdoing it somewhat after 26 cxb5 ♘xd5 27 ♖d1, so lose four. We are not that desperate to pick off the d5-pawn.

Finally, 25...♘e4 (d) is fine for one point because the a6-pawn is not going anywhere.

**25...♖a7 26 ♖f2**

26...♖xa6 (a) is logical for two points, as is 26...♖b8 (b) for one.

26...b5 (c) 27 cxb5 again is unimpressive (minus two), while 26...♘g4 (d) 27 ♖e2 scores nothing and can be discarded for verging on being 'aimless'.

**26...♖xa6 27 ♖b1**

a) 27...♖a4
b) 27...♖b8
c) 27...♔f7
d) 27...♘e4

27...♖a4 (a) will certainly feature at some stage and scores two points.

27...♖b8 (b) can be accused of being slightly passive and only scores one.

Bringing the king forward in anticipation with 27...♔f7 (c) earns one, but it is 27...♘e4 (d) which takes top honours of three. The ideal square for the knight, but notice that Black did not rush to place it there. Patience is a real virtue in chess.

**27...♘e4 28 ♖c2**

a) 28...♖a5
b) 28...♖f8
c) 28...♔f7
d) 28...♖a7

28...♖a5 (a) makes no sense after 29 ♗c1, so your total remains static.

28...♖f8 (b) illustrates progress as Black now has the f-file to himself (score two points). Notice how Black avoids exchanging rooks. This will leave White feeling cramped.

Again you cannot be criticised for wanting to utilise the monarch at this stage with 28...♔f7 (c), which scores one point. Nothing for 28...♖a7 (d), however, as the b-pawn could become a target.

### 28...♖f8 29 ♗c1

Firstly, two bonus points for the effective response to 29 ♖f1, when Black dances along the back rank with 29...♖b8 30 ♖b1 b5 31 ♗c1 b4.

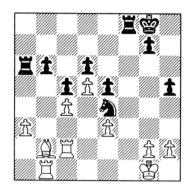

> a) 29...♖f7
> b) 29...♖f2
> c) 29...♖a7
> d) 29...h5

Nothing for 29...♖f7 (a) and minus three for 29...♖f2 (b) 30 ♖xf2.

Now on to the real moves... 29...♖a7 (c) is interesting and scores one point. If you intended to meet 30 ♖xb6 with 30...♖af7, threatening 31...♖f1 mate, then add a bonus. It is surprising just how dangerous the attack becomes but White does not have to take up the challenge. Instead 30 h3 leaves Black having to decide how to proceed.

29...h5 (d) scores two, with a bonus if you appreciate that this could enable Black to set up mate threats later.

### 29...h5 30 ♗b2

Did you check out 30 ♖2b2? Deduct a point if you were going to defend your b-pawn with 30...♖b8. On the contrary, two bonuses are yours if you saw 30...♘c3 31 ♖xb6 ♘e2+ leading to mate. For this reason White may be tempted to create an escape square with h2-h3, when ...h5-h4 and ...♘g3 in combination with ...♖f1+ and ♖h1 mate is an example of how 29...h5 is forward looking to potential mate threats.

> a) 30...h4
> b) 30...g5
> c) 30...♖a4
> d) 30...♔h7

30...h4 (a) and 30...g5 (b) score one, but White's last has enabled him to make an annoying challenge with 31 ♖f1.

30...♖a4 (c) ties White up for two points, with a bonus if you spotted the rather tasty tactic with 31 ♖f1 ♖xf1+ 32 ♔xf1 ♖xc4 33 ♖xc4 ♘d2+ etc.

30...♔h7 (d) doesn't quite merit an award.

### 30...♖a4 31 h4

Two bonus points if you half expected White to reduce himself to 31 ♗c1, when you sensed it was time to pounce with 31...♖a7 32 ♖xb6 ♖af7. At grandmaster (GM) level, White can resign after 33 g3 ♖f1+ 34 ♔g2 ♖8f2+ 35 ♖xf2 ♖xf2+ followed by 36...♖c2. As it is, White is not far from zugzwang (the state of worsening one's position by being obliged to move) and 31 h4 has hardly helped his position to gel.

> a) 31...♖f6
> b) 31...♖f5
> c) 31...g5
> d) 31...♘g3

31...♖f6 (a) is Timman's choice for three points. If you saw the opportunity to invade with ...♖g6-g4, then you may take a bonus.

Both 31...♖f5 (b) and 31...g5 (c) come into consideration for one point and 31...♘g3 (d) also earns one point on the condition that it was to prevent White confronting his opponent down the f-file.

**31...♖f6 32 ♔h2**

> a) 32...♘f2
> b) 32...♖f2
> c) 32...g6
> d) 32...♖g6

White has covered one of Black's winning tries, namely 32...♖g6 (d), which scores one point, when Black does not gain anything after 33 ♖g1 ♖g4 34 g3 ♘f6 35 ♖gc1.

One point also for 32...♘f2 (a), but two for 32...♖f2 (b), which seeks to weaken the c4-pawn further. You score a bonus if you realised that.

32...g6 (c) is non-productive over the board and for your total, while it seems that White has done enough to combat the previous threat.

**32...♖f2 33 ♖bc1**

> a) 33...♖xc2
> b) 33...♘d2
> c) 33...♖d2
> d) 33...♖xc4

33...♖xc2 (a) scores a nominal one, but it is 33...♖d2 (c) which causes maximum discomfort to White and scores three points. The rook is untouchable as 34 ♖xd2 ♘xd2 nets the c4-pawn.

Setting up a self-pin with 33...♘d2 (b) fails to score, but it's not disastrous after 34 ♔g1 ♖e2 35 ♗c3 ♘b3!.

Time to see what category your score is in.

The horrible 33...♖xc4 (d) 34 ♖xc4 ♖xb2 35 ♖xe4 reduces your total by four.

**33...♖d2 34 ♔h3**

> a) 34...b5
> b) 34...♖xc2
> c) 34...♖d3
> d) 34...♘f2+

34...b5 35 cxb5 (a) undoes the clamp that Black has on the situation and undoes your score by one.

34...♖xc2 (b) 35 ♖xc2 and 34...♘f2+ (d) are harmless to Black in each case (take one point), but I must question how you actually make progress.

34...♖d3 (c) continues to infiltrate and scores three points.

**34...♖d3 35 ♖e1**

Before we move on, there is a bonus if you were planning to end White's wriggling with 35 ♖e2 ♖d2.

> a) 35...♖b3
> b) 35...♖d2
> c) 35...♘d2
> d) 35...♖axa3

35...♖b3 (a) is fine for one point, but nothing for 35...♖d2 (b), which repeats after 36 ♖ec1.

There is not a case for giving up an exchange with 35...♖axa3 (d) 36 ♗xa3 ♖xa3, so dock one point from your total.

It is fitting to end on a final monster knight sortie: 35...♘d2 (c) scores three points and caused White to call it a day. One last bonus if you carefully checked out 36 ♖d1, when 36...♖xe3+ fits the bill.

**35...♘d2 0-1**

Less than 20: Work on erasing those negative scores from your total.

21-32: Not bad. This suggests a mixture of good ideas intermingled with the odd mistake.

33-44: An average club player's result. You have a sound base of ideas.

45-54: This is a powerful performance. Well done.

55+: Brilliant. You did not put a foot wrong. Have we heard of you?

# CHAPTER FOUR

## Rooks and Pawns versus Minor Pieces

The earliest example of this material imbalance which you may have come across often stems from opening moves looking something like this: **1 e4 e5 2 ♘f3 ♘c6 3 ♗c4 ♗c5 4 d3 ♘f6 5 ♘g5 0-0 6 ♘xf7 ♖xf7 7 ♗xf7+ ♔xf7**

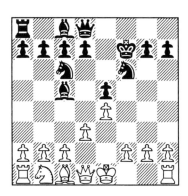

While each player has six points to his credit, Black's bishop and knight are far better suited to the middlegame position than the rook and pawn. There are no open files for the white rooks and the extra pawn will be irrelevant until any ending.

It is surprising how often this opening is wheeled out in junior chess as White tries to force the pace and then cannot understand why Black ends up with all the trumps.

I appreciate the saying 'the pawns tell the pieces where to go' for in this case it is clear that the black pieces happily settle on good squares after, for example, ...d7-d6, ...♔g8, ...♗g4, ...♕e8-h5 and ...♖f8 etc.

It is in unfamiliar positions where a player obtains a rook and two pawns for two minor pieces when it is harder to assess the situation. Also, as the game progresses and the ending approaches, the rook and pawns could prove stronger as rooks can zap from one side of the board to the other as they are sometimes not hindered by pawns acting as obstacles. This is illustrated in Game 17, although as the material dwindles towards the end Karpov manages to skilfully secure a draw with the minor pieces. In Game 16 Shirov supplies us with one of his fiery efforts. I think that I have chosen some entertaining games in this book, which is why he features highly. Apologies to him are due because he loses this game. The minor pieces triumph here, again with some excellent management. It does, however, take the most formidable of players to secure the full point. Good judgement and good knowledge are combined here.

On with the chapter. The first game is an old one, which again demonstrates on how to use the minor pieces effectively.

## Game 15
# Keres-Kottnauer
Moscow 1947

A game from one of the great players of the past.

**1 d4 ♘f6 2 c4 e6 3 ♘c3 ♗b4 4 e3 c5 5 ♗d3 0-0 6 ♘f3 d6 7 0-0 ♗xc3 8 bxc3 ♘c6 9 e4 e5**

This is not the only place in these multiple choice chess books where Black chooses Hübner's blockading plan in the Nimzo-Indian Defence.

**10 d5 ♘a5 11 h3 b6 12 ♗g5 h6 13 ♗e3 ♗a6 14 ♕e2 ♘xe4**

Black decides to enter complications.

**15 ♗xe4 f5 16 ♗c2**

White chooses to retain all his minor pieces at the expense of losing his rook and a couple of pawns. This decision leaves White a pawn or point down. An alternative, such as 16 ♗d3 e4 17 ♘d2 exd3 18 ♕xd3, leaves the point count even but gives Black an advantage as White is tied up and has doubled pawns.

**16...♗xc4 17 ♕d1 ♗xf1 18 ♕xf1 e4 19 ♘h2 ♕f6 20 ♗d2 ♖ae8**

The mist has cleared. Black is a point ahead but the position suits White's powerful minor pieces. The reader is now invited to select moves on White's behalf.

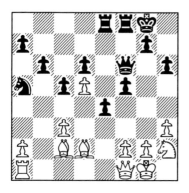

a) 21 c4
b) 21 ♖d1
c) 21 ♕e2
d) 21 ♕a6

First off, 21 c4 (a) loses one point because of 21...♘xc4, when the White queen cannot both defend her own rook and take the enemy knight. This is an example of an overworked piece, which can also be described as 'overloaded'.

You can have one point for 21 ♕a6 (d), which attacks a pawn, but 21...♖f7 is a simple way of defending it.

21 ♖d1 (b) scores one as it is safe. Furthermore, after 21...♖e5 22 c4 White has improved his chances and Black has himself prevented ...♕b2. Take a bonus if you appreciated that Black is preparing ...f5-f4, possibly by ...♖e7 and ...♖fe8. Therein lies the secret: White must block the advance of the potential passed pawn. Therefore, 21 ♕e2 (c) scores two points as it prevents Black's action.

**21 ♕e2 ♖e5**

a) 22 c4
b) 22 ♗f4
c) 22 f3
d) 22 ♗b3

22 ♗f4 (b) ♖xd5 loses one, while 22 ♗b3 (d) scores one. It is worth bearing in mind that after 22 ♗b3 ♘xb3 23 axb3 ♖xd5 24 ♖xa7 the point difference has not changed. Take a bonus of one if you saw that far.

22 c4 (a) scores zero if you took a wild guess without looking ahead. However, 22 c4 ♖xd5 scores a bonus of one if you noticed that Black has opened up the a1-f6

diagonal. More bonuses are on offer for seeing 23 ♖e1 ♖e5 24 ♗c3, and 23...♖d4 24 ♗c3 (two points for each one). Two more points for noticing 23...♖xd2 24. ♕xd2 ♘xc4, when Black hangs on to an extra point advantage. With dwindling material on the board, one must favour Black to be able to press for a win.

The remaining choice, 22 f3 (c), scores two points. When a piece is attacked, in this case the pawn on d5, White has to find some way of defending it. MCSB (Move, Capture, Support or Block) can sometimes give some assistance to finding a satisfactory reply. However, chess is such a fascinating game and not a simple one by any means. Therefore, you sometimes just have to calculate specific variations.

**22 f3 e3**

> a) 23 ♗xe3
> b) 23 ♗e1
> c) 23 ♗c1
> d) 23 f4

23 ♗e1 (b) scores two, while 23 ♗c1 (c) is not the best square for the bishop and scores one.

The counterattack on the rook with 23 f4 (d) loses one because of 23...♖xd5 24 ♗xe3 ♕xc3.

23 ♗xe3 (a) loses two, but there are some complications after 23...f4 24 ♘g4. Take a bonus of two if you had planned that, and 24...♕e7 25 ♕d3 deserves another bonus of two because of 25...fxe3 26 ♕h7+ ♔f7 27 ♗g6 mate. Add a bonus of one if you saw that mate. However, 23...♖fe8! will leave Black ahead – take a bonus if you saw that move. In this case I am assuming that you did not choose option 23 ♗xe3 as it could continue 23...♖fe8! 24 ♘f1 f4 25 ♕d3 fxe3 26 ♕h7+ ♔f7, which avoids any problems for Black and leaves him up on points. The attack does not finish with mate for White and so White should not pursue it.

**23 ♗e1 ♖xd5**

> a) 24 ♘f1
> b) 24 ♕xe3
> c) 24 c4
> d) 24 ♖d1

It has got to be 24 ♕xe3 (b), which scores one for recapturing the pawn.

24 ♘f1 (a) f4 scores nothing, as does 24 ♖d1 (d). Finally, 24 c4 (c) loses one because of 24...♕xa1 25 cxd5 ♕xa2.

**24 ♕xe3 ♖e5**

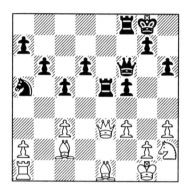

> a) 25 ♕f2
> b) 25 ♕d2
> c) 25 ♕d3
> d) 25 ♕f4

Four safe queen moves to choose between. 25 ♕f2 (a), 25 ♕d2 (b) and 25 ♕f4 (d) all score one, but 25 ♕d3 (c) scores two. White does not worry about ...c5-c4 because then the Black knight cannot use the c4-square from which to rejoin the main action. White himself threatens c3-c4, which explains Black's next. In addition, 25 ♕f4, which has the same function 25 ♕d3, only encourages ...g7-g5, which is why this fails to top score.

**25 ♕d3 ♕e6**

> a) 26 ♔f1
> b) 26 ♔f2
> c) 26 ♗g3
> d) 26 ♗f2

26 ♗g3 (d) scores two points and is best.

26 ♔f1 (a) and 26 ♗g3 (c) both score one point as they allow 26...♖e3 with a subsequent attack on the c3-pawn.

26 ♔f2 (d) ♖e8 scores zero as it leaves White with the problem of stopping Black infiltrating with his major pieces.

**26 ♗f2 ♖d5**

a) 27 ♕a6
b) 27 ♕b5
c) 27 ♕e3
d) 27 ♕f1

It is wrong to desert the kingside and play 27 ♕a6 (a) ♖d2 or 27 ♕b5 (b), both of which lose one.

27 ♕f1 (d) is safe but still fails to stop the black rook infiltrating with 27...♖d2. This scores zero.

27 ♕e3 (c) is best and is the only way to score a positive one point.

**27 ♕e3 ♕xe3**

a) 28 ♗b3
b) 28 ♗xe3

No real choice here. 28 ♗b3 (a) loses six, but recapturing the queen with 28 ♗xe3 (b) scores one. White is not losing a queen here; this is simply a swap.

**28 ♗xe3 ♖e8**

a) 29 ♘f1
b) 29 ♔f2
c) 29 ♗f2
d) 29 ♗f4

The Black rooks are making some effort to get to White's second rank. 29 ♘f1 (a) scores two points as this move prevents Black's idea.

29 ♔f2 (b) can have one point as it appears natural, but add an extra one if you observed 29...♖xe3 30 ♔xe3 ♘c4+. You score one more if you saw 31 ♔f2 ♖d2+ and ...♖xc2, when Black is two points up. Additionally, there is one for 31 ♔f4 g5+ 32 ♔g3 f4+, which picks up the bishop.

29 ♗f2 (c) and 29 ♗f4 (d) both lose one because they allow at least one rook onto White's second rank (29 ♗f2 ♖d2 or 29 ♗f4 ♖e2).

**29 ♘f1 ♔f8**

a) 30 ♗b3
b) 30 ♔f2
c) 30 ♗a4
d) 30 ♖c1

It's time to improve the position with 30 ♔f2 (b), which scores two points.

There's no point trying to win the black rook along the b3-g8 diagonal because Black has just moved his king. 30 ♗b3 (a) ♖d3 loses one because White's pawn on c3 comes under fire.

30 ♗a4 (c) and 30 ♖c1 (d) do not help White, but they are safe moves that do not allow Black to infiltrate and so they both get one point.

**30 ♔f2 ♘c4**

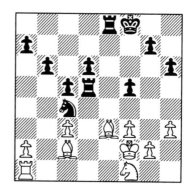

a) 31 ♗c1
b) 31 ♗f4
c) 31 ♖e1
d) 31 ♗b3

Did you find the backward move 31 ♗c1 (a) to top score with two points? Black's pieces are still unable to progress into the white position.

Not too much damage is done with 31 ♗f4 (b) or 31 ♖e1 (c), so one point for these, but the former does allow Black to improve with 31...g5.

The move to avoid here was 31 ♗b3 (d), which loses two points because of 31...♘xe3 32 ♘xe3 (32 ♗xd5 ♘xd5 is good for Black too) 32...♖d2+ 33 ♔e1 ♖b2! and Black has a very commanding position.

**31 ♗c1 ♖de5**

> **a) 32 ♗a4**
> **b) 32 ♗b3**
> **c) 32 ♗d1**
> **d) 32 ♗d3**

The key for White remains to prevent Black from infiltrating. Therefore, 32 ♗d3 (d) scores the maximum two points.

32 ♗d1 (c) is a poor move that scores minus one. Now the black knight is not attacked so Black can play 32...♖e1. It should also be mentioned that trapping the rook does not work because of 33 ♘e3? ♖1xe3 34 ♗xe3 ♘xe3. Here, as is recommended in previous comments, Black realises a clear advantage by exchanging off into a position where he has two extra pawns. White is actually in some trouble after 32...♖e1, especially as 33 ♗d2 is met by 33...♖xf1+!.

Alternatives such as 32 ♗a4 (a) ♖e2+ 33 ♔g1 ♖8e6 and 32 ♗b3 (b) ♖e2+ are not successful and do not score.

**32 ♗d3 ♘a5**

> **a) 33 c4**
> **b) 33 ♗f4**
> **c) 33 ♗b2**
> **d) 33 ♗d2**

White needs to develop. Black is trying to advance his pawns in order to limit White's pieces; the move ...d6-d5 is Black's next idea if it is allowed. For this reason, 33 ♗b2 (c) and 33 ♗d2 (d) score just one. 33 ♗f4 (b) is the move that was being sought after and it scores two points.

33 c4 (a) also scores one. It remains an interesting situation after 33...d5 34 f4 dxc4

35 fxe5 cxd3. If you noticed that Black might be able to do this, then take an extra point. It is interesting to note that this is a common theme in positions of rook and pawn (or pawns) versus minor pieces. By giving away an exchange but gaining a pawn, the material situation is now minor piece versus three pawns. Alternatively, Black can use White's lack of momentum to play 33...g5.

**33 ♗f4 ♖d5**

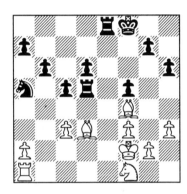

> **a) 34 ♗b5**
> **b) 34 ♗c2**
> **c) 34 ♖d1**
> **d) 34 ♗e2**

A straightforward idea again here. White must move the light-squared bishop and he must do so without losing time. Therefore, he must attack a black piece if he can. For this reason, 34 ♗b5 (a) top scores with two. The other choices all score one point as they are safe but they all allow Black time to improve his position. For example, 34 ♗c2 (b) g5 gains some space for Black and decreases the scope of White's dark-squared bishop.

**34 ♗b5**

At this juncture, it must be added that an advantage has passed to White. Black should not have wasted time shuttling his knight and rook to and fro.

**34...♖e6**

a) 35 h4
b) 35 &d7
c) 35 &e1
d) 35 a4

35 h4 (a) is a nice move, which stops 35...g5 and scores two points. Now White has well posted minor pieces that cannot be attacked or driven back.

The other moves all score one point. There is no purpose in attacking the black rook without good reason with 35 &d7 (b). So long as Black notices and plays 35...&e7, then it is White who is suddenly on the back foot due to the attack on the bishop and the forthcoming ...g7-g5.

**35 h4 c4**

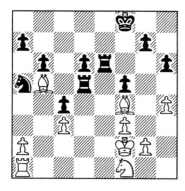

a) 36 a4
b) 36 &d7
c) 36 &a6
d) 36 &a4

White must move or support his bishop, but which? With 36 &a6 (c), some attempt can be made to run the bishop out of squares with ...b6-b5, but I cannot really see any problems for White as he has &b1 prepared and so you score one point. Inferior is 36 &a4 (d) because Black pushes forward with 36...b5, but you can have one anyway because it is safe. Also ruled out as best is 36 &d7 (b). Again you can take a point even though the familiar reply 36 &d7 &e7

beckons.

That leaves 36 a4 (a) to score a maximum of two, when White retains slightly more opportunities for his bishop than in choice (c), for example.

**36 a4 &d3**

a) 37 &d7
b) 37 &e3
c) 37 &g3
d) 37 &c1

37 &c1 (d) is an adequate defence of the c-pawn for one point. The other three choices all involve counterattacking Black's f-pawn. 37 &d7 (a) looks good at first sight, but some calculation is required to see that the move is really only ordinary and worth just one point. For example, 37 &d7 &f6 38 &e3 &e7 39 &c8 &d8, and either the bishop gets chased away from attacking f5 or White heads for an unclear ending with 40 &xf5 &xe3 41 &xe3 &xf5 42 &xd6.

37 &e3 (b) scores three points because &d7 is left until it is exactly the right moment. 37 &g3 (c) scores two. It is similar to &e3, with the downside that, importantly, the knight is not attacking c4.

**37 &e3 &xc3**

a) 38 &xf5
b) 38 &d7
c) 38 &d1
d) 38 &d5

Both the knight moves allow Black to attack. 38 &d5 (d) loses one point as White is not even taking a pawn. With 38 &xf5 (a), which scores one point, 38...&c2+ 39 &f1 &ee2 gives Black a great position and 39 &g3 &g6+ is no better for White.

38 &d1 (c) scores two points and is a sufficient way of winning a pawn back.

38 &d7 (b) is the star move worth three points. If you noticed that the rook from d3 has moved so White can meet 38...&e7 with 39 &xd6, then take a bonus of two points.

**38 &d7 &f6**

a) 39 ♗xf5
b) 39 ♘xf5
c) 39 ♖d1
d) 39 ♘d5

The reader should have been able to apply what has been read above in order to work out White's 39th move. 39 ♗xf5 (a) loses two points because of 39...♖xe3!. Take a bonus of two if you remembered or worked out that Black can correctly exchange his rook for White's two minor pieces. Therefore, 39 ♘xf5 (b) is correct and scores three points.

39 ♘d5 (d) does not score, once more because of 39...♖c2+ 40 ♔f1 ♖g6 with an attack for Black and his rooks.

39 ♖d1 (c) is adequate for one point.

**39 ♘xf5 ♖c2 +**

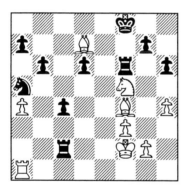

a) 40 ♔g3
b) 40 ♔e3
c) 40 ♔f1
d) 40 ♔g1

40 ♔g3 (a) is obviously bad and loses

two points in view of the aforementioned ...♖g6+.

40 ♔g1 (d) scores one, and so does 40 ♔e3 (b), when pieces ominously gather around the Black king after with 40...♖xg2 41 ♗xd6+. The only problem is that White has better with 40 ♔f1 (c), which scores three points.

**40 ♔f1 ♘b7**

a) 41 ♖c1
b) 41 ♖d1
c) 41 ♖e1
d) 41 ♖a3

41 ♖a3 (d) does not score.

41 ♖c1 (a) scores one. White does not give any pieces away but he relinquishes the pressure with after 41...♖xc1+ 42 ♗xc1 ♘c5.

41 ♖d1 (b) scores two and it is a sensible way of trying to win a pawn. However, White has better with 41 ♖e1 (c), which scores four points. If you planned this ahead, then take two extra points.

**41 ♖e1 1-0**

Black resigned at this point. Admittedly, he is a point up material-wise and so at first sight resignation seems to be premature. Perhaps the game was adjourned (as games were often played without blitz or quickplay finishes at that time and digital clocks had not been invented!) and the competitor playing Black, after considerable analysis, may have thought his chances hopeless at that level. For example, 41...c3 42 g4 ♔g8 43 ♖e8+ ♔h7 44 g5 hxg5 45 hxg5 ♖f7 46 ♗e6 ♖c7 47 ♗g8+ ♔g6 48 ♘h4+ ♔h5 49 ♗f7+ ♔xh4 50 ♖h8 mate.

Add up your points and see how you did.

Less than 15: Not a high score, but did you learn something?
15-28: Sorry, not consistent enough.
29-50: Fair play. Some difficult moves to find with the minor pieces.
51-70: Good! Presumably you prevented the black rooks from becoming active.
71+: Well Done! Following in the footsteps of one of the great players.

## Game 16
## **Kramnik-Shirov**
Linares 2000

**1 ♘f3 d5 2 d4 c6 3 c4 ♘f6 4 ♘c3 dxc4 5 a4 ♗f5 6 ♘e5**

Openings and variations come in and out of fashion. At the time of this game, White's 6th move was considered the main line of the Slav.

**6...e6**

This 'old', popular move almost 'forces' the sacrifice of a piece for three pawns that follows. More recently Black has found 6...♘bd7 to be worth investigating.

**7 f3 ♗b4 8 e4 ♗xe4 9 fxe4 ♘xe4 10 ♗d2 ♕xd4 11 ♘xe4 ♕xe4+ 12 ♕e2 ♗xd2+ 13 ♔xd2 ♕d5+ 14 ♔c2**

The now-retired English Grandmaster Matthew Sadler captured the mood here and I hope readers will allow me to pinch his idea and write, 'I hope that you are strapped in your seatbelts.'

**14...♘a6 15 ♘xc4 b5 16 axb5 ♘b4+ 17 ♔c3 cxb5 18 ♖d1 ♕c5 19 ♕e5 ♘d5+ 20 ♖xd5 b4+**

Such is grandmaster opening preparation. I believe this was Shirov's improvement on previously played games.

**21 ♔b3 ♕xd5**

White has given back an exchange and the result is that White has bishop and knight versus Black's rook and three pawns. This puts Black two points up. White's compensation is that Black's rooks are not connected. This is a tricky start position, particularly if you have never seen a position like this before.

> a) 22 ♕xd5
> b) 22 ♕xg7
> c) 22 ♗e2
> d) 22 ♖g1

22 ♕xd5 (a) is not bad for two points,

but after 22...exd5 23 ♘a5 ♔d7 both kings are appropriately active in the ending. Three points for 22 ♗e2 (c), after which White hopes for a better version of the endgame arising after 22 ♕xd5. For a bonus point you must have noticed that there is nothing to fear in 22...♕xg2 23 ♘d6+, when White is amassing a strong attack.

Taking a pawn with 22 ♕xg7 (b) is greedy and does not score because of the white king, which is exposed with queens on the board. Black has the mating line 22...♕d1+ 23 ♔xb4? ♖b8+ 24 ♔c3 ♖b3, which scores one point if you spotted it. Instead, White can try for the trap 23 ♔a2 0-0-0 (this move is also worth a point because there are now a lot of threats and White cannot develop) 24 ♘b6+. Now, in this position, not 24...axb6 25 ♗a6+ winning the queen with a discovered attack, but the calm 24...♔c7, which wraps things up nicely for Black.

In such a violent position 22 ♖g1 (d) must lose two points. There's no time for White to allow 22...♕d1+ and ...0-0.

**22 ♗e2 0-0**

> a) 23 ♕xd5
> b) 23 ♖d1
> c) 23 ♗f3
> d) 23 h4

You could have been excused for choosing 23 ♖d1 (b), but you lose a point if you did not notice 23 ♖d1 ♕xg2. If on the other hand you planned 24 ♖d3 with the threats of ♖g3 and ♗f3, then you can score two points. The problem is that 24...f6 25 ♕xe6+ ♔h8 26 ♗f3 ♕f1 does not win material for White. Instead, the white king will be exposed with queens and rooks on the board while the black king is safely tucked away into the corner.

23 h4 (d) straightforwardly loses one point after 23...♛xg2. Even worse is 23 ♗f3 (c) ♛d3+, which loses four points. Instead, now is the time to exchange queens with 23 ♛xd5 (a), which scores three points. A bonus is scored if you realised the significance of Black's previous move. In castling (not that he had a wide choice) Black has disadvantaged himself for the ending.

**23 ♛xd5 exd5**

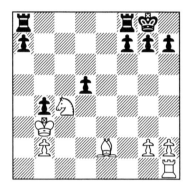

a) 24 ♘a5
b) 24 ♘e3
c) 24 ♘d6
d) 24 ♘d2

Care should be taken not to allow Black to develop the rooks with gain of time. 24 ♘a5 (a) scores two points. 24 ♘e3 (b) loses three points because of 24...♖ae8. 24 ♘d6 (c) and 24 ♘d2 (d) are not great, but you can have one point. In both instances Black has 24...a5.

**24 ♘a5 ♖fe8**

a) 25 ♗b5
b) 25 ♗f3
c) 25 ♖e1
d) 25 ♗g4

One point for 25 ♗b5 (a) and 25 ♗g4 (d). Two points for 25 ♗f3 (b), with another if you realise that it would be useful to

have pawn and bishop defending each other.

25 ♖e1 (c) loses three points and is destined to fail to the pin. After 25...♖ac8 the white king cannot even help out.

**25 ♗f3 ♖ac8**

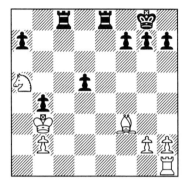

a) 26 ♗xd5
b) 26 ♖d1
c) 26 ♔xb4
d) 26 ♘b7

Black can more than adequately react to 26 ♘b7 (d) with 26...♖e3+ and ...♖c2 (unless White falls for 27 ♔xb4 ♖b8), so no points there for allowing such activity.

26 ♔xb4 (c) scores one for capturing the pawn, but again, 26...♖b8+ swings in Black's favour. 26 ♗xd5 (a) also deserves just one, but the top score is two points for 26 ♖d1 (b). If you realised that the bishop on f3 stops ...♖e2, then give yourself another point.

**26 ♖d1 ♖e3+**

a) 27 ♔xb4
b) 27 ♔a4
c) 27 ♔a2

I hope just having a choice from three alternatives did not mislead you.

27 ♔a2 (c) is okay for one point, but the king is supposed to be a fighting unit in the ending so it is 27 ♔a4 (b) that scores most highly with two points.

27 ♔xb4 (a) fails to 27...♖b8+ 28 ♔c5 ♖xb2. You can have a point for rejecting this option if you realised that White needs to keep the b-pawn in order to retain serious winning chances. I doubt anyone planned 29 ♘c4, but if you did you can have a point even though Black has 29...♖c2 30 ♖xd5 g6. In the end White achieves only what was expected in capturing the d-pawn, which has been on death row for a few moves.

**27 ♔a4 b3**

Black goes in search of counterplay. The passive 27...g6 28 ♖xd5 ♖e7 29 ♘c6 does not seem tempting.

> a) 28 ♘xb3
> b) 28 ♗xd5
> c) 28 ♖xd5
> d) 28 ♗g4

28 ♗g4 (d) loses three points to 28...♖e4+ 29 ♔xb3 ♖xg4.

You have not really understood the importance of active rooks if you selected 28 ♘xb3 (a) or 28 ♗xd5 (b), which each score just one point.

Best is 28 ♖xd5 (c) for two points. You score a bonus if you have spotted the idea of ♖d7 and ♗d5.

**28 ♖xd5 g6**

> a) 29 ♖d7
> b) 29 ♘xb3
> c) 29 ♖d4
> d) 29 ♖b5

One point for 29 ♖d4 (c). It does not do much but it is safe.

29 ♖d7 (a) scores three. I even hinted at this move in the previous comment. Inferior versions to this are 29 ♘xb3 (b) and 29 ♖b5 (d), which each score one point. A possible continuation is 29 ♖b5 ♔g7 30 ♖xb3 ♖xb3 31 ♔xb3 f5 32 ♘c6 ♖c7 33 ♔a4 g5, but in this race to obtain a queen Black has a comfortable amount of counterplay to draw by pushing the kingside

pawns and playing ...♖c2 when the time is right.

**29 ♖d7 ♖c2**

> a) 30 ♗d5
> b) 30 ♖xa7
> c) 30 ♔a3
> d) 30 ♘xb3

I apologise if you chose 30 ♗d5 (a). You may feel that you have been lead astray but you have not calculated some important variations, so just one point. Black is not forced to play 30...♖f2, but can go for the stronger 30...♖xb2 31 ♖xf7 ♖ee2 when White runs out of pawns. Similarly, Black mops up pawns on the seventh rank with 31 ♗xf7+ ♔h8 32 ♗xb3 ♖xg2.

30 ♘xb3 (d) also scores just one, but please deduct three if you chose 30 ♖xa7 (b) because of 30...♖xb2. With each of these choices Black captures White's b-pawn, which earns you a point if you understood this to be the one that Black is after. In the latter of these cases Black suddenly has a well advanced passed pawn himself!

It only leaves us to award two points for 30 ♔a3 (c) before we move on.

**30 ♔a3 ♔g7**

> a) 31 ♖xa7
> b) 31 ♗d5
> c) 31 ♘xb3
> d) 31 ♘b7

There's nothing better now than to round up the loose pawn. So two points for 31 ♖xa7 (a). You score another one if you realised that White must take the a-pawn at some stage in order to make a queen with the b-pawn.

One point only for 31 ♗d5 (b), unless you planned to meet 31...♖f2 by then taking on a7, when you score one more. One point also for 31 ♘xb3 (c).

31 ♘b7 (d) is erroneous, so nothing for that. If you chose this idea, then you are going after the wrong pawn, presumably with ♘d6 or ♘d8. Instead, you should have straightforwardly captured a free pawn as indicated above.

**31 ♖xa7 h5**

If Black had attempted to scare White with a passed pawn by playing 31...♖xf3 32 gxf3 ♖xh2, then he would have had to contend with 33 ♘c6 and a subsequent attack on the f-pawn.

---

a) 32 h4
b) 32 h3
c) 32 ♘xb3
d) 32 ♗d5

---

32 h4 (a) scores one point, but 32...♖c1 begs the question of how to defend the h-pawn because ...♖h1 is threatened. 32 h3 (b) is a better version of this and scores two points.

You score one for 32 ♘xb3 (c) and a bonus if you digested the information following Black's 31st move and saw 32...♖xf3 33 gxf3 ♖xh2, when a race to queen results.

32 ♗d5 (d) scores one, but it is not clear how to meet the threat of ...♖ee2 after 32...♖f2.

**32 h3 h4**

---

a) 33 ♗d5
b) 33 ♘xb3
c) 33 ♖b7
d) 33 ♘c6

---

The game could end in tears from

White's point of view after 33 ♘c6 (d). Please take off three points due to 33...♖xf3 34 gxf3 ♖xc6 35 ♔xb3 ♖f6. It is also Black's advantage after 35 ♖b7 ♖a6+ 36 ♔xb3 ♖f6.

33 ♘xb3 (b) scores one, but the threat to the precious b-pawn is too real after 33...♖f2. White cannot move the bishop and forget that it is protecting against the threat ...♖ee2. Yet leaving the bishop on f3 provokes ...♖fxf3 and we are back in a race to see who can promote a pawn first, only this time White starts in disarray with his knight pinned.

33 ♖b7 (c) scores two points. Give yourself one extra if you saw that taking on b3 with the rook defends against some of the outlined threats.

Order of moves is important here as can be seen in 33 ♗d5 (a), which scores just the one. Too late is 33 ♗d5 ♖f2 34 ♖b7 because Black has 34...♖e5 35 ♖b5 ♖ff5. Alternatively, 34 ♘xb3 ♖ee2 35 ♘c1 (hoping for 35...♖xb2 36 ♘d3) 35...♖d2 36 ♗f3 ♖xb2 is no good for White.

**33 ♖b7 ♖c5**

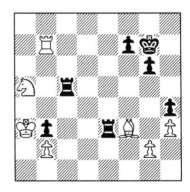

---

a) 34 ♘c6
b) 34 ♘xb3
c) 34 ♔a4
d) 34 ♔b4

---

You should not have fallen for the tactic after 34 ♘c6 (a), so lose two points. At least

34 ♘c6 ♖xf3 35 gxf3 ♖xc6 36 ♖xb3 ♔f6 is not as bad as last time it was pointed out.

After 34 ♘xb3 (b) there is a clever response in 34...♖a5+ 35 ♔b4 ♖a2. White loses an opportunity to make a queen, so no points.

34 ♔a4 (c) scores one point, but deduct two instead if you were adamant that you were taking on b3 with the rook no matter what Black played. The variation 34 ♔a4 ♖f5 35 ♖xb3 ♖xa5+ 36 ♔xa5 ♖xb3 leaves Black winning easily.

34 ♔b4 (d) top scores with two points, but the devil is in the detail.

**34 ♔b4 ♖f5**

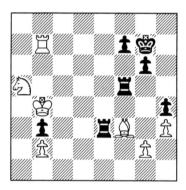

a) 35 ♗g4
b) 35 ♖c7
c) 35 ♘c4
d) 35 ♘xb3

Both players are manoeuvring in order to increase their chances when it comes to an out and out race to queen a pawn. One assumes that the black b-pawn will be taken at White's convenience.

35 ♗g4 (a) loses two points. After 35...♖f2 White has carelessly given away a pawn.

35 ♘c4 (c) does not score because the variation 35...♖f4 36 ♗d5 g5 37 ♔a3 ♖d3 shows only Black improving his position.

35 ♘xb3 (d) scores two points, but the sacrifice 35...♖fxf3 will end up with Black

having three connected passed pawns which will prove a 'tour de force'.

That leaves 35 ♖c7 (b) to notch up the maximum with three points. Another point is awarded for those readers who saw that 35...♖fxf3 36 gxf3 ♖xf3 (as indicated in the previous paragraph) can be met with 37 ♖c3. Another bonus is awarded for those players who realised that 34 ♔b4 rather than 34 ♔a4 was necessary in order to be able to take back on c3 without letting the black b-pawn through.

**35 ♖c7 g5**

a) 36 ♖c3
b) 36 ♘xb3
c) 36 ♘c4
d) 36 ♖c5

Some poor moves to avoid here. 36 ♖c3 (a) loses five points because of 36...♖xc3 37 bxc3 b2. The move 36 ♘c4 (c) is just lazy and allows 36...♖exf3 37 gxf3 ♖xf3 etc., which creates a dangerous passed pawn extremely quickly for Black.

36 ♖c5 (d) just loses time following 36 ♖c5 ♖xc5 37 ♔xc5. One point is scored here as it is a safe move.

That leaves 36 ♘xb3 (b) to score three points because now is the time to clear the way so that the b-pawn can run in order to touch down. Play can continue 36...♖exf3 37 gxf3 ♖xf3. A bonus is scored for remembering that 38 ♖c3 is important. Then, after 38...♖xc3 39 ♔xc3, the move 39...g4 is required by Black in order for White not be too casual. However, after 40 ♘c1 gxh3 41 ♘d3 h2 42 ♘f2 ♔f6 he can still win with 43 b4. I noticed one variation where the win only comes because White 'queens' just in time. There then follows a tricky, but technically winning, ending of queen versus pawns, viz. 43...♔e5 44 b5 ♔f4 45 b6 ♔f3 47 ♘h1 ♔g2 48 b7 ♔xh1 49 b8♕ etc. Black may instead prefer 38...♖f2, but after 39 ♔a3 White retains his passed b-pawn and therefore enough of an advantage to claim that he is still winning.

These variations justify White's choice of move. It is also worth noting that, materially, White is now a point up.

**36 ♘xb3 ♖f4+**

---

a) 37 ♔a3
b) 37 ♔a5
c) 37 ♔c5
d) 37 ♖c4

---

The white king is too far away from the action, but one point for 37 ♔a3 (a), even though I would expect the black pawns to gain speed and create some problems for White after 37...♖exf3 38 gxf3 ♖xf3 39 ♖c3 ♖xc3 40 bxc3 ♔f6. At least this is better than 37 ♔a5 (b) or 37 ♔c5 (c), which each lose three points as the knight on b3 will be hanging.

37 ♖c4 (d) scores three. It is the best move, a logical move, and the only satisfactory way to play.

**37 ♖c4 ♖xc4+ 38 ♔xc4 f5**

---

a) 39 ♘d2
b) 39 ♘d4
c) 39 ♗d5
d) 39 ♘c5

---

You can have a free point as I assume that everyone intended the recapture on White's 38th move.

Now for White's 39th, where Kramnik is looking to move the knight in order to get the b-pawn moving. Therefore, 39 ♗d5 (c) does not score at this stage – the wasted time could prove costly.

39 ♘d2 (a) is a bit too backward and does not look to support the pawn as best it can, so just one point here.

39 ♘c5 (d) scores two points, but the winner here is 39 ♘d4 (b) for three points. Black wants to play ...♔f6 and ...♔e5, but this immediate advance allows ♘c2 trapping the rook and winning the exchange. You can score a bonus if you saw this.

**39 ♘d4 ♔f6**

---

a) 40 b3
b) 40 b4
c) 40 ♔d5
d) 40 ♘c6

---

40 b3 (a) is the right idea, but it seems like you have slipped with your fingers, so just one point for 40 b3. Naturally 40 b4 (b) scores three points.

In general it is good to use the king to support the pawn, but 40 ♔d5 (c) allows Black to try for a tactic. So this only scores two points as 40 ♔d5 ♖e5+ 41 ♔d6 g4 42 hxg4 fxg4 43 ♗xg4 ♖e4 gives Black the edge. Instead, 43 ♗c6 h3 44 gxh3 gxh3 45 b4 h2 46 b5 ♖e1 is heading for a draw.

Another move to avoid was 40 ♘c6 (d), which loses two points. The sharp 40 ♘c6 ♖xf3 41 gxf3 g4, which earns you two points if you saw it, forces White to be on his mettle. Certainly 42 fxg4 fxg4 43 hxg4 h3 44 g5+ ♔xg5 45 ♘e5 ♔f4 is no good. This highlights the well-known maxim that knights are no good at stopping rook's pawns. Instead, 43 ♘d4 allows White another bite at the cherry, but he is making life difficult for himself.

**40 b4 ♖e1**

---

a) 41 b5
b) 41 ♘e2
c) 41 ♔c5
d) 41 ♘b3

---

41 b5 (a) scores four points and is best.

41 ♘e2 (b) is delicate and clever for one point. If you realised that the knight and bishop combine and stop ...♔f4, then add another to your score. Black could meet this with ...♖b1 (you can have a point for if you thought about that) and then ...♖b2 in order that he can make oscillatory checks on both b2 and c2. Ultimately, however, the white king zigzags up the board and seeks refuge in front of the b-pawn. When the pawn is on b7, White threatens ♔c7 in order to touch down. The move ♗c6 can be used as shelter from the last remaining check. If you too outlined this winning plan, then please add another point to your score.

41 ♔c5 (c) misses the mark and loses two points due to 41...♔e5 42 ♘c6+ ♔f4 and Black has been granted some counterplay. That is unless you really intended 42 ♘e2, in which case you score as in (b).

41 ♘b3 (d) definitely loses two points because Black can get a draw with 41 ♘b3 g4, although there is no need for White to give Black the chance to play 42 hxg4 fxg4 43 ♗xg4 ♖e4+, when Black is suddenly winning.

**41 b5 ♔e5**

a) 42 b6
b) 42 ♘c6+
c) 42 ♘b3
d) 42 ♘c2

42 ♘c6+ (b) scores four points and is the easiest and clearest way to win.

42 b6 (a) is unnecessarily longwinded, especially if Black reacts with the stiffest defence of 42 b6 ♖c1+ 43 ♔d3 ♖b1 44 b7 g4, so that scores just two points. If White then plays 45 hxg4 fxg4 46 ♗xg4 ♖xb7 Black will be able to draw, although at the right moment it might mean having to find the squares h5 and g3 respectively in which to place the king and rook. Instead, White must find 46 ♗c6 (or 45 ♗c6) and use a similar method to the game.

42 ♘c2 (d) scores three points. White can win by shielding the pawn from the rook with ♘b4 (have a point if you realised that). Whether or not you chose this option, you can have another point for seeing that the a6-square might also prove useful for the knight in order to support the b-pawn home.

It is obviously a bad slip for White to allow 42 ♘b3 (c) g4, so please deduct two points.

**42 ♘c6+ ♔d6**

a) 43 b6
b) 43 ♔d4
c) 43 ♗h5
d) 43 ♘b4

43 b6 (a) top scores with three points. Sometimes chess is intuition and 43 b6 is intuitively the move. One does not always have the time to justify everything by analysis so I have included the following variation only because there is an unusual and pretty forced mate at the end. I would expect the better players to see up to move 47 for White and then assess the situation as winning: 43...g4 44 b7 ♖b1 45 b8♕+ ♖xb8 46 ♘xb8 gxf3 47 gxf3 ♔e5 48 ♔d3 ♔f4 49 ♔e2 ♔g3 50 ♘c6 ♔xh3 51 ♔f2 ♔h2 52 ♘e7 h3 53 ♘xf5 ♔h1 54 ♘g3+ ♔h2 55 ♘f1+ ♔h1 56 f4 h2 57 ♘g3 mate.

I will score 43 ♔d4 (b) ♖b1 as no points, 43 ♗h5 (c) ♖g1 as minus one and 43 ♘b4

(d) g4 as minus two. Remember to try and find the very best moves. In this game you should try to avoid having to mate with bishop and knight and king versus king if you can. If you cannot avoid this, then what will be will be (but if you do not know the required technique, then you had better ask someone or look it up in an appropriate book).

**43 b6 ♖c1+**

> a) 44 ♔b5
> b) 44 ♔b4
> c) 44 ♔d4
> d) 44 ♔d3

44 ♔b5 (a) is the correct route for the king and scores three points. You score a bonus for seeing that Black wins a point with 44...♖c5+ and another for realising that White will subsequently promote.

The other choices all lose two points and allow 44...♖xc6, which should result in a drawn position of king and h-pawn versus a king that gets back in time. By continuing after the first of these errors, one can see some useful tricks to watch out for in king and pawn endings. Play through the moves that follow – they are instructive: 44 ♔b4 ♖xc6 45 ♗xc6 ♔xc6 46 ♔c4 g4 47 ♔d4 ♔xb6 (not 47...f4 48 hxg4 f3 49 ♔e3 as this wins for White!) 48 ♔e5 gxh3 49 gxh3 ♔c5 50 ♔xf5 ♔d6 with a draw.

**44 ♔b5 g4**

> a) 45 hxg4
> b) 45 ♗xg4
> c) 45 b7
> d) 45 ♗e2

It should be evident that 45 b7 (c) is best for four points. For the purpose of this book, we must investigate how bad the other moves are. 45 hxg4 (a) scores only two points because White only secures victory by playing deftly with the knight and bishop in the variation 45 hxg4 fxg4 46 ♗e4 ♖c5+ 47 ♔a6 ♖c3 48 b7 ♖b3 49 b8♕+ ♖xb8 50 ♘xb8 ♔e5 51 ♗b7 ♔f4 52 ♘d7 ♔g3 53 ♘f6 h3 54 gxh3 gxh3 55 ♔b5.

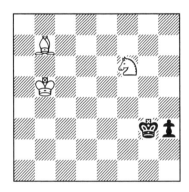

45 ♗xg4 (b) loses four points and 45 ♗e2 (d) loses three points. Both are blatant blunders and even with the latter Black has great chances to win after 45...♖c5+.

**45 b7 ♖b1+**

> a) 46 ♔a6
> b) 46 ♔c4
> c) 46 ♔a5
> d) 46 ♘b4

46 ♘b4 (d) was the move that Kramnik had planned some moves ago and you can award yourself two points for choosing it. I did point out this shielding idea previously so I will be harsh on the other three moves, which are all bad blunders. 46 ♔a6 (a) gxf3 47 gxf3 ♔xc6 loses seven points from your total, while 46 ♔c4 (b) gxf3 47 ♘b4 ♔c7 48

gxf3 ♗xb7 and 46 ♔a5 (c) gxf3 47 ♘b4 ♔c7 48 gxf3 ♔xb7 each lose five points.

**46 ♘b4 ♔c7**

> a) 47 ♔c5
> b) 47 hxg4
> c) 47 ♗xg4
> d) 47 ♘a6+

First we score the blunders of 47 ♔c5 (a), which loses five points, and 47 ♗xg4 (c), which loses four points. The illegal 47 ♘a6+ (d) can only be punished in a game by the embarrassment that you have moved into check. We certainly cannot positively reward such an oversight in this exercise, so sorry, but no points here.

47 hxg4 (b) is sensible for two points.

**47 hxg4 fxg4**

> a) 48 ♗xg4
> b) 48 ♗e4
> c) 48 ♗d5
> d) 48 ♗c6

No points for 48 ♗d5 (c) or 48 ♗c6 (d). The latter could continue 48...h3 49 gxh3

gxh3 50 ♔c5 ♖a1 51 ♔b5 ♖b1, which is heading for a draw by repetition.

White is still winning in after 48 ♗xg4 (a), but to begin with he must round up the pawn with the variation 48 ♗xg4 ♔xb7 49 ♔c5 ♔c7 50 ♘d3 ♖g1 51 ♗h3 ♔d8 52 ♔d5 ♔e7 53 ♔e4 ♔f6 54 ♔f4 ♖a1 55 ♔g4 ♖a4+ 56 ♔h5 ♖d4 57 ♘e1 ♖a4 58 ♘f3.

Simpler is 48 ♗e4 (b), which gains a valuable tempo on the rook and scores three points. 48...♖b2 49 ♔c4 leaves Black unable to salvage the position as he cannot make a sensible check (you can score one for seeing that). Also, White threatens the unstoppable ♘a6+ (you can also have a point for if you spotted that). Also worth a mention and a point is 48...♖b3 49 ♔a4. The variation 48...♖a1 49 ♘a6+ (I have already mentioned this move, so no more points) 49...♖xa6 50 ♔xa6 ♔b8 51 ♗d5 h3 52 gxh3 gxh3 53 ♗e4 h2 54 ♗h1 ♔c7 55 ♔a7 also wins. The theory of 'one diagonal' does not come into it here because the white king is so close to the b- pawn. However, had the white king been further afield, then it would have been handy from White's point of view that the bishop could cover h1, g2 and b7 simultaneously.

**48 ♗e4 1-0**

For a great many years, I found it very much easier to coordinate play with rooks rather than minor pieces. In my experience this feeling is a common one for other players. Thinking in straight lines is probably where most players begin their chess lives. As real novices, 1 h2-h4 and 2 ♖h1-h3 is a popular way to start but, as we can see, mastering bishop and knight play is essential.

How did you do in this technically superbly played game by White?

Less than 21: Perhaps you were bamboozled with the minor piece play.
21-39: Please practise and build up confidence playing with knight and bishop.
40-67: A sound player but perhaps you would have found it easier to play black.
68-85: A pass on this exercise with distinction. Well done!
86+: You did not let go. A really long, determined performance. Honours pass!

## Game 17
## Karpov-Kasparov
World Championship (Game 2), Moscow 1985

**1 e4 c5 2 ♘f3 d6 3 d4 cxd4 4 ♘xd4 ♘f6 5 ♘c3 a6 6 ♗e2 e6 7 0-0 ♗e7 8 f4 0-0 9 ♔h1 ♕c7 10 a4 ♘c6 11 ♗e3 ♖e8 12 ♗f3 ♖b8**

Grandmaster prophylaxis. The white king on h1 avoids a potential check on the g1-a7 diagonal. Black plays ...♖b8 in order to prepare ...b7-b6. At the same time he avoids any nasty treatment from White's light-squared bishop.

**13 ♕d2 ♗d7**

The stakes were high which also meant that there was heavy preparation going on. You are embroiled in a line of deep theoretical value.

**14 ♕f2 ♘xd4 15 ♗xd4 e5 16 ♗e3**

Now take over the pieces from one of the most aggressive players around. You are up against one of the most successful and positional players of all time.

> a) 16...exf4
> b) 16...♘g4
> c) 16...♗e6
> d) 16...♗g4

16...exf4 (a) scores two points, but it was important not to capture this pawn earlier

and allow the white bishop to recapture from its starting square c1.

16...♗e6 (c) adds protection to the d5-square and scores two points, but it is a provocative move that I would not recommend under normal circumstances because it gives White an additional method of play. Perhaps this, too, was all part of Kasparov's preparation.

16...♘g4 (b) and 16...♗g4 (d) both lose one because they allow White to crash through on f7.

**16...♗e6 17 f5**

> a) 17...♗c4
> b) 17...♗d7
> c) 17...♗c8
> d) 17...d5

17...♗c4 (a) was the choice of the ex-World Champion, so take three points for this. The move 17...♗d7 (b) scores one as a solid alternative, with an extra point available if you intend to re-route your bishop to c6.

17...♗c8 (c) fails to score, while 17...d5 (d) loses two points. Take a bonus if you rejected this central strike because of 18 ♗b6, which is crushing due to 18...♕c6 19 fxe6 d4 20 exf7+ ♔xf7 21 ♘d5 ♘xd5 22 exd5 ♕xb6 23 ♗h5+.

**17...♗c4 18 ♗b6**

> a) 18...♕c6
> b) 18...♕d7
> c) 18...♕c8
> d) 18...♗xf1

18...♕c8 (c) scores two, and an extra bonus if this was your favoured square for the reason that if Black arranges ...d5-d5, the f5-pawn will be loose after exd5.

One point each for the safe 18...♕c6 (a) and 18...♕d7 (b).

18...♗xf1 (d) is a bad mistake – minus six.

**18...♕c8 19 ♖fc1**

| |
|---|
| a) 19...♘d7 |
| b) 19...d5 |
| c) 19...a5 |
| d) 19...♘xe4 |

19...d5 (d) is a thematic Sicilian freeing pawn break and is worth three points here.

Lose one for 19...♘d7 (a) because it is embarrassing in the least to have to answer b2-b3 with ...♗b5 in order to be able to exchange the bishop fairly. One cannot believe anyone would be agreeable to such an idea.

At least you realised that your bishop on c4 is short of squares if you went for 19...a5 (c), but something has gone badly wrong if Black must shed a pawn, so no score.

The sequence 19...♘xe4 (d) 20 ♗xe4 begs the question 'and now?' The answer is, 'lose 2'.

**19...d5 20 b3**

| |
|---|
| a) 20...dxe4 |
| b) 20...♘xe4 |
| c) 20...♗b4 |
| d) 20...d4 |

I cannot distribute any points for 20...dxe4 (a), which still leaves your bishop bereft of squares after 21 ♘xe4, for example 21...♗d5 22 ♘xf6+ ♗xf6 23 ♗xd5. However, your score does go down by two if you did not realise that you have caused some minor complications by attacking the bishop on f3. You score a bonus for seeing 21...♕xf5 22 ♘xf6+ ♗xf6 23 bxc4 and another for 23...e4 24 ♗e2 ♕f2 25 ♗f2 ♗a1 26 ♗a1, which keeps the point count level even though the bishops should eventually triumph. (see the introduction to Chapter 3).

20...♘xe4 (b) 21 ♘xe4 dxe4 22 ♗xe4 loses two points, as does 20...d4 (d).

20...♗b4 (c) scores three points. I suspect it took an entourage of Russian grandmasters all night to give this line their blessing.

**20...♗b4 21 ♘a2**

| |
|---|
| a) 21...dxe4 |
| b) 21...♗a3 |
| c) 21...a5 |
| d) 21...♗d6 |

21...♗a3 (b) scores three; this looks to me like a case of process of elimination. I don't think it is fair to expect anyone to have seen this far ahead when Black originally played 17...♗c4, but if you did plan 20...♗b4 and saw 21 ♘a2 ♗a3 at the same time as your 17th, you deserve five bonus points.

In order not to lose material, Black's last two moves have been a case of attacking a white piece of at least equal value to the black one that was attacked. If you tried to get what you could for the bishop because you did not see 21...♗a3 (b) and you chose 21...dxe4 (a), then you score one. The alternatives both drop a piece and two points without a fight.

**21...♗a3 22 bxc4**

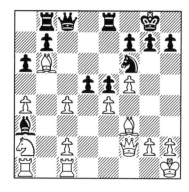

| |
|---|
| a) 22...♗b2 |
| b) 22...♗xc1 |
| c) 22...♕xc4 |
| d) 22...dxe4 |

22...♗b2 (a) is too slow and allows White a huge position with 23 cxd5. This loses two points.

22...♗xc1 (b) reveals Kasparov's intention of an unbalanced clash of pieces. Score two for pursuing this theme.

22...♕xc4 (c) and 22...dxe4 (d) both lead to a chaotic situations but it is not quite the best that Black can do, so just one point here.

**22...♗xc1 23 ♘xc1**

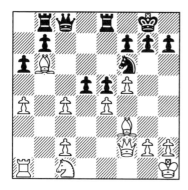

> a) 23...♕xc4
> b) 23...dxc4
> c) 23...dxe4
> d) 23...♘xe4

All score one with the exception of 23...♕xc4 (a), which gets double with two. Take a bonus if you are aware that the point count on the board is identical at the moment, short-lived though it might be...

**23...♕xc4 24 exd5**

> a) 24...♘e4
> b) 24...e4
> c) 24...♘xd5
> d) 24...♖bc8

24...♘e4 (a) scores one, as does the natural 24...♘xd5 (c) and 24...♖bc8 (d). Top score of three points, however, is awarded to the energetic 24...e4 (b).

**24...e4 25 ♗e2**

> a) 25...♕xc2
> b) 25...♕xd5
> c) 25...♕c3
> d) 25...♕c8

Which pawn to take? If the d-pawn ends up being a menace you may wish you chose 25...♕xd5 (b) for two points, but if you eliminated the c-pawn with 25...♕xc2 (a), you agree with Kasparov and can have three.

25...♕c3 (c) is safe enough for one, but 26 ♗d4 appears to be a strong response. Likewise, there is nothing wrong with 25...♕c8 (d) for one point, but Kasparov would no doubt have scowled at its lack of ambition.

**25...♕xc2 26 ♕d4**

Take a bonus point if you are getting ideas about back rank mates.

> a) 26...♖bc8
> b) 26...e3
> c) 26...h6
> d) 26...♕c8

No, I meant the back rank mating ideas were to be inflicted on White, not Black! Anyway, you can have one for the ultra-prophylactic 26...h6 (c).

26...♖bc8 (a) claims the open c-file for three points, with an additional two if you calculated that 27 d6 ♕xc1+ 28 ♖xc1 ♖xc1+ 29 ♗d1 e3 (one point) 30 d7 e2 (one point) 31 dxe8♕+ ♘xe8 is the end of the road for White.

26...e3 (a) must also have come into consideration – score two points for this move.

26...♕c8 (d) is just too wet to merit anything, I am afraid. Guessing Kasparov's moves should be avoided for you in future.

**26...♖bc8 27 h3**

> a) 27...♕xc1+
> b) 27...e3
> c) 27...♘d7
> d) 27...♖e7

27...♛xc1+ (a) 28 ♖xc1 ♖xc1+ loses its sting when White uses the escape square with 29 ♔h2. Deduct a point for not noticing the reason behind White's 27th.

27...e3 (b) coordinates Black's position in a pleasing way as all his pieces are actively placed with useful squares to frequent. As long as you have some idea of how to meet 28 d6, award yourself two.

27...♘d7 (c) is sensible for one, as is 27...♖e7 (d) with the intention of gradually rounding up the white d-pawn.

**27...e3 28 d6**

At the time this was considered to be the only way forward. We can now conclude that the position stemming from the opening is in Black's favour as Karpov's pieces are still lacking harmony. A brave concept from Kasparov as, generally speaking, a knight and bishop are considered superior to a rook and pawn, especially in the opening/middlegame.

> a) 28...♘d7
> b) 28...♛d2
> c) 28...♖e4
> d) 28...♘e4

28...♘d7 (a) is an extremely natural method for blockading the passed pawn and nets you two points.

Typically, Kasparov looks for a more aggressive path which he finds in 28...♛d2 (b). If you discovered his route too, accept my congratulations, take three points but don't forget that pride comes before a fall. If you didn't realise that 29 d7 can now be met by 29...♘xd7 due to the x-ray support from the queen on d2, I'll have one of those hard-earned points back.

28...♖e4 (c) and 28...♘e4 (d) both permit the d-pawn to push on to d7. In the first case 28...♖e4 29 d7 ♖d8 30 ♛xe4 ♛xe4 31 ♗xd8 ♘xd7 leaves Black struggling to save the situation despite having a queen, while 28...♘e4 leads to a straightforward loss of material that should have been avoided.

Those options cost you one and four points respectively.

**28...♛d2 29 ♘d3**

> a) 29...♖e4
> b) 29...♛xe2
> c) 29...♖c2
> d) 29...♘d7

It is true that rooks on the seventh rank can be extremely effective, but as with most things 'there is a time and there is a place'. In this case 29...♖c2 (c) reduces your score by four as 30 d7 ♖d8 31 ♗xd8 ♛xe2 32 ♘f4 is one example that stops it in its tracks.

29...♛xe2 (b) cannot be argued with and scores two points, while 29...♘d7 (d), which was largely expected during the match, scores a creditable one.

29...♖e4 (a) is even worse than before, so lose five.

**29...♛xe2 30 d7**

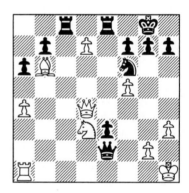

> a) 30...♖c2
> b) 30...♖ed8
> c) 30...♖cd8
> d) 30...♘xd7

Even Kasparov cannot find something unexpected here and indeed he liquidated the cheeky d-pawn without much thought with 30...♘xd7 (c), which is worth one point.

Everything else costs you four unless you

were torn between which rook to move in (b) and (c), when you lose eight.

**30...♘xd7 31 ♕xd7**

> a) 31...♕h5
> b) 31...h6
> c) 31...♕d2
> d) 31...♖c2

You can have three for 31...♕h5 (a) but this is conditional on you having checked out the threat of 32 ♗xe3, when you cannot capture with 32...♖xe3 due to 33 ♕xc8+. To then have stuck to your choice, I trust you found the response 32 ♗xe3 ♖cd8!. If not, you only score one for 31...♕h5.

One point for 31...h6 (b), which makes sense because Black does not want his rooks to be tied down to the 8th rank.

31...♕d2 (c) prepares to clear the path for Black's own passed pawn and scores the maximum of four.

The good news for those opting for 31...♖c2 (d) is that, if you weren't threatening mate on g2, you would have been penalised significantly higher than minus one for permitting 32 ♕xe8 mate.

**31...♕d2 32 ♖e1**

> a) 32...e2
> b) 32...h6
> c) 32...♕a2
> d) 32...♕c3

Score three points for 32...e2 (a), which

ensures that White must keep his eye on the dangerously advanced pawn.

32...h6 (b) again scores one, as does 32...♕c3 (d), but I cannot allow anything for 32...♕a2 (c), which relieves some pressure on the white knight and rook.

**32...e2 33 ♔g1**

With the white pieces now working together Karpov cleverly offers to watch the e-pawn with his king too. It is not easy to see how Black can press on...

> a) 33...♕e3+
> b) 33...♔f8
> c) 33...a5
> d) 33...♕g5

33...♕e3+ (a) would be fine if the white bishop were not on b6. Chess is a harsh game where it is possible to play 59 moves like a champion, but it only takes a single oversight to cost the game. As this blunder was so spectacular, it costs you nine points. If you were rushing due to a boiling kettle, a phone ringing (excluding your mobile that should have been switched off while you were concentrating) or a child crying, then you can reduce your loss to five.

33...a5 (c) scores two points and is not as random as it looks because Kasparov seeks to prevent Karpov clamping the queenside with a4-a5 himself. Award yourself a bonus of two if you wanted to tempt White to continue with 34 ♔f2, when 34...♖cd8! 35 ♗xd8 ♕e3+ is mate. Although unlikely to come to fruition against the likes of Karpov, such combinations will succeed time and time again in your average tournament.

Deduct two points for 33...♕g5 (d), which drops your e2-pawn due to 34 ♖xe2 ♖xe2 35 ♕xc8+ leading to mate. A relatively insignificant pawn biting the dust normally costs you one penalty, but I think you will agree that this was one juicy pawn that you were entrusted to look after.

33...♔f8 (b) scores one if you had the idea of ...♖c3. If not, then no points.

**33...a5 34 g3**

a) 34...♕g5
b) 34...♕h6
c) 34...♖a8
d) 34...♖f8

Five points for the star move 34...♖f8 (d), which Kasparov only noticed after the game. White now has no good way to deal with Black's threats, for example:

1) 35 f6 ♖c1! 36 ♖xc1 ♕xc1+ 37 ♘xc1 e1♕+ 38 ♔h2 ♕xc1.

2) 35 ♔f2 ♖c3 36 ♘e5 ♖f3+!! 37 ♔xf3 ♕xe1 (Kasparov).

34...♕h6 (b) makes use of a file, rank and diagonal, all in one go, and is worth three points. If you realised that the bishop on b6 is attacked, as well as the freshly weakened h3-pawn, add a bonus point too.

Take one point for both 34...♕g5 (a) and 34...♖a8 (c).

**34...♕h6 35 ♗f2**

a) 35...♕xh3
b) 35...♕c6
c) 35...♕f6
d) 35...♖cd8

Those of you who wanted to go with an earlier ...h7-h6 can feel smug right now for the natural 35...♕xh3 (one point) was not favoured due to the recurring trick 36 ♖xe2 ♖xe2 37 ♕xc8+, which culminates in a back rank mate.

Kasparov rightly decided that his powerful rooks and extra pawns would ensure his initiative carried into the ending, so 35...♕c6 (b) scores two points.

No points for 35...♕f6 (c) and 35...♖cd8, which both allow 36 ♖xe2.

**35...♕c6 36 ♕xc6**

a) 36...bxc6
b) 36...♖xc6

Kasparov's choice, 36...♖xc6 (b), scores two, while 36...bxc6 (a) gets one.

**36...♖xc6 37 ♖b1**

a) 37...b6
b) 37...♖d8
c) 37...♖c4
d) 37...♖c2

37...b6 (a) scores zero on its own, but you can have one for noticing 38 ♗xb6 ♖b8 and another for 38 ♖xb6 ♖xb6 39 ♗xb6 e1♕+.

37...♖d8 (b) would have been fine if that black h7-pawn had ever moved, but since 38 ♖xb7 ♖xd3 39 ♖b8+ again highlights your weak back rank, deduct one point.

If you counterattacked the white a-pawn with 37...♖c4 (c), Kasparov's style is rubbing off on you. Take two points for this.

37...♖c2 (d) sheds a pawn unnecessarily, so also shed one from your total.

**37...♖c4 38 ♖xb7**

a) 38...♖xa4
b) 38...♖c3
c) 38...♖d8
d) 38...h6

38...♖xa4 (a) is logical and scores one. 38...♖d8 (c) and 38...h6 (d) fail to score, while 38...♖c3 (b) drops one point.

**38...♖xa4 39 ♗e1**

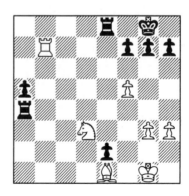

a) 39...♖a3
b) 39...♖d4
c) 39...h6
d) 39...g6

Three points for 39...♖a3 (a), which maintains pressure. A similar harassment on the white knight with 39...♖d4 (b) earns two.

I agree that 39...h6 (c) is becoming thematic, so two points if you thought it was about time too. I appreciate that you could also provide an escape square for the king with 39...g6 (one point), but 40 f6 could be a little awkward.

**39...♖a3 40 ♖d7**

| |
|---|
| a) 40...a4 |
| b) 40...♖e3 |
| c) 40...f6 |
| d) 40...♖a1 |

40...a4 (a) scores three points. Passed pawns must be pushed. Not many of my games have the luxury of two on the go, however.

40...♖e3 (b) constitutes another gross slip as the black king is caught on the back rank. You can't have many points if that has already happened to you, so take off five, but please don't feel obliged to fall below zero unless you have a strong conscience and prefer to take it on the chin. Whoever is looking over your shoulder will think that the lower the score the better and will be proud of you as you move into negative territory!

I don't fully trust 40...f6 (c) as it invites the white knight to invade with ♘f4 and ♘e6, but you can have one point because you would be free of the back rank curse.

Finally, 40...♖a1 (d) nets one point.

**40...a4 41 ♔f2**

This feels like the end of a chapter for at this point the game was adjourned. For the juniors reading this, it was not that long ago when games were stopped (no exciting quickplay finishes) and resumed some hours later or even the next day. The player whose turn it was would write his move down and seal it in an envelope, to be opened on resumption of the match.

Then, in the case of this world championship match, the various trainers and seconds would study the position for as long as possible and convey their findings to the 'rested' participants. This became more and more unsatisfactory as computers were introduced to the chess world, and now it has been phased out altogether in favour of longer playing sessions and time limits to suit.

Not that it effects anything, but your next choice was the sealed move.

| |
|---|
| a) 41...♖a2 |
| b) 41...♖a8 |
| c) 41...♖b3 |
| d) 41...h6 |

Both 41...♖a2 (a) and 41...h6 (d) are non-committal and safe for two points, while 41...♖a8 (b) relinquishes the e-pawn for no apparent reason and loses one. Kasparov actually went for better placement of his rook with 41...♖b3 (c), so award yourself three if you opted for this manoeuvre.

**41...♖b3 42 ♘c1**

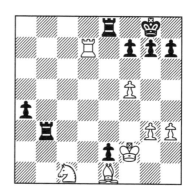

| |
|---|
| a) 42...♖bb8 |
| b) 42...♖b1 |
| c) 42...♖eb8 |
| d) 42...♖b5 |

The position is not without its complications despite the reduction in pieces. 42...♖bb8 (a) is entitled to one point. Take one extra if you planned to meet 43 ♘xe2 with 43...♖b2 and then to run your a-pawn as White is tied up defending his material. Three points for 42...♖b1 (b), which contains the same idea with the additional merits of attacking the knight on c1 and having been chosen by the great Kasparov.

Two points for 42...♖b5 (d), which also gives White something to think about (that is if Karpov's team did not get this far in their analysis).

42...♖eb8 (c) loses three as after 43 ♘xb3 axb3 White can stop the b-pawn reaching the b1-square with 44 ♗c3 f6 45 ♖d2.

**42...♖b1 43 ♘a2**

a) 43...♖a1
b) 43...♖b2
c) 43...♖a8
d) 43...♖b5

At the time, 43...♖a1 (a) was widely expected by the resident chess journalists so a well-deserved two points there.

Interestingly, Karpov had his first decent pause for a think after 43...♖a8 (two points), which suggests he might have been on his own for the first time since the game resumed. Take a bonus if you realised that 44 ♔xe2 fails due to 44...♖e8+.

43...♖b2 (b) does no harm and scores a point, but I am not sure if Black is making progress after 44 ♘c3 a3 45 ♖a7. Last, but not least, 43...♖b5 (d) also scores one. One of the most difficult tasks in chess is deciding between many tempting possibilities.

**43...♖a8 44 ♖e7**

a) 44...a3
b) 44...♖b5
c) 44...♖b2
d) 44...♔f8

44...a3 (a) and 44...♖b5 (b) increase your score by one, while you can have two for 44...♖b2 (c). It is only 44...♔f8 (d) that fails to score, for obvious reasons.

**44...♖b2 45 ♖xe2**

a) 45...a3
b) 45...♖xe2+
c) 45...♖ab8
d) 45...♖b5

Again, one point for the reasonable 45...a3 (a) and 45...♖ab8 (c), two for Kasparov's 45...♖xe2+ (b) and none for the now less effective 45...♖b5 (d).

**45...♖xe2+ 46 ♔xe2**

a) 46...♖a5
b) 46...a3
c) 46...♖e8+
d) 46...♔f8

If you want to attack the white f-pawn, you'll have to find another method next time. If you chose 46...♖a5 (a), deduct five points for overlooking the bishop on e1.

Three points for 46...♖e8+ (c), which cleverly makes the white king commit himself in one direction or the other. After 47 ♔d2 h5 it would be difficult for Karpov to defend his kingside pawns in the long term.

46...a3 (b) makes sense for one point, but activating the king with 46...♔f8 (b) is even more appealing for two.

**46...♖e8+ 47 ♔f2**

a) 47...♖e5
b) 47...a3
c) 47...h5
d) 47...g6

Two points for 47...h5 (c), with an extra available if you calculated that you are now threatening 48...♖e5 49 g4 hxg4 50 hxg4 ♖e4, which snares an enemy pawn.

47...♖e5 (a) and 47...a3 (b) are worthy moves for one point, but I cannot support 47...g6 (no points) since it permits White to exchange his vulnerable pawn on f5.

**47...h5 48 ♗c3**

a) 48...a3
b) 48...♖e4
c) 48...♖b8
d) 48...♔h7

All options notch up one point here with the exception of 48...♖b8 (c), which scores two.

**48...♖b8 49 ♗b4**

a) 49...♖d8
b) 49...♖c8
c) 49...♖e8
d) 49...♔h7

Two points for both 49...♖d8 (a) and 49...♖c8 (b); Black tries to penetrate with his rook. You score one for the respectable 49...♖e8 (c) and 49...♔h7 (d).

**49...♖d8 50 ♔e2**

a) 50...♖d5
b) 50...a3
c) 50...f6
d) 50...g6

It does not come naturally to disagree with Kasparov (or indeed most grandmasters) but I am going to award 50...f6 (c) two points and the actual text move 50...a3 (b) only one. He may be the ultra-aggressive and talented superstar but we all need to use our kings in the ending. In the game, although White cannot grab the a-pawn due to 51...♖a8, it could be vulnerable later.

Score one point for 50...♖d5 (a), but 50...g6 (d) again fails to score as liquidating pawns only makes life easier for White.

**50...a3 51 ♗c3**

a) 51...♖a8
b) 51...♖b8
c) 51...f6
d) 51...♔h7

51...♖a8 (a) seems a little pointless (no points) and we know that 51...♖b8 (b) is answered by 52 ♗b4, so nothing there either.

51...f6 (c) again scores two and a token one for 51...♔h7 (d). Award yourself two bonus points if you have been avoiding ...♔h7 because you looked further and decided that ...♔h6 would be met by ♗d2+, when the monarch's march into the action is severely set back.

**51...f6 52 ♗b4**

a) 52...♔h7
b) 52...♔f7
c) 52...♖d5
d) 52...♖a8

The pawns tell the pieces where to go and I think the previous ...f7-f6 invites the black king to step to f7, so no score for 52...♔h7 (a).

Three points to you for the logical 52...♔f7 (b) and two for the centralising 52...♖d5 (c). However, I cannot condone 52...♖a8 (no points), which defends the a-pawn unnecessarily at the moment.

**52...♔f7 53 ♘c3**

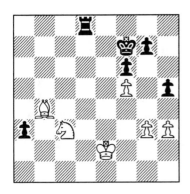

a) 53...♖a8
b) 53...a2
c) 53...♖b8
d) 53...♖e8+

It's still too tame, but this time 53...♖a8 (a) can have one point.

53...a2 (b) drops the all-important pawn and two points.

It is 53...♖b8 (c) that heads the rating list with two points. For those who thought that lost a pawn to 54 ♗xa3, note that Black has the retort 54...♖b3.

53...♖e8+ (d) is good enough for one point.

**53...♖b8 54 ♘a2**

a) 54...♖e8+
b) 54...♖d8
c) 54...♖b5
d) 54...g6

I am not sure you are making progress with 54...♖e8+ (a) or 54...♖d8 (b) but you can have one point as at least they are harmless.

54...♖b5 (c) scores two but still none for 54...g6 (d) for the same reasons as before.

**54...♖b5 55 g4**

a) 55...hxg4
b) 55...h4
c) 55...♖b8
d) 55...♖e5+

All moves strike me as reasonable here. The decision is whether to open the h-file with 55...hxg4 (one point) or retain the h-pawn with 55...h4 (one point) and hope to round up the blockading h3-pawn later.

Two points for 55...♖b8 (c) and one for 55...♖e5+ (d); both maintain flexibility and leave White guessing his opponent's next manoeuvre.

**55...♖b8 56 ♔d3**

a) 56...hxg4
b) 56...♖h8
c) 56...♖d8+
d) 56...♖c8

I can see you are trying to cut the king off from the queenside with the subtle 56...♖c8 (d) so have two points for your efforts. Top marks of three points, however, go to 56...♖d8+ (c) as Black is prepared to shed his a-pawn in order to infiltrate with the rook.

Take one point for both 56...hxg4 (a) and 56...♖h8 (b).

**56...♖d8+ 57 ♔c4**

a) 57...hxg4
b) 57...♖d1
c) 57...♖d2
d) 57...♖e8

If Kasparov had wanted the structure after 57...hxg4 (a), he would have done it by now so no points there.

Three points for 57...♖d1 (b), which sees the rook finally invading, while 57...♖d2 (c) is the first blunder I have introduced for a long time and costs you five.

57...♖e8 (d) scores one point but take a bonus if you rejected it due to 58 ♔d3, when again the black rook is kept at bay.

**57...♖d1 58 ♗xa3**

> a) 58...♖a1
> b) 58...♖h1
> c) 58...♖g1
> d) 58...hxg4

58...♖a1 (a) is a great concept that draws the white king far away from his precious kingside. If you had anticipated this scenario before, add five to your score. If it dawned on you only after having been given your list of four moves, you can still have four.

58...♖h1 (b) must be the second choice and scores two points. 58...♖g1 (c) is a further way of rounding up some pawns (one point), while 58...hxg4 (d) 59 hxg4 earns one as long as you were going to quickly follow up by hitting the weak g-pawn.

**58...♖a1 59 ♔b3**

> a) 59...hxg4
> b) 59...♖h1
> c) 59...♖g1
> d) 59...g6

I'm afraid I am going to be strict here. As the next job is to mop up the pawns as quickly as possible, taking one of them with check must be the key. Therefore you score two points for 59...♖h1 (b) but no points for the alternatives.

**59...♖h1 60 gxh5**

> a) 60...♖xh3+
> b) 60...g5
> c) 60...♔e8
> d) 60...♖h2

Again, only 60...♖xh3+ (a) is worth one point, while the others are inferior.

**60...♖xh3+ 61 ♘c3**

> a) 61...♖xh5
> b) 61...♖f3
> c) 61...g5
> d) 61...♔g8

I am sorry if your knee jerk reaction here was to go for 61...♖xh5 (a). You can certainly have one point for it, but it is 61...♖f3 (b) that keeps White tied down slightly longer and takes the honours with two points. A bonus is available for noticing 61...♖xh5 62 ♘e4 ♖xf5? 63 ♘d6+.

No score for 61...♔g8 (d) and minus two for 61...g5 (c). I suggest you brush up on the 'en passant' rules too.

**61...♖f3 62 ♗c1**

> a) 62...♔g8
> b) 62...♖h3
> c) 62...g5
> d) 62...♖xf5

62...♔g8 (a) and 62...♖h3 (b) can be discarded and score no points, but 62...g5 (c) is going to cost you three since there was previously a huge hint about 'en passant'.

62...♖xf5 (d) is the best move and is rewarded with one point.

**62...♖xf5 63 h6**

> a) 63...g6
> b) 63...g5
> c) 63...gxh6
> d) 63...♖f1

Black does best to try and maintain his connected pawns, so 63...g6 (a) scores three and 63...g5 (b) scores two. If you opted for 63...g5 over 63...g6 due to the variation 63...g5 64 ♘e4 ♚g6 65 h7 ♚xh7 66 ♘xf6 ♖xf6 67 ♗xg5 forcing a draw, you deserve an extra bonus of one. If, on the other hand, you did not know that a king and rook against a king and bishop is a draw, far from punishing you for this lack of information, I award you three extra for daring to take on the challenge of this exercise with so little chess experience. There is not room to complete a study of such endings in this book but, just so the information is a little more complete, I should add that it is important for the successful defender not to get his king caught near the corner that is of the same colour as the bishop.

I am in a generous mood, so both 63...gxh6 (c) and 63...♖f1 (d) score one.

**63...g6 64 ♘e4**

> a) 64...♚e6
> b) 64...♖h5
> c) 64...♖f3+
> d) 64...♖e5

The spectators were certainly treated to an eventful game this time. There are still tactics going on, for example 64...♖e5 (d) 65 ♘xf6! as 65...♚xf6 66 ♗b2 even wins for White. Take one off your total if you chose (d).

64...♖f3+ (c) only drives the white king where he wants to go, so no points there, but one for 64...♚e6 (a) and two for 64...♖h5 (a), which attempts to round up the remaining white pawn.

**64...♖h5 65 ♗b2 ½-½**

At this point Kasparov admitted his winning hopes were finally snuffed out. There is one last bonus on offer if you saw that 65...f5 is precisely met by 66 h7 ♖xh7 67 ♘g5+.

All is done except, if you are not too exhausted, you can examine how you did in the usual way.

Less than 20: Avoid those blunders and your scores will pick up.

20-39: You must have had successes at club level. Most of your moves are sound.

40-64: Kasparov is one of the most brilliant players to grace the chess circuit. This is a respectable attempt at emulating the flamboyant Russian grandmaster.

65-89: I would expect a county or regional player to achieve this high level. It was not an easy encounter to comprehend.

90-109: An excellent all-rounder. You coped well with both the tactics and positional elements.

110+: Either you have memorised this game from earlier or you are a potential candidate for the world chess championship.

# CHAPTER FIVE

## Endgames Made to look Easy

There are books to persuade us that anything can be made to look easy these days!

With club games sometimes adjudicated or tournament games with quickplay finishes, it is rarely possible to concentrate on a delicate and subtle ending of one's own. Indeed, I believe that the ending is an area of the game that, and I think most commentators would agree, is studied and written about less than any other area of the game. For the beginner, this means that time is most probably spent on trying to get a playable position from the opening. Sometimes rote learning methods are employed to teach children attacking openings that 'win', whereas there is no concentration on checkmating with king and queen, rook, two bishops, or bishop and knight versus king. Furthermore, a competent young player can play king and pawn endings at great speed and extremely poorly. Some of the most complex chess around can be discovered in such endings, so it is important not to underestimate the concentration level that is required as more pieces get exchanged.

There is a view that although more experienced players in England can perhaps play a game with better foundations than lower-graded players, they possess less knowledge and understanding of more complex endings (such as bishops of opposite colour or rook endings) when compared to some of their foreign counterparts who study endings and technique from an early age. I know that I can play through endings occurring between top players and know that I am not even vaguely understanding the depths of their moves. As if to disprove the rule, there are one or two players who thrive on reaching endings, which they feel are their strength. Their opponents lack their experience and succumb from equal positions.

Game 19 is perhaps an example of a stout defence. A lesser player than Bronstein could have easily underestimated the significance of some of White's tries. Blunders here are of the form of wasting a move, or swapping off the wrong pawn (for example, because you are giving your opponent a passed pawn).

Another school of thought could be that these endgame specialists are lazy and prefer not to have to analyse deep lines in the middlegame. As I have indicated, I have respect for experts in any area of the game and one cannot exactly suggest that endgame players are taking a short cut as their games could last hours longer than other players' games!

In this chapter we examine just some possibilities. When writing this chapter I thought about positions that had a reasonable number of pieces exchanged. Of course, at some stage there is a grey area. I would normally put positions with just queens exchanged in a 'queenless middle-games' box. However, such games invariably continue and enter a later middlegame or early ending phase. The exact moment when the ending has been reached is not important and so naturally comments and games in other chapters of this book would have also been at home here. Once again, the game of chess is found to be rich in possibilities so that it cannot be easily categorised into separate boxes. Instead, all the different compartments overlap. For example, see Georgiev-Smirin (Game 6), when Black employed some technique to win in the ending. Also, see Kramnik-Shirov (Game 16), when we saw a longer demonstration of ending technique, but the imbalance in material encouraged me to place the

game there.

I have selected the last two games in this chapter because the material found at the end of them is commonplace in games of chess. Indeed, there are a number of rook and pawn ending themes that run throughout the ending of Games 19 and 20. For the beginner, your decision making will be helped if, at the right time, you can apply the well-known maxim that 'rooks belong behind passed pawns'.

First, though, we witness Game 18, which demonstrates that endings can be full of tactics that require calculation and are not necessarily about delicate technique that some people misname by calling it 'boring'. Perhaps you are one of these people and, if that is the case and you really do think that you will enjoy this chapter less than the others, then at least give the games a try. As a matter of fact, you have experienced some endings in this book already and this chapter can only add to that and prove most valuable. You never know, you might be fascinated by some new ideas.

## Game 18
## Ki.Georgiev-Timoshenko
### France 2001

**1 d4 ♘f6 2 c4 g6 3 ♘c3 ♗g7 4 e4 d6 5 ♗d3 0-0 6 ♘ge2 ♘c6 7 0-0 a6 8 f3 ♘d7 9 ♗c2 ♖b8 10 ♗g5 ♘a5 11 b3 c5 12 dxc5 dxc5 13 f4 ♘c6 14 e5 f6 15 ♗h4 fxe5 16 f5 gxf5 17 ♕d5+ ♔h8 18 ♗xf5 ♘f6 19 ♕xc5 ♘d4 20 ♗xf6 ♖xf6 21 ♗e4 b5 22 ♘g3 ♘e6 23 ♕a7 ♕d4+ 24 ♕xd4 exd4 25 ♘d5**

After a typically tactical King's Indian Defence opening, the smoke has subsided and we have reached a position late into the middlegame with equal material. Black has a couple of central passed pawns and the bishop pair, but at the moment White has a strong grip on the centre. How would you proceed from Black's point of view? You are playing alongside a highly respected grandmaster who competes all around the world.

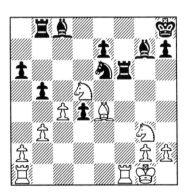

a) 25...♖h6
b) 25...♖f8
c) 25...♖xf1+
d) 25...bxc4

25...♖h6 (a) immediately drops you two below zero as 26 ♘f5 leaves Black floundering. 25...♖f8 (b) lets White pick off the e-pawn, so no score there. The third

e-pawn, so no score there. The third way to try and mess up Timoshenko's position is with the over-ambitious 25...bxc4 (d), which loses two points since 26 ♘xf6 cxb3 27 ♘d5 d3 28 ♖ab1 proves the idea to be unsound.

Those who went for the time saving 25...♖xf1+ (c), kick off your score with two points.

**25...♖xf1+ 26 ♖xf1**

a) 26...bxc4
b) 26...♘c5
c) 26...♗f8
d) 26...♖b7

Three points for 26...bxc4 (a), which enables Black to take advantage of the open b-file and weakens the white c-pawn.

26...♘c5 (b) is interesting and scores two points. There is no doubt that White can grab a pawn with 27 cxb5 (27 ♘xe7 is likely to transpose to the text) 27...♘xe4 28 ♘xe4 ♖xb5 29 ♘xe7 ♖e5 30 ♘xc8 ♖xe4, but take two bonuses if you realised that this would ensure Black plenty of compensation due to the d-pawn and the powerful bishop.

26...♗f8 (minus two) is too passive for comfort and take a bonus if you saw that 27 ♖f7 is an effective response. 26...♖b7 (d) sets you back one point for similar reasons.

**26...bxc4 27 bxc4**

a) 27...♖b7
b) 27...♗f8
c) 27...♘c5
d) 27...♘g5

Counterattacking rather than grovelling is the key to this position, so minus one for 27...♖b7 (a) and minus two for 27...♗f8 (b).

Timoshenko looked no further than

27...♘c5 (c). This scores three, while 27...♘g5 (d) is similar and scores one. The latter idea does not block White's c-pawn and does not aid the advance ...d4-d3.

**27...♘c5 28 ♘xe7**

> a) 28...♗e6
> b) 28...d3
> c) 28...♘xe4
> d) 28...♗g4

No one gets penalised here so it just a question of what your preference scored.

28...♗e6 (a) certainly comes into consideration and scores one point, but take a bonus if you rejected this due to the retort 29 ♗d5.

28...d3 (b) is tempting and scores two because Black's advanced pawn will definitely put the opposition under pressure after 29 ♘xc8 ♗d4+ 30 ♔h1 ♖xc8, despite the pawn deficit.

The bishop pair is often at its most devastating on an open board and against a pair of knights. This situation fits the bill so three points for 28...♘xe4 (c).

Finally, 28...♗g4 (d) can't be bad and scores one.

**28...♘xe4 29 ♘xe4**

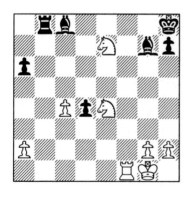

> a) 29...♗e6
> b) 29...♗g4
> c) 29...d3
> d) 29...♗e5

With 29...♗e6 (a), Black spots the perfect diagonal and scores two.

29...♗g4 (b) earns one. There is also a bonus point available if you analysed 30 c5 ♖e8, but White can take the sting out of this skewer with 31 ♖b1 ♖xe7 32 ♖b8+ ♗f8 33 ♖xf8+ ♔g7 34 ♖f4, which scores another bonus.

29...d3 (c) scores one and one extra if you saw the beautiful variation 30 ♖d1 ♗d4+ 31 ♔f1 ♗g4 32 ♖xd3 ♖b1+ leading to mate. If you were aware that this is in no way forced and actually opted for a different line you may take another bonus. 30 ♘xc8 ♗d4+ 31 ♔h1 ♖xc8 32 ♘d2 appears one way for White to set up an adequate defensive stance.

29...♗e5 (d) is one to avoid due to 30 ♖f8+ ♔g7 31 ♖xc8. This costs the advocates three points.

**29...♗e6 30 ♘d5**

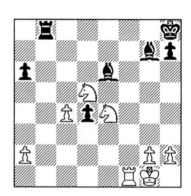

> a) 30...♗xd5
> b) 30...♖c8
> c) 30...♖b2
> d) 30...d3

30...♗xd5 (a) gives away most of Black's trumps in one fell swoop as well as giving White a menacing d-pawn. No score there.

30...♖c8 (b) gets two points as a thematic way to undermine the knight on d5, and it also highlights the vulnerability of the white c-pawn.

30...♖b2 (c) obeys the general rule that rooks belong on the seventh rank. For that I will award one point. However, on specific criteria, take a bonus if you assessed that 31 ♘c5 ♗xd5 32 cxd5 would give Black too many problems and too little counterplay with his own passed pawn.

Three points for 30...d3 (d), which opens up the diagonal for Black to spring a timely check on d4.

**30...d3 31 ♘g5**

> a) 31...♗g8
> b) 31...♔g8
> c) 31...♗d4+
> d) 31...♗xd5

Take one point for 31...♗g8 (a), with a bonus for those who judged that it was not the ticket to success as 32 ♘f3 would cover key squares from White's point of view.

Don't forget to watch out for the odd blunder such as 31...♔g8 (b); this scores minus three.

31...♗d4+ (c) sends the white monarch into the corner, which provides back rank mate possibilities and means that the king to be less able to stop the enemy d-pawn in some variations. An important intermezzo for three points.

Again, 31...♗xd5 (no points) is not necessary and lets White somewhat off the hook.

**31...♗d4+ 32 ♔h1**

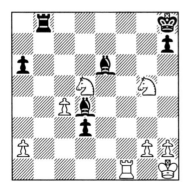

> a) 32...♗xd5
> b) 32...♗g4
> c) 32...♖e8
> d) 32...d2

It would be satisfying to simplify here with 32...♗xd5 (a) 33 cxd5 d2, followed by ...♖c8 and ...♖c1. However, no points for this due to the strength of the opposing d-pawn, for example 34 d6 ♖c8 35 d7 etc.

32...♗g4 (b) heads the list with two points, with a bonus for the taking if you worked out that Black is now threatening to run his d-pawn.

32...♖e8 (c) drops two. Did you miss 33 ♘c7?

32...d2 (d) 33 ♘xe6 ♖e8 34 ♘xd4 ♖e1 forms part of a pleasant dream but lacks reality. Deduct one from you total if you went for 32...d2 and one more if it was based on this flawed variation. Add one if you were able to refute the above line with, for example, 34 ♘dc7.

**32...♗g4 33 h3**

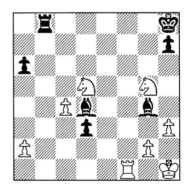

> a) 33...♗e2
> b) 33...♗h5
> c) 33...h6
> d) 33...d2

33...♗e2 (a) nets you two points, as does the steady 33...♗h5 (b).

33...h6 (c) costs two since White has 34 ♘f7+ before picking off the black bishop.

The ultra ambitious (or careless!) 33...d2 (d) 34 hxg4 ♖e8 35 ♘f3 turns the tables in White's favour, so diminish your score by three if you chose this.

**33...♗e2 34 ♖f7**

> a) 34...♗g7
> b) 34...d2
> c) 34...♖b1+
> d) 34...h6

I can fully understand if you went for the piece retreat 34...♗g7 (a), which scores one point.

34...d2 (b) drops two, but only for the inconvenience of having walked into a perpetual check (or mate if you try and run), i.e. 35 ♖xh7+ ♔g8 36 ♘e7+ ♔f8 37 ♘g6+ ♔e8? (37...♔g8 secures a draw) 38 ♖e7+ ♔d8 39 ♘e6+ ♔c8 40 ♖c7 mate. If you foresaw all this, you deserve two extra points. If, for this reason, you went for 34...♖b1+ (to vacate the b8-square for your king to secure his escape), then take three points. If you stumbled on 34...♖b1 for your own reasons, take two.

34...h6 (d) is a worse version of 34...d2, so deduct three. White should not even take the perpetual in this case. In effect, he has an extra move that he can utilise to threaten mate with 35 ♖xh7+ ♔g8 36 ♘e7+ ♔f8 37 ♘e6 ♔e8 38 ♘f5.

**34...♖b1+ 35 ♔h2**

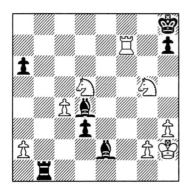

> a) 35...♗g1+
> b) 35...♗e5+
> c) 35...d2
> d) 35...♗g7

35...♗g1+ (a) fails to score as it takes the bishop off the important a1-h8 diagonal, which enables White to meet 36 ♔g3 d2 with 37 ♖xh7+ ♔g8 38 ♘f6+ ♔f8 39 ♖f7 mate.

35...♗e5+ (b) helps Black cover many key squares and is the key to your score increasing by three.

35...d2 (c) is too early as 36 ♖f8+ ♔g7 37 ♘e6+ ♔h6 38 ♘xd4 d1♕ 40 ♖f6+ allows White perpetual checks and mating nets all over.

No points for 36...♗g7 (d), which is now more risky as 37 ♖d7 gives White the opportunity to harass Black on the back rank.

**35...♗e5+ 36 g3**

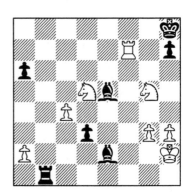

> a) 36...♖h1+
> b) 36...♗f3
> c) 36...d2
> d) 35...♗g7

36...♖h1+ (nil points) 37 ♔xh1 d2 38 ♘e3 holds up the d-pawn for the time being.

36...♗f3 (b) may threaten mate for one millisecond, but still drops two as I'm not sure if you have anything planned after 37 ♘xf3.

Timoshenko judged that it was finally time to put his cards on the table with 36...d2 (c), which scores four points. I trust that you have checked out all of White's checks...

36...♗g7 (d) gets the same comments and score as in the previous notes, i.e. zilch.
**36...d2 37 ♖xh7+ ♔g8 38 ♘e7+ ♔f8 39 ♘g6+**

No choice for the last two moves, but if you envisaged this position in your head then score a bonus. Score nothing for having reached it by playing the moves on the board for if you are to gain maximum benefit from these exercises, it is necessary for your brain to do all the calculating as a lot of chess takes place in the mind. I appreciate this is nigh on impossible but I don't want to get you into bad habits!

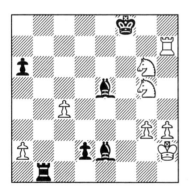

> a) 39...♔e8 and you would offer a draw.
>
> b) 39...♔e8 and if you were offered a draw, then you would decline.
>
> c) 39...♔g8 and you would offer a draw.
>
> d) 39...♔g8 and if you were offered a draw, then you would decline.

39...♔e8 (b) scores three points. You can have one point if you played 39...♔e8 accompanied with a draw offer. You can have one point for choice (c) too. However, choice (d) scores more generously in that if

you are doing this exercise with a clock and you wanted to get a few more moves in before the imaginary time control at move 40, then you score three points. Instead, if you were just guessing, then you score just the one.
**39...♔e8 40 ♖e7+ ♔d8 41 ♘e6+ ♔c8 42 ♘xe5**

First of all, as the forced sequence has pushed us forward, award yourself three bonus points if you realised before move 40 that White had this at his disposal and is now threatening mate with 43 ♖c7+ ♔b8 44 ♘c6+ ♔a8 45 ♖a7 mate.

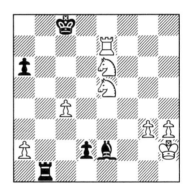

> a) 42...♖h1+
> b) 42...d1♕
> c) 42...♗f3
> d) 42...♖b7

42...♖h1+ (a) is a wonderful concept for two points, but White does not have to capture on h1. There follows 43 ♔g2 ♗f3+ 44 ♔f2 d1♕ 45 ♖c7+ ♔b8 46 ♘d7+ ♔a8 47 ♘b6+ ♔b8 48 ♘d7+ etc. with a draw. Take one bonus if you saw Black's 43rd and two more if you calculated this through to the end.

Lose four points for 42...d1♕ (b), especially as we have already discussed that White intended 43 ♖c7+ ♔b8 44 ♘c6+ ♔a8 45 ♖a7 mate. That leaves 42...♗f3 (c) as Black's best for three points. Furthermore, if you analysed (a) or (c) correctly when choosing Black's 39th, then add three to your score (six if you calculated both variations).

The embarrassing 42...♗b7 (d) 43 ♖e8 mate sets you back three points.

**42...♗f3 43 ♖e8 + ♔b7 44 ♘c5 +**

Nearly home and dry but a little bit more accuracy is required before White will let up.

> a) 44...♔a7
> b) 44...♔c7
> c) 44...♔b6

44...♔a7 (a) and 44...♔c7 (b) both cause the white attack to eventually run out of steam, so two points.

44...♔b6 (c), on the other hand, drops three as your advantage disintegrates on 45 ♖b8+ ♔xc5 46 ♖xb1 d1♕ 47 ♖xd1.

**44...♔a7 45 ♖e7 +**

> a) 45...♔a8
> b) 45...♔b8
> c) 45...♔b6
> d) 45...♖b7

45...♔a8 (a) and 45...♔b8 (b) are sufficient for one point, but 45...♔b6 (c) cuts down on any white counterplay and scores two.

Reduce your total by four if you thought 45...♖b7 (b) was the answer, as 46 ♘xb7 d1♕ 47 ♘xf3 ♕xf3 suddenly permits White rather a lot of material for the queen.

**45...♔b6 46 ♘cd7 +**

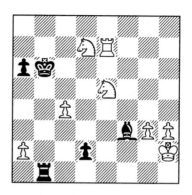

> a) 46...♔a7
> b) 46...♔b7
> c) 46...♔a5
> d) 46...♔c7

46...♔a7 (a) 47 ♘c5+ repeats the position once, but is only costly if you plan to do so once more and relinquish a draw. Score minus four if you intended to take the draw. 46...♔b7 (b) 47 ♘c5+ gives you a second bite at the cherry but it does not engender my confidence, so no points too.

Two points for 46...♔a5 (c), after which the end of the checks is in sight. Score a bonus if you pursued 47 ♘xf3 d1♕ 48 ♖e5+ ♔b4 to the bitter end. You score another for noticing mate is imminent with 49 ♖e1 ♖b2+.

Finally, minus one for 46...♔c7 (d) 47 ♘c5+, leaving the black king in trouble.

**46...♔a5 0-1**

Now you can see which comment applies to you below.

Less than 16: Stick to safe, natural moves and your scores should improve.

16-25: Encouraging signs but your score must be handicapped by the odd mistake.

26-35: Only a decent amateur player could score in this range so I commiserate if you are about to go pro.

36-44: Well done. A near perfect interpretation of Timoshenko's play.

45+: Excellent scoring. You covered everything and understood all aspects of the position.

## Game 19
## Smagin-Bronstein
Moscow 1982

You can play through the moves if you like, or else just start from the diagram.

1 e4 e5 2 ♘f3 ♘c6 3 ♗c4 ♘f6 4 d3 h6 5 c3 d6 6 0-0 ♗e7 7 ♘bd2 0-0 8 ♗b3 ♘h7 9 ♘c4 ♗f6 10 ♘e3 ♘e7 11 h3 ♔h8 12 d4 ♕e8 13 ♗a4 b5 14 ♗c2 ♗b7 15 ♖e1 ♘g6 16 ♘g4 ♕e7 17 a4 a6 18 ♗d3 c6 19 ♘e3 ♕c7 20 ♘f5 ♖ad8 21 ♕c2 ♖fe8 22 ♗e3 ♘hf8 23 axb5 axb5 24 ♖a7 ♘e6 25 g3 ♘e7 26 ♘xd6 ♕xd6 27 dxe5 ♗xe5 28 ♘xe5 ♕xe5 29 ♖xb7 ♘c5 30 ♗xc5 ♕xc5 31 ♗f1 ♔g8 32 e5 ♕d5 33 e6 fxe6 34 c4 ♕f5 35 ♕xf5 ♘xf5 36 cxb5 ♘d6 37 ♖b6 ♘xb5 38 ♗xb5 cxb5 39 ♖bxe6 ♖xe6 40 ♖xe6 ♖d2 41 b3 ♖b2 42 ♖e3 ♔f7 43 ♔g2 g5 44 g4 ♔g6 45 ♖d3 b4 46 ♔g3 ♖c2 47 f4 ♖c3 48 ♖f3 ♖c1 49 fxg5 hxg5 50 ♔f2 ♖b1 51 ♖e3 ♔f6 52 ♔f3 ♖d1 53 ♔e4 ♔e6 54 ♖d3 ♖e1+ 55 ♔d4 ♖c1 56 ♖f3 ♖c2 57 ♖e3+

Now choose your defence carefully.

a) 57...♔f6
b) 57...♔f7
c) 57...♔d7
d) 57...♔d6

Award yourself two points for 57...♔f6 (a), but none for 57...♔f7 (b), which gives away ground. Likewise, the retreat 57...♔d7 (c) scores zero, but you can have one for 57...♔d6 (d) as long as you did not plan to meet the reply 58 ♔e4 with 58...♔e6, when the discovered check 59 ♔d3+ nets the rook.

**57...♔f6 58 ♔d5**

a) 58...♔g6
b) 58...♖c3
c) 58...♖b2
d) 58...♖d2+

It is vital to realise that Black's main hope lies in harassing White's third rank here. So no points for 58...♔g6 (a), when 59 ♖e4 ♖c3 appears on the critical square one move too late and allows White to remain a pawn ahead with excellent winning chances after 60 ♖xb4 ♖xh3.

58...♖c3 (b) is the only move to score in positive territory, so take two if you opted for this.

58...♖b2 (c) loses one point as the white king can start rounding up the b-pawn with the reply 59 ♔c4. Also, take off one point for 58...♖d2+ (d), which is careless and allows White unnecessary access to the c4-square.

**58...♖c3 59 ♔e4**

a) 59...♖xe3+
b) 59...♖xb3
c) 59...♖c8
d) 59...♔e6

Exchanging rooks with 59...♖xe3+ (a) 60 ♔xe3 ♔e5 61 ♔f3 ♔d4 62 h4 gxh4 63 g5 loses both the ending and one point for not analysing the outcome, plus a further two for bad judgement. Rook and pawn endings with a pawn difference can often be drawn, but king and pawn endings, as a general rule, nearly always lead to victory for the side with the extra material.

59...♖c8 (c) asks White how he can make progress and scores two, while 59...♔e6 (d) can be rejected on pure calculation after 59...♔e6 60 ♖xc3 bxc3 61 ♔d3. If you failed to reach this conclusion, drop two points.

Whoops! If you chose 59...♗xb3 (b), take off four.

**59...♖c8 60 ♖d3**

> a) 60...♖c3
> b) 60...♔e6
> c) 60...♖e8+
> d) 60...♖h8

60...♖c3 (a) reaches the same outcome as 59...♔e6 and loses double the amount (four points this time), not just because I am peeved that you are not reading my hard grafted notes, I promise.

White is threatening 61 ♖d6+ ♔e7 62 ♖b6, so therefore 60...♔e6 (b) makes a lot of sense and makes you two points to add to your score.

60...♖e8+ (c) 61 ♔d5 ♖c8 62 ♖d4 ♖c3 63 ♖xb4 ♖xh3 is difficult for Black but not totally without hope. Score one point for this and the same for 60...♖h8 (d), which tries to tie the white rook down to the third rank. 60...♖h8 61 ♔d5 would be likely to transpose to (c) anyway.

**60...♔e6 61 ♖d4**

> a) 61...♖h8
> b) 61...♖f8
> c) 61...♖c1
> d) 61...♖b8

61...♖h8 (a) fails to score now because the white king is so well poised to snaffle the g-pawn after 61...♖h8 62 ♖xb4 ♖xh3 63 ♖b6+ ♔f7 64 ♔f5. Black must still rely on clever tricks to hold his position together

and so it is with 61...♖f8 (b) that you score top marks of two. Take two bonus points if you had spotted the trick 62 ♖xb4?? ♖f4+ 63 ♔d3 ♖xb4, when Black has turned the tables.

61...♖c1 (c) does Black's position no favours, so lose one point.

61...♖b8 (d) is rather passive, but score one for being resilient.

**61...♖f8 62 ♔e3**

> a) 62...♖h8
> b) 62...♖b8
> c) 62...♔e5
> d) 62...♖c8

At least the h-pawn will drop with check this time so take one for 62...♖h8 (a), but none for 62...♖c8 (c), which transposes to the unpleasant 63 ♖xb4 ♖c3+ 64 ♔e4 ♖xh3 65 ♖b6+ etc.

Having driven the white king back a square, now is the time to defend the weak pawn on b4 so take two points for 62...♖b8 (b).

62...♔e5 (c) puts up no resistance so lose one.

**62...♖b8 63 ♖c4**

> a) 63...♖b7
> b) 63...♔d5
> c) 63...♔e5
> d) 63...♔e7

White is now planning to invade with 64

♔d4 or 64 ♔e4 and as 63...♖b7 (a) does nothing to prevent this, it scores zilch.

63...♔d5 (b) scores two, while 63...♔e5 (c) scores one as White can kick the black king back with 64 ♖c5+.

63...♔e7 (d) looks wrong, feels wrong and is wrong. Be thankful it is just the king moving backwards here and not your score!

**63...♔d5 64 ♔f3**

> a) 64...♖b5
> b) 64...♖b6
> c) 64...♔e5
> d) 64...♖f8+

There is a real waiting game going on here as both sides vie for position. White has now changed direction and has headed for the kingside.

64...♖b5 (a) scores one point, but you must agree that it is no fun for Black after 64...♖b5 65 ♔g3 ♔e5 66 h4 gxh4+ 67 ♔xh4. The move 64...♖b6 (b) is similar and is awarded one.

64...♔e5 (c) takes on White at his own game and heads for the action. Have three points if you chose this line of defence: 64...♔e5 65 ♔g3 ♖d8 66 ♖xb4 ♖d3+ 67 ♔g2 ♖d2+ 68 ♔f3 ♖d3+ 69 ♔e2 ♖xh3. Only take two if you went for 64...♔e5 out of gut instinct but didn't realise 65...♖d8 was so effective.

64...♖f8+ (d) leads to a worse version of (c) after 64...♖f8+ 65 ♔g3 ♖e8 66 ♖xb4 ♖e3+ 67 ♔g2 ♖e2+ 68 ♔f3 and deserves nothing.

**64...♔e5 65 ♖c5+**

> a) 65...♔d6
> b) 65...♔e6
> c) 65...♔f6
> d) 65...♔d4

One point for 65...♔d6 (a) 66 ♖xg5 ♖c8 67 h4 ♖c3+ 68 ♔f4 ♖xb3, but neither 65...♔e6 (b) nor 65...♔f6 (c) score due to White's strong response 66 ♔e4 in both cases.

Congratulations if you realised that now was the time to activate your king with 65...♔d4 (b); take two points.

**65...♔d4 66 ♖xg5**

> a) 66...♖h8
> b) 66...♖f8+
> c) 66...♔c3
> d) 66...♔d3

Three options are just too slow here, namely 66...♖h8 (a) 67 ♖h5, 66...♖f8+ (b) 67 ♖f5 and 66...♔d3 (d) 67 ♖c5. There's no improvement to your position and therefore no improvement to your score. 66...♔c3 (c), on the other hand, is valued at three and the race is on...

**66...♔c3 67 h4**

> a) 67...♔xb3
> b) 67...♖e8
> c) 67...♖f8+
> d) 67...♖h8

67...♔xb3 (a) is the move for two points as it is a sure bet that it will be useful. Why consider anything else here? This is the stage where the essence is speed and it is quite interesting that when reaching such positions, some players visibly speed up the time taken on their moves as if it were a real race. I'm sure these top players know that only long thinks would reveal their best chances, however.

67...♖e8 (b) and 67...♖f8+ (c) 68 ♖f5 fail

to score, but I'll let you have one for 67...♖h8 (d).

**67...♔xb3 68 ♖c5**

| |
|---|
| a) 68...♖h8 |
| b) 68...♔a4 |
| c) 68...♔a3 |
| d) 68...♔a2 |

Again 68...♖h8 (a) can have one point, but getting on with pushing the b-pawn home will give White most to think about. It is possible that White would like to come behind the b-pawn with his rook at some stage, so leaving the black rook on b8 is logical.

It is perhaps hard to distinguish between any of the following three squares for the black king, but in order to avoid being checked back in front of the b-pawn, top marks of three go to 68...♔a4 (b). If you went for 68...♔a3 (c) or 68...♔a2 (d), increase your total by one.

**68...♔a4 69 h5**

| |
|---|
| a) 69...♖b5 |
| b) 69...♔b3 |
| c) 69...b3 |
| d) 69...♔a3 |

One move should have hit you as a necessity here. Hopefully it was not 69...♖b5 (a), which ends disastrously with 70 ♖xb5 ♔xb5 71 h6 b3 72 h7 b2 73 h8♕ b1♕ 74 ♕b8+. Drop three if you opted for 69...♖b5 and take a bonus point if you rejected it for the reason given.

If you chose 69...♔b3 (b), no, you cannot claim threefold repetition if you are the only player to repeat his moves. Dock three from your score and book up in claiming a draw using the threefold repetition rule.

If you chose 69...b3 (c), I'm glad you have the 'BO' situation under control. Take two points for playing the 'Blatantly Obvious'.

69...♔a3 (d) wasn't particularly good last move so it certainly doesn't score now as

time is valuable. I am sorry; you do not score here.

**69...b3 70 ♖c1**

| |
|---|
| a) 70...b2 |
| b) 70...♖h8 |
| c) 70...♖g8 |
| d) 70...♔a3 |

70...b2 (a) is extremely sensible and nets two points. However, the two connected passed pawns will win for White. For example, 70...b2 71 ♖b1 ♔b3 72 h6 ♔c2 73 ♖xb2+ ♖xb2 74 h7 ♖b8 75 g5.

All credit to you if you rejected and noted something like the line in the preceding paragraph. The star move is contained in 70...♖h8 (b), which scores four and holds up the advance of White's pawns.

70...♖g8 (c) does not have the same effect after 71 h6 so no score there.

70...♔a3 (d) is likely to prove useful and earns one point.

**70...♖h8 71 ♔g3**

| |
|---|
| a) 71...b2 |
| b) 71...♔a3 |
| c) 71...♖d8 |
| d) 71...♔b4 |

Three points for 71...b2 (a), which is again natural as Black would like to quickly win his opponent's rook and then head back to stop the enemy pawns with the aid of his king.

71...♔a3 (b) can have one point but no score for the wayward 71...♖d8 (c) or 71...♔b4 (d).

**71...b2 72 ♖b1**

> a) 72...♔a3
> b) 72...♔b3
> c) 72...♖b8
> d) 72...♖c8

It is not easy to distinguish between 72...♔a3 (a) and 72...♔b3 (b) so they each score two. If you went for the same as the grandmaster in the game, take an extra point for (b).

No points for 72...♖b8 (c), which is not the idea. Black must defend the pawn with his king and use the rook more effectively.

72...♖c8 (d), on the other hand, doesn't defend the pawn at all and drops one.

**72...♔b3 73 ♔h4**

> a) 73...♔a2
> b) 73...♔c2
> c) 73...♖a8
> d) 73...♖c8

73...♔a2 (a) is along the right lines and you can score one for the thought. The problem is that after 74 ♖xb2+ ♔xb2 75 g5 ♔c3 76 g6 ♔d4 77 g7 ♖g8 78 h6 ♔e5 79 ♔g5 ♔e6 80 ♔g6

Black is just too slow to stop the 'Space Invaders' landing. 73...♔c2 (b) can transpose to the variation already discussed and

also scores one. Award yourself an extra point if you considered the possibility of White trying to gain extra time with 74 ♖h1 b1♕ 75 ♖xb1 ♔xb1 but realised this was futile on further inspection as Black has 74...♖d8 75 h6 ♖d1 76 ♖h2+ ♖d2 77 ♖h1 ♖d1.

73...♖a8 (c) was how Bronstein saw fit to maximise his chances and this scores four. I could not conceive any difference between that and 73...♖c8 (d) at first, but then it dawned on me that if I were to bring the king to c3 later and then suddenly want my rook to return to c8, they might just be in each others way. So, to give recognition to the most flexible choice, take three for 73...♖c8.

**73...♖a8 74 g5**

> a) 74...♔a2
> b) 74...♔c2
> c) 74...♖a1
> d) 74...♖a4+

74...♔a2 (a) and 74...♔c2 (b) both score one again, but the most effective method for rounding up the rook is 74...♖a1 (c), which scores four points.

I can see that it is tempting to drive back the white king with 74...♖a4+ (d) 75 ♔g3 and then play 75...♖a1 76 ♖xb2+ ♔xb2 so you can have one point for this. However, the white king can later play to f4 and cold shoulder the black king so that it cannot get back easily to stop promotion.

**74...♖a1 75 ♖xb2 +**

> a) 75...♔xb2
> b) 75...♔c4
> c) 75...♔c3
> d) 75...♔a3

75...♔xb2 (a) scores three but zilch for the others. You can't afford to go to sleep now.

**75...♔xb2 76 ♔g4**

76 g6 ♖g1 holds the pawns up and if 77 h6 ♖g1 stifles their progress sufficiently to

enable the black king to come back and defend for a draw, so now we can appreciate the effects of Black bringing his rook round to a1. Score an extra point if you were at first surprised by the apparent lack of urgency of White's 76th move, but then worked out the consequences of pushing either pawn prematurely.

a) 76...♖f1
b) 76...♖g1+
c) 76...♖h1
d) 76...♚c3

76...♖f1 (a) is a bit too subtle at this stage to score. Cutting the white king off does nothing to hold up the connected pawns and leaves the black king watching from a great distance. 76...♖g1+ (b) does not help your score either as you are obliging the monarch to go where he wants to go, i.e. 77 ♚f5 ♖f1+ 78 ♚e5 ♖g1 79 ♚f6 ♖f1+ 80 ♚g7 ♚c3 81 h6 ♚d4 82 h7 ♖h1 83 h8♛ ♖xh8 84 ♚xh8.

76...♖h1 (c) slows White up and scores three points. The continuation 77 h6 ♚c3 78 ♚f5 ♚d4 79 g6 ♖h5+ 80 ♚g4 ♖xh6 secures the draw. 76...♚c3 (d) is likely to lead to a similar defence and scores three.

**76...♚c3 77 g6**

a) 77...♖h1
b) 77...♖g1+
c) 77...♖a4+
d) 77...♚d4

77...♖h1 (a) cuts out many of the opponent's responses and therefore makes it easier to calculate the ensuing lines to the death. Add three to your total if you were tempted by the same variation as our grandmaster.

I am nervous about irrelevant checks that end up suiting White so no points for 77...♖g1+ (b) on account of 78 ♚f5 ♖f1+ 79 ♚e6 ♖e1+ 80 ♚f6 ♖f1+ 81 ♚g7 ♚d4 82 h6 ♚e5 83 h7 ♖h1 84 h8♛. Likewise 77...♖a4+ (c) 78 ♚g5 surely helps White

and therefore no score for this.

77...♚d4 (d) certainly makes a lot of sense and scores one, but I am not at all sure that you will be in time to control the pawns. Don't forget that two connected pawns on the sixth rank cannot be stopped by a rook.

**77...♖h1 78 ♚g5**

a) 78...♖g1+
b) 78...♖xh5+
c) 78...♖a1
d) 78...♚d4

78...♖g1+ (a) and 78...♖a1 (c) don't help and fail to score. Things are not so desperate that you have to test your opponent on mating with king and queen versus king, so minus four for 78...♖xh5+ (b).

That leaves 78...♚d4 (d) for two points as the only move to scupper White's winning dreams.

**78...♚d4 79 g7**

a) 79...♚e5
b) 79...♖g1+
c) 79...♖a1
d) 79...♖b1

79...♚e5 (a) scores three as top class resistance. A bonus is available if you had 80 g8♛ ♖g1+ planned.

If you chose 79...♖g1+ (b) with a sincere attempt at defence in mind, have one point. If you just fancied throwing in a check, you fail to score. Again, the white king will run forward to find a haven with 80 ♔f6 ♖f1+ 81 ♔g6 ♖g1+ 82 ♔h7.

Neither 79...♖a1 (c) 80 h6 nor 79...♖b1 (d) look up to much so nil points there.

**79...♔e5 80 ♔g6**

> a) 80...♔e6
> b) 80...♖g1+
> c) 80...♖h2
> d) 80...♔d6

80...♔e6 (a) drops five due to 81 g8♕+.

80...♖g1+ (b) scores two points and follows the consistent plan.

80...♖h2 (c) loses one since the forcing line 81 g8♕ ♖g2+ 82 ♔f7 ♖xg8 83 ♔xg8 ♔f6 84 h6 allows your opponent to show off his skills at mating with an extra queen.

80...♔d6 (d) not only leads to the same conclusion as the previous line but looks bizarre into the bargain so take off two.

**80...♖g1+ 81 ♔f7**

There is a bonus point on offer if you intended to meet 81 ♔h7 with 81...♔f6 and noted that 82 g8♕ ♖xg8 83 ♔xg8 ♔g5 secures a draw.

> a) 81...♔f5
> b) 81...♖g5
> c) 81...♖f1+
> d) 81...♖a1

81...♔f5 (a) is all well and good if White proceeds with queening the pawn as you have the same defence as in the previous comment. However, it is 82 h6 that should cause concern so no score.

81...♖g5 (b) requires you to lessen your total by three since 82 g8♕ wraps things up for White. The white king is too close to the action and Black loses the rook in the ensuing queen versus rook ending.

81...♖f1+ (c) scores three and take a bonus of three if you have worked all the variations out to a draw. You had better wait until the end before you do the maths in case you only thought you knew all the

answers. Believe me, there is still life left in the position and plenty of opportunities for Black to go wrong.

81...♖a1 (d) is still pointless but this time costs you three.

**81...♖f1+ 82 ♔e7**

> a) 82...♖g1
> b) 82...♖a1
> c) 82...♖h1
> d) 82...♖f6

The accurate 82...♖g1 (a) tops up your score by four, whereas 82...♖a1 (b) and 82...♖f6 (d) are unimpressive and decrease your total by two each.

82...♖h1 (c) can have a generous one as you may have heard that computers can put up a rather stubborn defence of rook against a queen. If your microchips had been looking forward to trying it out, well done for spotting the opportunity.

**82...♖g1 83 h6**

> a) 83...♖xg7+
> b) 83...♔f5
> c) 83...♖g6
> d) 83...♖a1

83...♖xg7+ (a) tends to suggest that you have forgotten which way the pawns are travelling so lose two.

83...♔f5 (b) is interesting but, due to 84 ♔f7 ♖a1 85 g8♕ ♖a7+ 86 ♔f8 ♔f6 87 ♕g2, winning for White, it does not score.

The black rook is doing a Houdini effort at stopping the enemy pawns and 83...♖g6 (c) is no exception for three points.

Take off one for 83...♖a1 (d). I know this move has featured a lot and I hope you didn't have your heart set on it coming into the equation.

**83...♖g6 84 ♔f7**

> a) 84...♖xh6
> b) 84...♖xg7+
> c) 84...♖f6+
> d) 84...♔f5

There are many ways to still spoil this ending but let's concentrate on the saving 84...♖f6+ (c) for four points. You can have one for 84...♖xh6 (a) as Black has the move after White 'queens', but really it is a lost game for Black. Other options fail to score.

**84...♖f6+ 85 ♔e8**

If you were aware of 85 ♔g8 and had the response 85...♖xh6 86 ♔f7 ♖h7 or 86 ♔f8 ♖g6 lined up and intended to sacrifice your rook for the pawn, take two bonus points.

> a) 85...♖xh6
> b) 85...♖g6
> c) 85...♖e6+
> d) 85...♖a6

Three moves objectively lose whether you are a computer or not. Therefore, an award of three points goes to 85...♖e6+ (c). Generously, 85...♖xh6 (a) gets one point.

Nothing for anything else and think yourself lucky there are no negatives to carry on to your score.

**85...♖e6+ 86 ♔d8**

> a) 86...♖d6+
> b) 86...♖xh6
> c) 86...♖g6
> d) 86...♖a6

Again, the top-scoring move is a check; 86...♖d6+ (a) scores four. A bonus point is available if, before reading the answer below, you can work out what happens if the white king goes to c7 next move.

So that White does not end up with two queens or queen and king versus king, I shall again show that I am a soft marker and award one point for 86...♖xh6 (b). Naturally, the alternatives do not score.

**86...♖d6+ 87 ♔c8**

If you had 87 ♔c7 covered with 87...♖g6 you can have the promised bonus.

> a) 87...♖c6+
> b) 87...♖a6
> c) 87...♖g6
> d) 87...♖xh6

You must have got the hang of this perpetual check by now so two points for 87...♖c6+ (a). I will not penalise 87...♖xh6 (d) but the other two choices each force you to deduct one from your total.

**87...♖c6+ ½-½**

White cannot hide from the checks unless he goes in front of the pawns, which prevents him from pushing them, or he goes so far away from them that ...♖g6 is adequate for Black. It is interesting to note that if the white king were on, for example, the bizarre a1-square, then the position would actually be winning for White!

Now add up your score.

0-10: Rolling a dice might serve you just as well next time.

10-20: Subtlety is not your strong point.

20-30: You coped with this ending reasonably well for an amateur.

40-50: Your powers of judgement are well equipped for endings.

60-70: Well played. This was a difficult ending and you hardly put a foot wrong.

70+: Were you totally honest? You have scored like a world champion.

---

*Game 20*
## Smyslov-Bronstein
Budapest 1950

---

**1 d4 d5 2 c4 c6 3 ♘f3 ♘f6 4 ♘c3 e6 5 ♗g5 dxc4 6 e4 b5 7 e5 h6 8 ♗h4 g5 9 ♘xg5 hxg5 10 ♗xg5 ♘bd7**

This line is great fun (in particular for the spectators) and one of the sharpest to emerge from the deceptively quiet Slav Defence. I heard a tale once that a talented club player, who had never studied a chess book, made up this line as White as he went along in a critical club match and could not understand why his opponent was responding in seconds to each of his carefully calculated moves. Needless to say, Black knew his theory, duplicated a sharp variation and won with ease.

**11 g3 ♗b7 12 ♗g2 ♖g8 13 ♗xf6 ♘xf6 14 exf6 ♕xf6 15 a4 b4 16 ♘e4 ♕f5 17 ♕e2 0-0-0 18 ♕xc4 ♗g7 19 ♕xb4 ♗xd4 20 0-0 ♕e5 21 ♔h1 a5 22 ♕c4 ♖h8 23 ♖fe1 ♕h5 24 h4 ♕g4 25 ♕e2 ♕xe2**

This is perhaps the first indication of why I put this game in this chapter.

**26 ♖xe2 ♔c7 27 ♖c1 ♖d5 28 ♘c3 ♖c5 29 ♖ec2 ♔b6 30 ♘e4 ♖xc2 31 ♖xc2 ♖d8**

The board has cleared somewhat and

taking stock, we can see that White has an extra pawn while Black can claim to have compensation in the form of his bishop pair. The reader is now invited to take over and play as White.

> **a) 32 ♘g5**
> **b) 32 ♖d2**
> **c) 32 ♘d2**
> **d) 32 ♖c4**

If you are already aware that your h-pawn's queening square is covered by the bishop on d4, kick start your score by one.

32 ♘g5 (a) is worth two, and one for the similar 32 ♖d2 (b) c5 33 ♘g5 ♖d7.

32 ♘d2 (c) cleverly heads the knight to c4 so take three for this. No score, however, if you didn't realise that this leaves the pawn on f2 temporarily without defence. Incorporated into the three points is the assumption that you analysed 32...♗xf2 33 ♘c4+ and were highly satisfied that Black could not muster up anything from here.

32 ♖c4 (d) ♗xb2 simply drops a pawn and a point.

**32 ♘d2 ♔c7**

> **a) 33 ♘b3**
> **b) 33 ♘c4**
> **c) 33 ♔g1**
> **d) 33 h5**

One point for 33 ♘b3 (a), which leaves the knight slightly out of play after 33...♗b6. The c4-square must be the most effective place for this minor piece, so two points for 33 ♘c4 (b).

One point for 33 ♔g1 (c), which can't be bad either. It is only 33 h5 (d) which costs you a point since now 33...♗xf2 is possible.

**33 ♘c4 ♖a8**

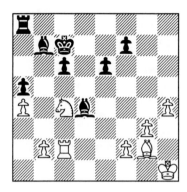

a) 34 f4
b) 34 ♔g1
c) 34 b3
d) 34 ♖d2

34 f4 (a) seeks to prevent Black expanding with ...e6-e5, ...f7-f5 and ...e5-e4 and is awarded two points. The three viable alternatives all score one.

**34 f4 f6**

a) 35 ♗f3
b) 35 ♗h3
c) 35 ♖e2
d) 35 ♔h2

35 ♗f3 (a) and 35 ♗h3 (b) are fine for one point.

35 ♖e2 (c) is interesting and scores one, but I wonder how you were going to meet 35...♗a6? If you intended to slink back to c2, no points, but if you spotted the elaborate 36 ♖xe6 ♗xc4 37 ♖xc6+ followed by rounding up the black bishop on c4, take two well-deserved bonuses. There is also one bonus available for those who calculated that 35 ♖e2 e5 36 fxe5 fxe5 37 ♘xe5 doesn't actually net a pawn due to 37...♖e8 at the end.

You must be motoring if you covered all the tactics for option (c) and then chose 35 ♔h2 (d) for a further three points. It cannot be misguided to activate your king at this stage (see Game 9 for an additional and

similar example of how to use the king effectively).

**35 ♔h2 e5**

a) 36 f5
b) 36 fxe5
c) 36 ♖d2
d) 36 g4

36 f5 (a) is natural enough for one point, and award yourself a bonus if you intentionally tried to keep the position blocked in order to suit your knight and shut down the scope of the enemy bishop pair. That is invariably a useful concept to remember.

36 fxe5 (b) is the text move and scores three. There are probably several factors going to make the decision, including that now White has two connected passed pawns and Black's e-pawn is isolated.

36 ♖d2 (c) fails to lift your total as 36...♗a6 37 b3 ♗xc4 38 bxc4 ♗e3 lets Black right back into the game.

36 g4 (d) exf4 is as bad as it looks so deduct one.

**36 fxe5 fxe5**

a) 37 ♗e4
b) 37 ♔h3
c) 37 g4
d) 37 ♗h3

Blockading the passed pawn with 37 ♗e4 (a) may not be strictly necessary now, but is always a sound option and scores two.

37 ♔h3 (b) can have one, the forthright 37 g4 earns two, but nothing for 37 ♗h3 (d), which banishes the bishop to an inferior diagonal.

**37 ♗e4 ♗c8**

a) 38 ♗f3
b) 38 ♘d2
c) 38 ♘a3
d) 38 ♖g2

38 ♗f3 (a) drops one as it invites Black to strengthen his position with 38...♗f5 39 ♖d2 ♖d8 40 ♘xa5 e4 with counterplay.

38 ♘d2 (b) is flexible and scores two.

38 ♘a3 (c) makes full use of Black's last move for three points. They say 'knights on the rim are dim' but this horse intends to leap back into action with ♘b5+ – a bonus is scored for noticing this. There is not a lot Black can do to stall this plan either as the c-pawn badly needs some attention too. This observation gives you another bonus point.

Take one point if you chose 38 ♖g2 (d) with the intention of pushing the g-pawn, and one if you rejected this on account of 38...♗g4.

**38 ♘a3 ♗d7**

a) 39 ♖e2
b) 39 ♘b5+
c) 39 b3
d) 39 ♔g2

I cannot see much point in 39 ♖e2 (a) ♗g4, but it is safe enough for one and admittedly you could always repeat the position once with 40 ♖c2 ♗d7. The answer is that Black should play 39...♖b8. Also scoring one are the harmless 39 b3 (c) and 39 ♔g2 (d).

Really, I gave you a massive hint in the notes to White's 38th and you could perhaps do with concentrating harder when you read them if you did not find the consistent 39 ♘b5+ (b), which top scores with three.

**39 ♘b5+ ♔b6**

Decision time now. Whether or not to go into a single bishop and rook ending. Again on basic principles, it is often a relief to rid your opponent of the bishop pair and endings with the same-coloured bishops do not have the same drawish stigma attached to them as opposite-coloured bishop endings.

a) 40 ♘d6
b) 40 ♘a3
c) 40 ♘xd4
d) 40 g4

Where is this knight heading? Surely not back to c4. I am reluctant to over-praise 40 ♘d6 (a) so it can have a token point.

I hardly think 40 ♘a3 (b) ♖f8 can be described as progress for White, so nil points there.

40 ♘xd4 (c) makes sense and scores two because the bishop was really quite powerful occupying a central square.

Entering some complications with 40 g4 (d) is to be commended if Black has to continue 40...♗xg4, when you have rightly concluded that 41 ♖xc6+ ♔b7 42 ♖g6+ wins for White. And what a hero to notice that 40 g4 cxb5 allows the white bishop to gobble up the loose rook on a8.

However, I am afraid that your plan backfires as Black has 40 g4 ♖h8! 41 ♘xd4 ♖xh4+ 42 ♔g3 ♖xg4+ 43 ♔f3 exd4. The bonus is for players who chose to avoid 40 g4 for this reason. Subtract one if 40 g4 was listed in your campaign.

**40 ♘xd4 exd4**

a) 41 ♖d2
b) 41 ♖c4
c) 41 h5
d) 41 ♖f2

41 ♖d2 (a) fails to score as it allows Black to advance with 41...♔c5. The move 41 ♖c4 (b), on the other hand, carefully pressurises the d-pawn while shutting off the monarch. You score two for this.

41 h5 (c) and 41 ♖f2 (d) are respectable for one point.

**41 ♖c4 ♖b8**

a) 42 ♖xd4
b) 42 ♔g2
c) 42 b4
d) 42 ♗c2

One point for 42 ♖xd4 (a), which is indeed the first move that springs to mind. If it were not for 42...♔c7 43 ♖d2 ♖b4, regaining the pawn, no doubt White would not need to search elsewhere.

Nothing for 42 ♔g2 (b) c5 and minus one for the awkward 42 ♗c2 (d) c5 43 h5 ♗e6, trapping the white rook.

Three points this time go to 42 b4 (c) as White seeks to go two pawns ahead.

**42 b4 ♖e8**

a) 43 b5
b) 43 ♗xc6
c) 43 ♖xd4
d) 43 bxa5+

Just to make sure you were aware of Black's last threat, 43 b5 (a) drops three on account of 43...♖xe4.

43 ♗xc6 (b) ♗xc6 44 bxa5+ ♔c7 45 ♖xd4 obliterates the remaining enemy pawns, but do you really want to run the risk of defending king, rook and bishop against king and rook? Deduct one for this.

43 ♖xd4 (c) can have one point as long as you planned to meet 43...axb4 with 44 ♖xb4+ ♔c5 45 ♖b7 in preference to 44 ♖xd7 ♖xe4, when Black's pawns appear far more menacing.

43 bxa5+ (d) keeps White firmly in control and scores two.

**43 bxa5 + ♔c7**

a) 44 a6
b) 44 ♖xd4
c) 44 ♗d3
d) 44 ♗g2

44 a6 (a) costs you a bishop and three points after 44...♖xe4.

Two points for 44 ♖xd4 (b), which gives White a healthy three pawn advantage, but you are seeing ghosts if you thought you had to play safe with 44 ♗d3 (one point). Black is not dead and buried after 44...♖e5.

No score for 44 ♗g2 (d) ♖e2, which leaves a sensation of White having lost control. The following is an illustration of how the position could continue on a downhill slide: 45 ♖xd4 c5 46 ♖c4 ♗c6 47 ♖xc5 ♖xg2+ 48 ♔h3 ♖a2.

**44 ♖xd4 c5**

a) 45 ♗g6
b) 45 ♖c4
c) 45 ♖d5
d) 45 ♖d2

45 ♗g6 (a) would hardly be appealing for White after 45...cxd4 46 ♗xe8 ♗xe8 but since it is catastrophic on 45...♖e2+ 46 ♔g1 cxd4, diminish your score by five.

45 ♖c4 (b) solves all White's temporary problems and scores one.

Minus two for 45 ♖d5 (c) ♖xe4 46 ♖xc5+, which unnecessarily gives Black the better chances. Even more likely now than when it was last mentioned is the possibility that Black can round up the pawns for free and then have a go at winning rook, bishop and king versus rook and king. According to theory, that ending should be a draw but there are some positions where the defender is badly orientated and can lose by force. Also, there are other examples of games where strong players have misplayed and lost from a drawn position.

45 ♖d2 (d) ♖xe4 is a worse version of (c) so debit three from your total.

**45 ♖c4 ♗c6**

a) 46 ♗xc6
b) 46 ♗g6
c) 46 ♗g2
d) 46 ♗f5

Two points for 46 ♗xc6 (a), which is the

simplest way to proceed as two connected passed pawns are killers.

It is possible to keep the bishops on with 46 ♗g6 (b) or 46 ♗f5 (d) for one point as long as you appreciated that Black can cause no damage with 46...♖e2+.

46 ♗g2 (c) ♖e2 has already been touched upon in a previous variation. This time take off three points.

**46 ♗xc6 ♔xc6**

| a) 47 g4 |
|---|
| b) 47 h5 |
| c) 47 ♔h3 |
| d) 47 a6 |

Get them rolling with 47 g4 (one point) or the speedy 47 h5 (b) for three. The pawns will need support from the king at some stage so 47 ♔h3 (c) also scores positively, this time with two points.

Nothing for 47 a6 (d) as the doubled a-pawns will be no problem for Black.

**47 h5 ♔d5**

| a) 48 ♖h4 |
|---|
| b) 48 ♖g4 |
| c) 48 ♖c1 |
| d) 48 g4 |

Minus one for 48 ♖h4 (a) c4, which will cause White to have to think again after 49 h6 c3, and 48 ♖g4 (b) c4.

48 ♖c1 (c) is designed to hold up the c-pawn for as long as possible, so take two.

Running with the pawns is premature as confirmed by a loss of four points with 48 g4 (d) ♔xc4 49 g5 ♔d4 50 g6 ♖g8.

**48 ♖c1 ♖e4**

| a) 49 ♔h3 |
|---|
| b) 49 ♔g2 |
| c) 49 ♖d1+ |
| d) 49 h6 |

49 ♔h3 (a) heads the list for two, while 49 ♔g2 (b) heads the wrong way and fails to score.

49 ♖d1+ (one point) ♖d4 leads to some interesting king and pawn endings but there seems little point pursuing the outcome of these when Black can sidestep them with 49...♔e5. The a4-pawn is not important here and you were misguided if you thought that you should save it (perhaps you wanted to bide time and were hoping to be able to choose ♖a1 on move 50 because ♖a1 was not a choice on move 49).

49 h6 (d) ♖e6 50 h7 ♖h6+ illustrates an important method of rounding up a run-away pawn and costs you one point.

**49 ♔h3 ♖xa4**

| a) 50 g4 |
|---|
| b) 50 h6 |
| c) 50 ♖f1 |
| d) 50 ♖d1+ |

Both 50 g4 (two points) and 50 h6 (three points) disclose the correct plan, but the laborious 50 ♖f1 (c) fails to score.

White could legitimately seek to keep an eye on the c-pawn from behind with 50 ♖d1+ (d) ♔e4 51 ♖d8 ♖xa5 52 g4 c4 53 ♖c8. This scores one point.

**50 h6 ♖xa5**

| a) 51 ♔h4 |
|---|
| b) 51 ♔g4 |
| c) 51 g4 |
| d) 51 h7 |

If you are physically sweating or at least concerned that your pawn advantage is down to one, take off a bonus. You will soon become aware that the two connected pawns are worth significantly more than their material value.

Just because we are in an ending does not mean we should switch off from considering routine ideas. You score a bonus if you are aware that the black king has more flexibility now that c5 is defended by the rook. You score another bonus for realising that the defence is only temporary because, for example, 51 g4 ♔e6 allows 52 h7 ♖a8 53 ♖xc5. That only leaves me to award two points for whatever move that you chose since they each have a place here.

**51 h7 ♖a8**

a) 52 ♔h4
b) 52 ♔g4
c) 52 g4
d) 52 ♖d1+

Some diligence is now required as both 52 ♔h4 (a) ♖h8 and 52 g4 (c) ♖h8 shed the h-pawn and a point from your score.

52 ♔g4 (b) is best for three, and you can have one for 52 ♖d1+ (d) as long as you were not just playing for time and hoping for some hints in the notes.

**52 ♔g4 ♖h8**

a) 53 ♔f5
b) 53 ♔f3
c) 53 ♖h1
d) 53 ♖d1+

If the h-pawn disappears, so do our winning chances. Hence nothing for 53 ♔f5 (a) or 53 ♔f3 (b).

53 ♖h1 (c) is most efficient for two,

while again 53 ♖d1+ (b) gets one on the condition that you were intending to defend the h-pawn on the following move.

**53 ♖h1 c4**

a) 54 ♔f5
b) 54 ♔g5
c) 54 ♖h5+
d) 54 ♔h5

54 ♔f5 (a) and 54 ♔g5 (b) reveal the winning plan and both score two.

Minus one for 54 ♖h5+ (c), which is fruitless as you will have to retreat.

54 ♔h5 (d) is the only way out of the given choices that spoils a well executed game. Take away six for missing 54...♖xh7+.

**54 ♔g5 c3**

a) 55 ♔h6
b) 55 ♔g6
c) 55 ♔f6
d) 55 g4

Now it doesn't matter which square you utilise out of 55 ♔h6 (a) or 55 ♔g6 (b) – both score two.

55 ♔f6 (c) and 55 g4 (d) both score one as they don't change the fact that White is heading for victory, but I suspect you would not have made a great executioner.

**55 ♔g6 c2 1-0**

56 ♔g7 or 56 ♖c1 wraps things up for White. For interest, one can note how the white king defends the h-pawn. If the white king were only on g4 now, then Black would have the deflecting ...c1♛ or, better still, ...♖xh7. The latter is a very useful tactic to be able to recall.

How did you do?

Less than 15: Concentrate on safe moves first and foremost and you will improve.
16-29: You obviously chose many decent moves and are a respectable club player.
30-40: Competently played. You touched on most of the correct ideas.
41-49: Well done. You certainly got to grips with this ending.
50+: Your ending technique was impeccable. Congratulations.